# About CHARACTER COUNTS!
## and the Josephson Institute of Ethics

No one automatically develops good character. Young people especially need guidance and example—from parents, always, but also in our increasingly fragmented world from schools, businesses, and other community institutions acting in concert. In a pluralistic society, effective "character education" is based on the enduring values that we all share, regardless of cultural, political, religious, and socioeconomic differences.

These are the operating beliefs of a nationwide, grassroots education initiative called CHARACTER COUNTS!. A diverse alliance of human-service and educational organizations, the CHARACTER COUNTS! Coalition works to reinforce young lives with core ethical values called the "Six Pillars of Character": trustworthiness, respect, responsibility, fairness, caring, and citizenship. With over 250 members, the Coalition reaches millions of young people. Some 40 states and almost 1,000 cities, counties, school districts, and chambers of commerce (plus the U.S. president and Congress) have endorsed CHARACTER COUNTS! and its approach to nonpartisan, nonsectarian character education. To draw attention to their character-education efforts, communities across the country celebrate the third week of October as CHARACTER COUNTS! Week.

The Coalition—a project of the Joseph & Edna Josephson Institute of Ethics—is guided by an independent, volunteer Council of Advisors. National programs are supported by grants, membership dues, training fees, and the sale of videos, curricula, and other creative products—such as this book.

Through projects like CHARACTER COUNTS!, the Josephson Institute encourages people to make principled decisions and carefully consider the effects of their choices. The nonprofit Institute has also conducted programs for more than 100,000 leaders in government and the armed forces, in business and journalism, in law and law enforcement, and in education and the nonprofit community. To help individuals live more ethically, the Institute seeks to:

- Stimulate moral ambition

- Heighten the ability to perceive the ethical dimension of choices

- Teach how to formulate optimal ethical responses

- Show how to implement these responses intelligently

Further, the Institute seeks to enhance the ethical quality of organizational conduct by inspiring leaders to:

- Identify the ethical obligations arising from positions of authority

- Consider the impact of all institutional actions on all stakeholders

- Create workplaces that reward the ethical and discourage the unethical

More information about CHARACTER COUNTS! and the Institute is available online (www.charactercounts.org or www.josephsoninstitute.org) or from the Institute: 4640 Admiralty Way, Suite 1001, Marina del Rey, CA 90292–6610, tel: (310) 306–1868.

---

*Note:* CHARACTER COUNTS!℠ is a service mark of the CHARACTER COUNTS! Coalition, a project of the Josephson Institute of Ethics.

*The*
# POWER
*of*
# CHARACTER

*The*

# POWER

*of*

# CHARACTER

*Prominent Americans Talk About
Life, Family, Work, Values,
and More*

*edited by*
Michael S. Josephson
*and*
Wes Hanson

*a publication of*
the Josephson Institute of Ethics
and the CHARACTER COUNTS! Coalition

JOSSEY-BASS
A Wiley Company
www.josseybass.com

Published by

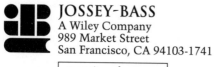

**JOSSEY-BASS**
A Wiley Company
989 Market Street
San Francisco, CA 94103-1741

www.josseybass.com

Jossey-Bass books and products are available through most bookstores. To contact Jossey-Bass directly, call (888) 378-2537, fax to (800) 605-2665, or visit our website at www.josseybass.com.

Substantial discounts on bulk quantities of Jossey-Bass books are available to corporations, professional associations, and other organizations. For details and discount information, contact the special sales department at Jossey-Bass.

We at Jossey-Bass strive to use the most environmentally sensitive paper stocks available to us. Our publications are printed on acid-free recycled stock whenever possible, and our paper always meets or exceeds minimum GPO and EPA requirements.

Interior design by Paula Schlosser

In Chapter 19, the Lancaster Laboratories' mission statement is reprinted from an essay by Earl Hess in *The Content of America's Character,* with the permission of Madison Books, Inc.

In Chapter 21, Floyd's dilemma is based closely on an experience shared by a participant in a 1995 seminar at the Leo Burnett Company in Chicago, and is used with permission.

In Chapter 34, Stephen L. Carter's comments are printed with his permission.

CHARACTER COUNTS!℠ is a service mark of the CHARACTER COUNTS! Coalition, a project of the Josephson Institute of Ethics.

Photo credits are on page 388.

LIBRARY OF CONGRESS CATALOGING-IN-PUBLICATION DATA

  The power of character : prominent Americans talk about life, family, work, values, and more / edited by Michael S. Josephson and Wes Hanson.—1st ed.
   p.  cm.
  Includes index.
  ISBN 0-7879-4172-7 (cloth)
  1. Character. I. Josephson, Michael S., date. II. Hanson, Wes, date.
  BJ1521 .P68 1998
  170—ddc21           98-25534

HB Printing 10 9 8 7 6 5 4 3        FIRST EDITION

# CONTENTS

# PREFACE

M ARK TWAIN ONCE REMARKED that everyone *talks* about the weather, but nobody does anything about it. Human character can seem a little like that—familiar but vaguely beyond our grasp.

This collection of essays, a project of the nonprofit Josephson Institute of Ethics, challenges the notion that we are powerless over our basic ethical makeup, our character. The more than forty contributors to this book make it clear that character, unlike cloud cover, is something we can do a great deal about. Indeed, they illustrate repeatedly that nothing could be more important for the quality of our individual and communal lives than consciously and continuously nurturing good character in ourselves and in others. And they show us how.

These authors have made their names in various fields: from business, politics, and media to academia, law, and laundry. They were asked to participate not only for their accomplishments but also for their diverse perspectives on the importance of character and how it can be developed. They received no payment for their considerable efforts. Proceeds from the book benefit the Josephson Institute, established by former businessman and law professor Michael Josephson to heighten public awareness of ethical issues and to provide ethics education programs for media, corporate, human service, and government organizations. This book is another way in which the institute seeks to be of service, to provide people with tools to live more ethically.

Several of the authors who have worked with the institute mention in their essays the CHARACTER COUNTS!ᔆᴹ youth initiative. One of the institute's most successful projects, this program emphasizes a nonpartisan, grassroots approach to teaching core values, which are called the Six Pillars of Character (trustworthiness, respect, responsibility, fairness, caring, and citizenship). The program has been adopted by schools and communities nationwide and has been heralded by Congress, the president of the United States, and most state governments. It is supported by a coalition of member organizations, including the American Federation of Teachers, the National Education Association, Little League Baseball, 4-H, the American Association of Retired Persons, the National Council of La Raza, Boys & Girls Clubs of America, Big Brothers Big Sisters, Goodwill Industries, the National Association of Secondary School Principals, the National Association of State Boards of Education, the YMCA, and the American Red Cross. More information about CHARACTER COUNTS! and the institute is available on the Internet at http://www.charactercounts.org or at http://www.josephsoninstitute.org.

The lesson of this book, as with the CHARACTER COUNTS! coalition, is that people working together *can* make a difference in the moral atmosphere. We thank the contributors for generously donating the time and insight necessary to make this book a success. And we thank you for your interest in character—your own, your children's, and your world's.

*Marina del Rey, California*                                        Wes Hanson
*July 1998*

# INTRODUCTION

S UPPOSE YOU SAVED the life of a leprechaun, and in gratitude, he said he would give the man your daughter will marry one exceptional quality of your choosing. This man could be very smart, enormously rich, remarkably good-looking, unusually strong and athletic, highly creative and artistic, or singularly competent—or he could possess extraordinary *character*. What would you choose? Now suppose you were picking a principal for your kid's school, or a business partner, or your own boss: what quality would you choose?

I would pick character every time. When we have to relate to, work with, and depend upon someone, nothing is more important than personal ethical virtues like honor, reliability, trustworthiness, and kindness.

But what if you were choosing a surgeon to save your life, a general to save your city, or a president to lead you through a depression or a war? I would still pick character, but I would place heavier emphasis on a different set of virtues, virtues like courage, tenacity, integrity—and, of course, competence.

The Greek philosopher Heraclitus tipped us off more than 2,500 years ago that "character is destiny." A person's true self—that enigmatic bundle of habits, dispositions, and attitudes called character—can influence more than that person's own life, of course, and this too has been known for millennia. History is largely known to us, after all, through the acts and thoughts of great heroes and villains whose character shaped their times. But as important as it is to understand how powerful character is in influencing events, it is more important to recognize how powerful *we are* in molding our own character and, therefore, in controlling our destiny. Character may determine our fate, but character is not determined by fate.

To clarify and enrich our understanding of character, this book offers the perspectives of a diverse group of thoughtful and accomplished people. As they write about spirituality, community building, business, leadership, role models, and just life in general, the contributors to this volume help us know what to look for as we pursue the morally good life.

## Character Is Dynamic

Character is often thought of as something fully formed and permanently fixed very early in life. This implies that we have little to do with who we are, that what we call character is essentially a composite of hereditary traits, tendencies and temperaments, and environmentally imposed values and attitudes. Psychoanalytic claims that the personality (a concept related to but different than character) is essentially formed by the age of six and old aphorisms such as "A leopard can't change its spots" and "You can't teach an old dog new tricks" depict character as etched in stone, something to understand and accept, not something that can be altered or improved. Even Popeye says, "I am what I am." The hidden message: don't expect me to be more, better, or different.

Many of the chapters in *The Power of Character* challenge this fatalistic notion in favor of a more dynamic concept of character. There is no doubt that the good and bad habits that become our virtues and vices are strongly influenced by both heredity and environment. But in no sense is anyone predestined to be good or bad, nor is a person's character permanently fixed by external circumstances.

Describing a person's character is like taking an inventory of that person's dominant habits of thought and action at a *particular time.*

Of course it's not easy to change our ways. Our habits of heart and mind are well entrenched, rooted in durable dispositions and beliefs. Yet just as a mountain is constantly being reshaped by weather, our character can be reformed by our choices. Our human capacity to reason and choose makes the formation of our character an ongoing process. Each day we can decide to be different. Each day we can decide to change our attitudes, reevaluate and rerank our values, and exercise a higher level of self-control to modify our behavior. Yes, character is the cause of our actions, but it's also the result of our actions. As Aristotle said, "we are what we repeatedly do." Hence the power to control our actions is the power to control our character, and the power to control our character is the power to control our lives.

## What It Means to Have Character

To better understand the power of character, however, it's important to understand the nature of character and the central role it plays in our everyday lives. Everything we do and say ultimately arises from and reveals our character. In addition to a proper concern for improving our character, we should care about the character of others. If we know a person's character, we can better predict how he or she is likely to respond to temptation, adversity, and success. It helps us make better judgments when we know about the character of the people we date and marry, do business with, and elect as our political leaders.

In recent years, public discussion about the character of various politicians, business executives, journalists, sports stars, and even children has dominated national media coverage. It would be a mistake to underestimate the profound impact on our national consciousness of stories of unspeakable acts of violence and callousness by youngsters and of the never-ending barrage of scandals among high-profile leaders and celebrities. More and more we are called upon to evaluate individuals and understand events in terms of character.

So we must be careful to recognize the different ways that the word *character* is used. Sometimes we use the term strictly in a descriptive sense, as if we were describing a particular "nature" or established pattern. Although we can talk about a person's character without making moral judgments, most of the time we use the term in the context of praising or scorning a person.

When we say a person "has character" or that we want to "build character" in youngsters, the idea of *good* character is implied. A person who has character is thought to be especially worthy, virtuous, or admirable in terms of moral qualities.

The chapters in this book reveal three qualities that are essential to good character. First, people of character have good principles. They believe in honor, integrity, duty, compassion, justice, and other ethical values. People of character also possess two emotional or psychological qualities that help them live up to their values: conscience and courage. Conscience is an internalized sense of right and wrong, a virtuous inner voice that unceasingly reminds us of our moral obligations and urges us to live up to them. A strong conscience will not be denied. It enforces its moral judgments by rewarding good behavior with good feelings of pride and self-esteem, and it imposes penalties for bad behavior, in the form of shame and guilt. But even good principles and a vigilant conscience aren't always enough. Many of us know when we are doing something wrong, and we know we'll feel bad afterward—but we still do it. Thus, the third quality possessed by people of good character is moral courage, or willpower, something to help us do the right thing even when it's costly, risky, or unpleasant.

Character, then, is moral, or ethical, strength. *Your* strength. And *your* future.

*Marina del Rey, California*                               Michael S. Josephson
*July 1998*

# part one

# LESSONS
## *for*
# LIVING

MICHAEL S. JOSEPHSON, ending two decades as a law professor and as CEO of a legal education and publishing company, resigned his tenure and sold his business in 1987 to found the nonprofit Joseph & Edna Josephson Institute of Ethics in honor of his parents. Since that time, he has contributed more than $1 million to the institute and has served as its president without compensation. In 1993, he founded the CHARACTER COUNTS! Coalition, one of the nation's largest and most influential character development organizations. Presented with the America's Award for Integrity by former president Ronald Reagan in 1996, he consults with some of the country's largest companies and government agencies. His daily radio commentaries and media appearances have made him one of the nation's most sought-after commentators on ethics and character.

*1*

# Being Good:
# Easier Said Than Done

*Michael S. Josephson*

O NE OF MY FAVORITE CARTOONS pictures a man checking in with the gatekeeper of heaven. The gatekeeper, who has a large book in front of him, says: "Edward the Good, huh? Well, Eddie, we'll be the judge of that." It's a great reminder that in the end, what will matter is our character, not defined by what we think of ourselves or even by what others think of us but by enduring principles of what is good and right.

As a full-time ethicist (can you believe there even is such a thing?), I collect these sorts of cartoons and worry about these kinds of issues. I've worked with politicians and police officers; journalists and generals; attorneys and accountants; the CIA, FBI, and IRS; and quite a few Fortune 100 companies. Through it all, two lessons stand out: (1) most people want to be ethical—and they think they are, and

(2) ethics is easier said than done—the hardest part is not knowing what's right but doing it.

I'm aware that some might see irony in a man trained as a lawyer in Los Angeles in the 1960s expecting to be taken seriously on issues of ethics and character. I admit it: when I graduated law school in 1967, my strongest moral conviction was: "It's wrong to be judgmental." After all, there are at least two sides to every question. Besides, in a world where people in some cultures eat dogs, others eat snails, and still others eat their enemies, who am I to judge? As a lawyer, law professor, and businessman, I found this a convenient perspective. It made no demands on me and excused me from making demands on others.

All this changed when I became a father. Detachment and value neutrality hardly seem to be the road to good parenting. How could I answer questions about lying, cheating, fidelity, violence, and racism with, "Well, son, what's the downside risk?" Or, "Let's do a cost-benefit analysis." And I certainly wasn't going to say, "Whatever works for you." If I was to teach values to my son (and, later, my four daughters), I had to decide what values I wanted to teach. I needed a moral philosophy beyond "do your own thing." That meant I had to overcome my knee-jerk ethical relativism and my deep-seated aversion to making moral judgments.

Like most parents, I care a lot about the kind of people my children will become, and I want to be worthy of their pride and emulation. As a father, what I say, what I do, what I demand, and what I permit take on special importance because with my every word and action I fulfill or fail my duties as a role model and teacher. This means I have had to get pretty serious about character—my character, my children's character, the character of the people my children will date and marry. Looking at the world through the lens of parental love and duty, I've become pretty judgmental. I want my kids and the people they associate with to be good, decent people—trustworthy, respectful, responsible, caring, and fair.

My "parent" perspective has not only fueled my desire to improve my own character; it has also clarified my thinking about right and wrong. Now, when I face an ethical temptation or dilemma, I envision my kids looking over my shoulder, and I try to do the thing that best supports the moral lessons I've tried to teach them. In the groups I work with as an ethicist, people often have rationalizations for their less-than-ethical behavior. No matter the group, I've found that the parent perspective is the most powerful tool I have to cut through these rationalizations and influence change. Would you behave any differently if you looked at your choices in reference to the following questions?

- What values do I want to see in my children?
- Is my conduct consistent with the way I want my children to think of me?
- What would the kind of people I want my children to marry do?
- What kind of world do I want my children to live in?

For my own part, I'm very much a work in process, struggling to recognize and overcome a full inventory of moral shortcomings. I'm certainly not where I want to be, but I'm better than I used to be. As I try to develop, I find two life prescriptions especially useful: first, remember what's really important; second, be vigilant—look out for self-righteousness, self-delusions, and selfishness.

## What's Really Important

I was on a radio talk show and had just quoted some dismal statistics to support my claim that there is a growing hole in our "moral ozone." A man named Bill called in and said that my views were naive and unrealistic. He said that he had had to cheat in high school to get into college, that he had cheated in college to get a job, and that he occasionally cheats on his job to get ahead. He said my statistics only convinced him he needs to do a better job of teaching his son to cheat. It wasn't the response I had in mind.

Well, why *should* a rational person be honest, be fair, and play by the rules in a world full of cheaters who prosper, liars who go undetected, and thieves who enjoy the spoils of their dishonesty? Why should people restrain themselves with abstract rules of ethics when those around them, including their most prominent leaders, do as they please to get what they want?

To begin to answer that question I have to ask the question, What's really important? and an old story comes to mind. Ben had just came to town as a new clergyman. Unfortunately, his first official duty was to conduct a funeral service for a fellow he had never met. Ben asked the congregation if anyone would say something good about the deceased. There was no response, so he asked again. After a long pause, a voice from the back said, "Well, his brother was worse."

If you died tomorrow, what would people say about you? Would it make you proud of the way you lived? Consider this old saying, "If you want to know how to live your life, think about what you'd like people to say about you after you die—then live backwards." Thinking about how we will be remembered can help us keep our priorities straight. It did for Alfred Nobel, who had the extraordinary opportunity to read his own obituary. It seems that after Alfred's brother died, a newspaper mistakenly printed Alfred's death notice. Though the article was positive, describing him as a brilliant chemist who made a great fortune as the inventor of dynamite, Nobel was horrified to be memorialized in such utilitarian terms. Determined to leave a more positive legacy, he bequeathed his considerable wealth to the establishment of the Nobel Prizes.

Perhaps people like Bill are not concerned with postmortem analyses of their lives. Well, they don't have to wait that long to experience the impact of character. At the turn of the century, two English politicians got into an intense debate. When one of them began name calling, the other said, "Sir, I will treat you as a gentleman. Not because you are one, but because *I* am one." This exchange yields a crucial insight. The importance of what we *do* goes well beyond what it gets us—it determines what we *are*. And for most people, that's important. As Lily Tomlin puts it, "the problem with the rat race is that even if you win, you're still a rat."

For most of us, the quest to satisfy individual wants and needs is not enough. In *When Everything You Ever Wanted Isn't Enough*, Harold Kushner writes: "Our souls are not hungry for fame, comfort, wealth or power. Our souls are hungry for meaning, for the sense that we have figured out how to live so that our lives matter, so that the world will be at least a little bit different for our having passed through it."

The Declaration of Independence uses the famous phrase, "We hold these truths to be self-evident." I think the value of good character—much like the value of beauty, love, and faith—is self-evident. Our quest to achieve good character can be, but doesn't have to be, justified by reasons. The urge to seek it is the best part of our human nature.

## The Need for Vigilance

Wanting to be a good person is very important. But it isn't sufficient. If we are not vigilant, our natural tendencies to put our self-interest first combine with the economic and social pressures we feel, and as a result, instead of asking, "What *should* I do?" we start searching for plausible reasons to justify what we *want* to do. A person of character must look out for and overcome three very human tendencies that undermine good intentions: self-righteousness, self-delusion, and selfishness.

*Self-Righteousness.* Self-righteousness is a big problem for me and others I know. I am referring to our tendency to overestimate both our moral insight and the ethical quality of our conduct. In my seminars I often ask attendees to think of the most ethical people they know. Then I ask, "How many people who know you well would probably name *you*? Almost all? At least half? Just a few?" Usually a majority say that at least half the people they know well would put them on their short list of ethical paragons. That's not very likely.

The tendency to have an inflated view of our own moral standing is probably the result of wishful thinking. Josephson Institute surveys show that 95 percent of us *want* others to think of us as highly ethical. So, when we judge our own character, we tend to base our opinion only on our good intentions, our most virtuous habits, and our most noble acts. We then become smug about the strength of our own character, and this can transform us into self-righteous scolds, invoking others to be "more like me." Excessively high self-esteem creates a moral complacency that blinds us to our shortcomings and the reality that none of us are as good as we could be.

*Self-Delusion.* An even more potent corrupter of character is self-delusion, the capacity to anesthetize the conscience with rationalizations and excuses. This tendency to contrive reasons to justify what we have done or want to do spawns an endless variety of rationalizations. Here are a few of the more common ones, ones that all of us have probably had to deal with at some time.

*If it's legal, it's ethical.* During a workshop for a Fortune 100 company, I made what many would think was an uncontroversial point: "There is an ethical duty as well as a legal obligation to keep promises." However, an executive on the company's managing board objected strenuously. He said, "It's a business, not an ethical decision, whether the company should live up to a promise. It's common practice for companies to breach contracts that are no longer advantageous as long as they're prepared to deal with the legal consequences."

The executive was able to take this narrow legalistic position because he had compartmentalized ethics into personal and business domains. This allows people who would never condone lying, cheating, or promise breaking in a personal setting to delude themselves into thinking that in a business the standards of the marketplace supersede traditional standards of ethics. But when we do this, we adopt a form of ethical relativism that confuses *descriptions of how people actually behave* with *prescriptions for how they ought to behave.* When we are people of character, we know that real ethics is about the *ought,* not the *is.* Though the ethical challenges we face in the workplace may be different from those in our personal lives, the principles of ethical conduct that apply to these challenges do not change. There is no such thing as *business ethics*—there is only *ethics.*

*Others are worse.* I had been asked to conduct an ethics seminar for the California Senate. (I think I was their punishment because in the prior year three senators had gone to jail.) Knowing that this would be a tough audience, I conducted extensive preprogram interviews with senators and senior staff. I was flattered when one staffer said, "I'm really glad you're coming to Sacramento." I asked why, and he replied, "Because they lie a lot here." When I didn't seem surprised, he added, "I hardly ever lie." From his tone it was clear he did not regard this as an admission of moral weakness. It was, in fact, a claim of superiority. He seemed to take to heart the expression "in the land of the blind the one-eyed man is king." In a culture where lying is epidemic, the merely occasional liar seems like a saint. I call this rationalization the *doctrine of relative filth*—"I'm not so bad as long as there are others who are worse."

*Being basically honest.* After a workshop a fellow came up to me and said, "Some of the things you said today made me feel a little uncomfortable. I don't always tell the truth, but I realized I'm basically honest." I suppose the idea underlying this rationalization is that nobody's perfect and being basically honest ought to be good enough. It reminds me of the cartoon in which one man says about another, "I don't mind him being honest, but I find his insistence on scrupulous honesty to be offensive." People who are content being basically honest are admitting that when the stakes are high enough, they are willing to be dishonest. Doesn't that mean they are basically *dis*honest? I once heard that a former presidential press secretary told a university audience that he believed in *always* telling the truth to the press. That way, he said, they will believe you when you have to lie. Telling the truth most of the time does not establish the virtue of honesty. After all, the best liars rarely lie. That's the secret of their success.

*It's the system.* While speaking to about sixty generals in charge of Pentagon spending, I asked whether they thought we got the most out of our defense dollar. "We do a pretty good job, but this is a political process," I was told. In other words, members of Congress tend to treat the defense budget as a public works fund to help their districts and strengthen their own political positions. One general said: "It's not a good system but that's the way it is, the way it always was, and the way it always will be." I protested, "But isn't it your ethical duty to ignore the politics and see that every dollar is spent wisely? After all, you're a *general.*" "Perhaps," he said, "but I'm only a one-star."

"I'm only a one-star" is a wonderful metaphor for the shield of powerlessness that we use to excuse our personal complicity with bad practices. Yes, there are powerful systemic forces that can make it difficult for us to do the right thing. In the last analysis, however, ethics is our individual responsibility. The "system" is ultimately the creature of our individual choice rather than its master, and the ethics of an organization or society can be improved only in increments— one person and one decision at a time.

We must never underestimate the power of leadership willing to do the right thing. What we need as each of us strives to develop his or her character is realistic idealism. As Edward Everett Hale observed:

I am only one, but still I am one.
I cannot do everything, but still I can do something;
And because I cannot do everything
I will not refuse to do the something that I can do.

*Selfishness.* The last major counterforce to good character is simple selfishness. I have discussed ethics with high-level executives who seemed supportive of all my statements about ethics—that is, until I got down to specific situations where scrupulous truth telling, promise keeping, and good-faith compliance were so contrary to common practice in their industry that such virtuous behavior could be a major disadvantage, resulting in losing business or cutting profits. At that point, I think they concluded that I wasn't very realistic. I've had the same experience with politicians, bankers, law enforcement officers, lawyers—you name it. Everyone is for ethics until it begins to exact a cost.

It is a fact that our desire to lead a good and honorable life must compete with the less noble but very powerful instinct to do what we think is best for ourselves. Pursuing self-interest—happiness, health, love, sex, security, money, status, power, freedom—is a natural preoccupation of most people. If we recognize this truth about ourselves, we can also recognize that the moral challenge is to carry out our pursuit with character, to treat ethics as a ground rule, not an option, even when the standards of ethics impede our ability to get what we want.

## The Way to Begin

Often I'm told that I'm "lecturing to the choir," that the people who are willing to hear me speak or read what I write are already more concerned with character than most. Yet this is precisely the group that can and will make the difference. The future of our families, neighborhoods, and country does not require the moral reformation of villains and rogues. It will be quite enough if good people are willing to try harder, to be better, and to do more.

OSEOLA MCCARTY astounded the nation with her gift of $150,000 to set up a scholarship for needy students, money saved from eight decades of work as a washerwoman, teaching everyone who heard her story the true meaning of generosity, grace, and humility. This unassuming woman, who had rarely left the town where she was raised, appeared on a Barbara Walters Special as one of the Most Fascinating People of 1995, on the front page of the *New York Times,* and in almost every other major publication and show, here and abroad. Harvard and others rushed to confer honorary degrees upon this woman who dropped out of school in the sixth grade to care for her family. Among her awards are the Presidential Citizens Medal, Wallenberg Humanitarian Award, and Community Heroes Award of the Urban League. She has published a collection of her sayings: *Simple Wisdom for Rich Living.*

*2*

# Living the Clean, Clean Life

*Oseola McCarty*

G OING ALL OVER the country, everywhere free, it surprised me, it really did, all the fuss about me giving my money away. I wasn't expecting that. People all thought it was great, the way I gave that much to the university for the children's education. I didn't know nothing else. I didn't have any brothers and sisters. I was just one child. I wanted to do for the other children.

Some people say I am a hero. No, I am just a plain, common, ordinary person. I don't want to be on a pedestal.

I didn't get an education. I went to work. People complain they have too much work to do, they don't have enough time. I like to work. It's company for you. And besides that, it gives you independence. You won't have to depend on other people so much; you can do for yourself. It's just good, that's all I can say. You won't be

---

*Note:* © 1998 Oseola McCarty.

looking for nobody else to do something for you. You just do it your-self. It makes me feel good about myself.

There are a lot of different ways to live your life. For me, living a good life is living a clean, clean, pure life. I believe in living a Chris-tian life, not too rushed, neither too slow. Where I got my values, I can't explain all of that. My family's dead now, but in my family we all tried to be loving to each other. Peaceful, quiet. My grandmother was sweet to me. But my mother taught me the difference between right and wrong. She would spank me if I did something wrong; yes, she would. Well, I tried to be good! I did the best I could.

The lessons I learned from my mother and my aunt were go to church and share the Lord the best I can. Treat everybody the way I want them to treat me. People would be happier if they treated other people the way they wanted to be treated. They sure would. It would be a better world than it is now.

Some complain about what's wrong with the world and blame other people. You need to look at yourself first. You need to change your own ways first. That way you know you are making a differ-ence in at least one life. If everybody did that, we would be all right.

The world is different now. People live faster than they used to, and they are learning more. Getting weaker and wiser. Every gener-ation gets weaker and wiser. You leave off a lot of things you *should* do and do what you *should not* do. When you get wiser, why, things you didn't know, you know them now.

The difference is in the people. Some people live fast lives; some live a common life. Our flesh is weak. And we can't go around that and can't go over it and can't go under it. We have to go straight on through with the Lord. Lord in front and you follow. I've tried to lead a clean, Christian life. I love the Christian life. I did the best I could.

Ever since I've been big enough, I've gone to work. At first, they had to stand me up on a box. Washing and ironing. Working, work-ing, working all I can. That makes you feel good.

Work is a blessing. It is a consolation to you. And you can work when you're old. Being old doesn't mean you can't work, although

I can't work the way I used to. I had a lot of sickness. I am right-handed, and I just used that one hand for everything I did. Everything I went to do, why, that right hand would have to do it for me. So that makes the difference. I want to work, but I can't, because of the arthritis, so I'm retired.

All my traveling helped me in a way. I saw a lot of things I would have never seen. I saw water I have never seen. I saw beautiful flowers. I saw oranges and grapefruit on the trees. Lemons. But I didn't learn anything new from the new people I met. No, I sure didn't.

Tell you the truth, some people expect too much of the other person. They should do some things for themselves. Some people don't want to do nothing but just sit down. Of course, I had to sit down because of the arthritis! I would tell other people to work, feel independent, don't depend on other people to do so much for you. Do for yourself. You've got to take care of yourself. That's the way I feel. It would help other people if they felt like that. That's my belief. Whatever you've got to do, just go on and do it.

You've got to plan for the future. You can't rely on other people or the government too much. You have to take responsibility for yourself. If you want to feel proud, you've got to do things you can be proud of. You can't get something for nothing. I know some people try.

Everybody should save money because it's so much help to you. You won't have to depend on nobody but yourself. You can meet your bills, spend some, save some. And keep on and on.

I don't like to waste nothing. Use it up until it wears out. I had some help in saving my money. I got clothes from the people I worked for. I only paid for groceries and some little things. But I was happy with what I had. It never bothered me that other folks had more. You can't live other people's lives. You have to live your own life. However it is. Why, if it's good or it's bad or it's just ordinary, you have to live that life to suit yourself. That's the way *I* feel.

Save some, spend some, and give some to other people. It's better to give than to receive. I got everything I thought I wanted. Washing and ironing was the way for me to make my living. I didn't mind that I didn't have an education. I am proud that I worked hard and my money will help children who have also worked hard. I want to leave something positive for the world.

I think getting an education is the way for people to go if they can. That's God's best for us. I gave my money to the school because you got to work and make your money to live, but if you get a good education, why, in place of working for a small amount of money, you go ahead and make big money. Then you can spend some of it, save some of it, and enjoy some of it—and give some of it. That's where money comes in handy for everybody.

DR. LAURA SCHLESSINGER, or Dr. Laura as she is known to
millions of listeners worldwide, dispenses no-nonsense moral
advice through the nation's airwaves. The nation's top radio
host (and first female winner of the Marconi, awarded by the
National Association of Broadcasters to the "broadcaster of
the year"), she has also written the best-selling *Ten Stupid
Things Women Do to Mess Up Their Lives*; *Ten Stupid Things
Men Do to Mess Up Their Lives*; and *How Could You Do
That?! The Abdication of Character, Courage and Conscience*.
The Reverend Robert Schuller calls her "a power voice for
positive values without equal in our time." Her secret? She
"preaches, teaches, and nags" about *moral* health, not *mental*
health. A licensed marriage and family counselor with a doc-
torate in physiology, she has served on the faculties of the
University of Southern California and Pepperdine University.

# 3

# Character, Courage, and Conscience

## Dr. Laura Schlessinger

I BEGAN MY TALK RADIO program career simultaneously with my training in marriage, family, and child therapy. My education as a psychotherapist focused on interpersonal pressures and challenges and unconscious motivations as the sources of people's behaviors and of their problems coping with life. The training did not exactly say that people were not at all responsible for their conditions, but it did emphasize that external situations and internal angst produced an almost inexorable force that became an explanation, if not an excuse, for all inappropriate, self-defeating, even destructive behaviors.

Consequently, in my early radio dialogues I tried to provide insights concerning the origins of each caller's uncomfortable, frustrating, and

*Note:* This chapter is adapted from *How Could You Do That?* (HarperCollins, 1996). © 1998 Laura Schlessinger.

sometimes downright scary predicament. For example, "Your father abandoned you at a young age and of course you'd be scared to trust men. That explains your promiscuity."

Neat package. Too neat. It worried me. First, I was bothered by the notion that just because a bad experience happened, it necessarily caused the person's present problems. Reality doesn't support that position. All people experiencing that same bad event do not have the same reaction or quality of life. Second, I worried that blaming something in the past and revering their victimhood was only helping people stay stuck. As a result I changed from talking about experience as cause-and-effect to speaking about it as a possible influence. Experiences are influential but by no means determinative of future actions; and feelings are important information but not irresistible forces.

It struck me that even profound anger, hurt, and fear are not automatic trip wires for specific reactions. Human beings control and redirect emotions all the time, often overriding them with conscious determination—even when they have to pay a considerable emotional price.

The bottom line is that regardless of the facts of our past and our perceptions and beliefs about ourselves based on the past, we can and must make decisions to act that involve something more special about us as human beings than our emotional reactions.

With this realization I began to develop a profound respect for the choices humans are capable of making. Callers were teaching me about the tenacity of spirit and nobility of purpose with which people can choose to behave, where sacrifice and suffering are seen as part of the elevation of the soul in accomplishing something truly special: being human.

The thing that separates human beings from other animals is morality. Without morality we are no more than termites seeking survival and gratification at every moment and at all costs. With morality we transcend instinct and the simple equation of learned responses.

More and more I began to see that the problems people sought to solve, resolve, or avoid in the first place needed to be viewed from the perspective of right and wrong. This view is anathema to much of the psychological establishment. In the modern world, feelings reign supreme, values are relative, and there is no judgment and little challenge. I started talking about honor, integrity, and ethics in tandem with the more traditional psychological approach and *bang!* My radio show took off and became an international phenomenon.

The basic premise of the program and my books is that regardless of our emotional angst or tremendous temptation, we must get back to the three C's—*character, courage,* and *conscience*—in order to be fully human and to benefit the most from our life experience.

Applying these qualities to our everyday lives is, apparently, more difficult than it seems. People's number one response to my reminders of cause and effect, common sense, values, ethics, morality, and fair play is, "Yeah, I know, but. . . . At that moment, they abdicate character, courage, and conscience. The "but" is followed by all sorts of attempts to justify the action with words like "unhappy," "confused," "frightened," "in love," "scared to risk being uncomfortable," "feeling lonely," "feeling needy," "feeling anxious."

(By the way, in using the word feeling, most people think they are on sacred ground, because popular psychology has elevated feelings from information to irresistible force.)

Victim status is the modern promised land of absolution from personal responsibility. Nobody is acknowledged to have free will or responsibility anymore. Everyone is the product of causation.

The excuse that really gets my hackles quivering is "I'm only human." *Only* human? As if one's humanness were a blueprint for instinctive, reflexive reactions to situations, like the rest of the animal kingdom.

In the classic film *The African Queen,* Charlie (Humphrey Bogart) attempts to explain a drunken evening by saying it was, after all, only human nature. Rosie, the missionary (Katherine Hepburn), peers over her Bible and aptly retorts that we were put on the earth to rise above nature.

I see being human as our unique opportunity to use our mind and will to act in ways that elevate us above the animal kingdom. In contrast to all other creatures on earth, only humans measure themselves against ideals. We are elevated above all other creatures because we have a moral sense: a notion of right and wrong and a determination to experience significance in our lives through actions that are selfless and generous.

We demonstrate our humanity by the value we give to behaviors that emphasize commitments over rights and a respect for our obligations to others. Humans are the only creatures on earth who take pleasure in resisting temptation, easy and fast gratification, and constant pleasure seeking. We respect, admire, trust, and love those whose struggle between self-interest and commitment tilts toward commitment—and honor, duty, compassion.

I think human beings can actually derive pleasure from not getting something, someone, or someplace the easy way. We can find it profoundly satisfying to forgo immediate pleasures, to benefit another at some expense to ourselves—even if no one knows we've done it.

## Character

Yes, I believe human beings can derive pleasure from having character. For humans, brute strength and stealth are not enough. We value reputation, respect, admiration, and the long-lasting happiness that comes from the sacrifices, pains, and efforts that go into forging character.

It is the absence of character that explains the problems so many of my callers have. What does it mean when we say someone lacks character? It suggests that in his inner battle between self (interest/indulgence) and obligation toward others (fairness/sacrifice), the person will lean toward self. Therefore, we can't count on that person to do the right thing or to honor commitments.

Character is the capacity to rise above immediate self-interest. After all, integrity, honesty, and honor may not yield immediate reward or gratification. Nor does the absence of these qualities always bring punishment or scorn. In fact, connivers and cheats often gain power and wealth. Therefore, morality must be its own reward.

Tony, for example, a single, twenty-nine-year-old caller, told me his career would take off if he simply concentrated his time, efforts, and resources on his goal. The problem was that about two years ago his older sister and her husband had died, leaving two children, now ten and thirteen. Another of Tony's sisters had taken the children, but then, because she didn't have the money and space to handle the additional responsibility, they had all moved in with Tony.

"Look" Tony complained, "I feel sorry for them, I really do. But isn't it my turn at life? I have so much I want to accomplish and this is the time. I don't think I'm being selfish, just practical. What do you think?"

Instead of giving him my opinion, I asked him one question: "If I could project you fifteen years into the future and you could look back at this time in your life, what would you want to see yourself having done?"

Sighing deeply and choking back tears, Tony replied, "Continue to help them."

Clearly, successfully resisting self-indulgence requires character and a value system that judges some behaviors as being better than others.

That is where courage comes in. Thoroughly living life requires initiative, risk taking, sustained action against the odds, making sacrifices for ideals and for others, and leaps of faith. People who lead such lives report being happy, hopeful, and exhilarated, even when they fail.

## Courage and Conscience

Courage is to life what broth is to soup. It is the context that gives experiences, events, and opportunities special richness, flavor, and meaning. Courage gives vibrancy to our values. Many people espouse certain values about sex, abortion, honesty, and the like until the problem is their own. Then, because of particular circumstances, selfish needs, and uncomfortable feelings, those values become optional.

I believe too many people use statements like "OK, I made a mistake" or "But I'm only human" or "I'm not perfect!" instead of "I did wrong" to escape a guilty conscience. The speakers hope or believe they cannot or should not be condemned. Using these protective clauses, they demand to be excused.

We wish to be excused because guilt (internal pain caused by disappointing ourselves) and shame (public awareness of our transgressions and the threat of condemnation and punishment) are painful emotions. So we go through verbal and psychological contortions of blame and rationalizations.

Conscience is our capacity to judge ourselves in moral terms and to conform to those standards and values that we make part of our inner being. Conscience is not simply a source of negative feelings of guilt and shame; it also can reward us with feelings of pride (in our fulfillment of goodness), compassion, empathy, and love.

One way to reinforce conscience is to ask: "Would I want this act open to public scrutiny?" If our answer is no, then no amount of justification is going to purify our conscience.

## Character Is About Choice

Human beings are not tightly programmed by instinct like lower animals. Therefore, we are charged with the seemingly overwhelming responsibility of making judgments and choosing between behaviors. The path to solid, supportive, healthy relationships, self-respect, and a quality life begins with the usually painful decision to do the right thing.

To help us make such decisions, here are some rules liberally paraphrased from "The Morals of Chess," written in 1779 by Benjamin Franklin:

- *Foresight*. Look into the future and consider the consequences. Think about the real advantages to yourself, then wonder about the impact on others and how that might reflect back on your life. Imagine how you might righteously defend your position.

- *Circumspection*. Examine the bigger picture: the dangers, the possibilities, the probabilities. Be braver about options that scare you.

- *Caution*. Don't make moves in haste or in passion. Keep to the rules and guidelines of etiquette, law, and the commandments. And understand that once you have made your move, you set into play a series of events over which you may not have recourse, from which you might suffer in your soul, as well as your life.

Why is there such an inner struggle between the human being as an instinctive animal and the human being as an elevated being capable of making choices? Simple. The conflict is all about immediate gratification. Conscience appears to get in the way of the pleasure of immediate gratification.

It would help if we could clear up the modern-day confusion between the concepts of happiness and pleasure. A balance between happiness and pleasure is a great formula for a satisfying life. Conversely, confusing happiness with pleasure has been devastating to individuals, families, and inevitably, society.

Pleasure is a discrete and enjoyable experience: eating a sugar-covered donut, having great sex, listening to music, getting a foot rub, watching an absorbing movie. As satisfying as pleasure is, it is also transitory and superficial. Pleasure is an event. In contrast, happiness is a process. Pleasure is material. Happiness is spiritual. Pleasure is self-involved. Happiness involves others.

When individuals disregard the process of their lives and focus mostly on the seduction of the pleasurable moment, their self-centered actions often generate pain for others and destroy their own ultimate potential for self-esteem and personal achievement.

There is a profound difference between doing what feels good right now and doing what we know to be morally good right now. The main thrust of too many lives is an overemphasis on feeling good instead of doing good.

Albert Einstein said, "The most important human endeavor is the striving for morality in our actions. Our inner balance and even our very existence depends on it. Only morality in our actions can give beauty and dignity to our lives."

ROBB ARMSTRONG takes on family life, careers, and everyday challenges in *JumpStart*, one of the few nationally syndicated cartoons to focus on middle-class African American life. Real life, his wife, Sherry, his daughter, Tess, and his son, Rex, serve as inspirations, he says, and he credits his late mother's love and willpower, more than his talent and good eraser, for his success. Serious about helping kids set goals for themselves and stay in school, Armstrong also uses his cartoons at speaking engagements at schools, churches, and libraries. His characters have appeared in American Diabetes Association messages and as boosters for the American Cancer Society's Great American Smokeout, on Gibson Greetings cards, and in "The Fabulous Funnies," a television special on the history of comics. He received the 1995 Wilbur Award for the communication of family values from the Religious Public Relations Council.

# 4

# Drawing Lessons from Life

*Robb Armstrong*

I CREATE THE COMIC strip *JumpStart,* which is nationally syndicated in three hundred newspapers. I base a great deal of the material in *JumpStart* on the ordinary goings-on of my real-life family. My wife, Sherry, my daughter, Tess, and my infant son, Rex, deserve most of my salary for inspiring the majority of what I write about Marcy and Joe and my other comic strip characters. (Justice prevails, since they end up getting the majority of what I earn, anyway.)

Most of whatever I do that is not based on my family comes from other external stimuli, like the TV, news media, and conversations eavesdropped on in crowded elevators. That still leaves about 10 percent of my material unaccounted for. This is stuff I have simply made up. In other words the unsuspecting public is exposed to my unfiltered opinion about once a week. Because of this, my character is a *very* big issue, and I'm happy for this opportunity to explain myself.

If a person makes a career of communicating publicly, then a lot of what that person says should contain arguable truth. Civilization itself depends upon that. I consider *JumpStart* nothing if not true. The issue of character goes beyond the things a person says publicly, however, even beyond what a person writes in daily newspapers. Character is what a person *is*. It is a word that begs the question, What reason do you have for existing?

Tough question. It is almost unfair to ask it until after a person's entire life has been lived (which makes getting an answer pretty difficult). The question reminds me of a cartoon I wrote about Elvis Presley. The Elvis postage stamp was being considered at the time, and I created a *JumpStart* scenario in which Marcy is asked by a neighbor, "Which Elvis would make the best stamp? The 1950's Elvis or the Las Vegas Elvis?" Marcy wonders aloud whether a guy who killed himself with drugs should be on a stamp at all. The neighbor interjects, "No, no ... you're thinking about fat, bloated Elvis. Nobody would dare put *him* on a stamp!" If character were a consideration in putting a person's likeness on a postage stamp, Elvis would never make the cut. But when pitted against personal popularity, character rarely stands a chance.

Not only was the stamp selection committee unconcerned about the character issue, so were the two dozen irate Elvis-worshipers who wrote me the most inflammatory letters I have ever received in my nine-year career. Here is an excerpt from one of the letters:

> Dear Mr. Armstrong,
> You should be shot for saying such horrible things about the King of Rock and Roll. You better apologize. We Elvis fans are all over. If you don't apologize, we will find you and destroy you.

This letter was written by an eleven-year-old girl.

## Being Funny or Being True

When I created *JumpStart* in 1989, I was about as close to the character issue as this poor child. At the time I was interested only in reaching a lifelong goal of obtaining a contract to write and draw a syndicated comic strip. I had been interested in cartooning since my mother convinced me that my rudimentary crayon sketches of Fred Flintstone looked just like the real thing. I pursued my interest through high school, and in college I penned *Hector*, a daily strip for Syracuse University's student newspaper, *The Daily Orange*.

The figure of Hector was a grim creation, born of the grief I felt after losing my mother to cancer. I transferred a lot of anger into him so that I could function normally. By 1981 college newspaper standards, Hector was a smash hit. He was a cynical, rebellious, self-obsessed cartoon character who seemed to touch a chord with a disturbing number of the student population. Because of the overwhelming approval that my rantings received, I quickly realized that I wasn't suffering alone. I saw, through my cartooning, an opportunity to connect emotionally with great numbers of people. My feelings about the world weren't merely validated; they were deemed necessary. There was suddenly a broader purpose in my existence. My point of view felt oddly integral to the machinations of campus life. Almost everyone I met, including professors, praised or excitedly criticized my work.

Hector even helped remove from me the suffocating stigma Ralph Ellison wrote about in *Invisible Man*. I began to believe that I *mattered*. Even though I and Hector are African American, I relied on broader human issues than race to fuel my creativity. I instead learned to use the power of example and the accessibility of humor to point out the truth in our lives. And, yes, sometimes I have been known to scold people about racial intolerance in a sneaky way that seems funny at first.

*JumpStart* bears little resemblance to *Hector*. I have deliberately crafted characters that seem likeable. Their appearance of niceness allows them access beyond our invisible barriers of mistrust that protect us from people of the flesh-and-blood variety. I exploit this opportunity to speak in cartoon parables on character issues routinely these days, but in the early years I focused on being "funny," and missed many opportunities to really reach people.

In my college years, people responded well to cartoons that focused more on truth than on humor. Hearing from a fan, "Today's strip is *sooo* true!" always meant more to me than, "Today's strip is so funny!" When I went for funny, there was always the risk that somebody would find what I was saying unfunny, humor being the subjective phenomenon that it is. That was a valuable lesson, which is why most of the strips I do now are based on true experiences I've had. The more true a strip is, the greater the likelihood that someone will cut it out of the newspaper and stick it on the fridge. To a cartoonist, this is the equivalent of the Nobel Prize.

## Developing Our Own Character First

Character is a spiritual concept to me. Only through my own maturity and spiritual growth can I accurately live it and report on it. The cartoon people in *JumpStart* aren't examples of perfect character, just as I am not. We all tend to mature *after* we make fools of ourselves—not before. I have found that it is only after I have run out of mistakes that I can assess my own character. But what I have learned is a working definition of character that at least gives me something tangible to pursue.

Good character develops in time, from long-term, selfless service to others. Moreover, examples of strong character are surprisingly plentiful. Those who wish to believe it is scarce are spending too much time looking for it in Washington and Hollywood. Instead, step outside that frame and consider the single mom with two kids in college and elderly parents to attend to. Consider the new dad who volunteers to change a dirty diaper instead of turning into Harry Houdini with the first whiff. Consider the talented teacher who chooses to share her gift with the kids who are most desperately in need of it—even if that means she must risk her life to do so.

But even looking right outside my front door for strong character is having to look too far. I believe that I have a responsibility to seek it only in my bathroom mirror. The characters in my strip are far from perfect because I don't want my readers to separate my characters from themselves in any way. If I paint the characters as being above life's fray, I do it at the peril of the strip itself. I want people who read my strip to recognize that although Joe and Marcy make mistakes, they're still OK because they keep trying to be good people. What readers seem to like about *JumpStart* is the absence of malice in my main characters. I once did a strip showing a very pregnant Marcy standing on a crowded public bus. Nobody offers her a seat, and she is saddened by how inconsiderate the human race has become. Just before she loses hope, a kind person offers her a seat. Marcy takes the seat, then looks up to discover the kind person is nine months pregnant. It seems we just can't relate to the suffering of others until we have been there ourselves.

As I mentioned earlier, much of what Marcy does, my wife, Sherry, has done. One of the things I am most grateful for is being married to a woman who is spiritual. Her faith has made my faith stronger. This has had a profound impact on the types of messages I convey in my strip. (Church is a great place to get material!)

The Bible is jam-packed with character-building truths that I try to weave into *JumpStart*. I almost hate to let the world in on my secret, but with Sherry, Tess, Rex, and God providing me with so much material, I'm nothing more than a glorified note taker.

It's easy to scare people off a comic strip by dealing with religion. I have avoided trouble by, again, showing how fallible my characters are even in their spiritual lives. My characters are always late for church (as are my real-life family and I), and they struggle with organized religion. In fact, when Joe's best buddy states that he doesn't go to church because of his problems with organized religion, Joe encourages him by saying, "You'd like our church. It's not organized at all!" And because they have a toddler, Joe and Marcy often show up with enough toys, games, and children's books to take up an entire pew—but they forget to bring along the Bible!

I am an ordained deacon in my church, but I struggle too. Selfishness is the antithesis of strong character, and I battle an addiction to selfishness that I often think I have lost for good. Then I read my Bible and realize that every person is in a similar battle. Christianity deals with selfishness consistently and directly. My faith connects me to others so that when I speak on emotional issues like child rearing, marriage, and aging, I speak with the kind of compassion that can come only from a person who is down in the trenches with everybody else. God keeps me humble. And humility is a sign of good character (or so I've heard).

## Sending Messages About Race

Race issues weigh heavily on almost every *JumpStart* strip I have ever written. Yet I have apparently hidden my race agenda well, and often an African American reader will ask, "How come you don't deal with race at all?" I respond by asking that reader what kind of individuals populate my strip. The reader will often answer, "The cop and nurse seem like nice people. Hardworking parents who take their careers and their roles as parents seriously. They appear to be in love too." There you have it. That makes my strip the most militant pro-black statement in newspapers—flying right in the face of all that negative stuff you read on the front page.

One of the reasons my heavy message about race goes undetected is because I approach race from the standpoint of character. It's an unexpected vantage point. As long as Joe and Marcy come across as decent human beings, they have overcome the stigma that suggests that African Americans lack humanity. Once readers identify with them, they also *trust* them, which is what most people want out of the society at large. In other words, my message is undetected but not unreceived.

I once drew a strip showing Joe approaching a black militant on the street. The guy is waving a sign, "End Racism." The militant yells at Joe, "Wake up, my Brother! Racism is everywhere! It's in the schools! It's in the churches! It's in the government!" Joe asks if it's

in the militant's bathroom mirror. The militant yells, "I don't know! Haven't checked!"

Are we so busy looking for racism on the outside that we forget to look on the inside? After all, the only place where we have a fighting chance of obliterating racism is in that bathroom mirror. To develop good character we must be humble and always look to improve ourselves even as we try to improve the world.

It is so easy to go through life frustrated because of prejudice and mistreatment. It's understandable to want to climb to the highest cliff and yell to nobody in particular, "Understand me!" Sadly, that desire leads to a life of unfulfillment and hurt. The only real choice we have is to climb that cliff and yell, "Let me try to understand you!" That understanding is what I am trying to do. *JumpStart* says a lot about my aspirations for my character—and yours.

**JOHN NABER,** a sports commentator and motivational speaker, won four gold medals and one silver medal at the 1976 Olympic Games in Montreal, setting four world records in the process. During his athletic career he won twenty-five national college titles and a record ten NCAA individual titles, leading his team to four undefeated seasons and winning the 1977 Sullivan Award as the nation's outstanding amateur athlete. In Los Angeles in 1984, he carried the Olympic flag in the opening ceremonies and was elected into the U.S. Olympic Committee Hall of Fame. In 1996, he was elected president of the U.S. Olympians, an association of over six thousand American Olympic alumni, and was chosen in a *USA Today* poll as the male captain of a team of the country's greatest Olympic champions. He serves on the advisory board of the CHARACTER COUNTS! All Stars, a group of athletes who appeal to young people to live ethical lives.

*5*

# Accepting the Rules of the Game

## *John Naber*

I WAS A RECENT high school graduate competing in the
U.S. National Swimming Championships, hoping to
earn a berth on the 1973 World Championship Team. Other than
the Olympic Games, the World Championships are the most significant competition in swimming. I was favored to win the 100-meter
backstroke. The race was especially important because the fastest
100-meter backstroker would also earn the right to swim on the U.S.
4 × 100-meter medley relay. The U.S. relay team was so strong that
I knew if I made the team I would almost certainly win at least one
gold medal at the Worlds.

I remember it all so well. The stadium lights that night were
bright, casting multiple shadows on the pool deck and making wet
bodies glisten in the cool night air. Moths swirled around the lamps

---

as crickets made their nighttime music, punctuated by the crowd's cheers and the occasional bang from the starter's pistol. The turn judges at the far end of the pool were dressed in their snappiest volunteer whites. The crowd was buzzing with excitement.

A quick start, and I was off. At the end of the first lap, I reached for the wall behind my head and initiated the spin. My feet swung around and found the wall and pushed off. I popped up to the surface in time to see the official standing over my lane raise her arm, signaling an infraction. I swam the rest of the distance angry and afraid. What had happened? Hadn't my hand touched the wall, as it was required to on the turn? It must have! Perhaps the official was signaling something else in an adjacent lane. My mind was racing faster than I was down the pool. I swam a smooth second lap and touched the finish line well ahead of the rest of the field.

Applause from the stands washed over me as other swimmers patted me on the back and congratulated me. But I couldn't hear a word they said. I was preoccupied by a conference that was taking place at the far end of the pool. When it was over, the head referee walked up to me and said, "I'm afraid you've been disqualified. The turn judge says she didn't see you touch the wall." A gasp came from the crowd as my shoulders dropped and my chin hit my chest. I could hear a rumble of conversation sweep through the bleachers. They hadn't seen anything wrong with my race. Perhaps the official had made a mistake.

My coach, Mike Hastings, ran over and pulled me aside. He asked, "Do you want to fight this thing? Do you want me to protest the call?" If I wanted this title, I would have to dispute the official's decision, and it would be her word against mine. Mike felt I could win. My head was swirling. After all, there was a potential world title at stake here. Maybe I didn't graze the wall as I usually do, but that wouldn't have given me any material advantage over the other swimmers. Besides, shouldn't America be represented in the Worlds by its fastest swimmer?

Even though I was a young man, I knew how I handled this situation would follow me the rest of my life. It would say something about the kind of person I was—and intended to be.

That fateful day, so many years ago in Kansas City, might very well have been a turning point in my life. My decision whether to fight the judge's call or to accept her decision was made in the blink of an eye. I knew what I had to do. My parents didn't raise a cheater. With moist eyes I looked at my coach, the man who was offering a way out of my disappointment, and I said, "Mike, I didn't touch the wall." Slowly I lifted myself out of the pool, and with a wet towel over my shoulder, I began a long slow march back to the team's area beneath the bleachers. My friends gave me wide leeway. They didn't know what to say. What *can* you say to a young man who just beat the field to the wall and then finds he doesn't get to walk to the awards stand?

Friends and even strangers wanted me to cry foul, to claim an injustice. They wanted me to rant and rave about how I had been robbed or how the ref was probably blind—anything that showed an attitude. But the truth was I had broken a rule. I should be held accountable.

This kind of test is repeated over and over in competitive sports. For instance, my friend the champion swimmer Bruce Furniss was disqualified from his final career race for missing a turn. He could easily have told the judge that he had touched the wall, and he would have been believed. His entire career (which included two Olympic gold medals and multiple world records and collegiate, national, and world titles) would be tainted by this disqualification. But his decision was simple. "The fact that you're in the arena means you accept the rules of the game," he says.

Bruce credits this thinking to his parents, his church, and his role models and their influence on his character—on the kind of person he is as reflected in the decisions and choices he makes. There was never any misunderstanding in his mind about the rules or what they meant. "Football fields have sidelines and end zones so that you know when you go out of bounds," he says, "and it's important that the better the athlete is, the more those rules have to be enforced. If the rules are bent for the best, what does that teach the rest?"

## Lessons for Us All

That's a good question for all of us. We are living in a time where top performers are judged by different standards. It's as if they are above the law as long as they keep winning. So we have steroid use, trash talking, and general anarchy on the playing field. We're seeing more and more examples of this on television and in the papers; players can assault coaches and officials, and "everybody's doing it" is the catch-all justification for unacceptable behavior. "Winning is everything" is the rallying cry, not just in sports but in business and in life in general.

Now, is being a good person—what we might call a person of character—just about obeying the rules? No, of course not. Character isn't about doing what you have a right to do (adherence to the rules) but about *doing what is right*. Rules and regulations exist for a reason, however. They may not necessarily make us better people, but they do provide some order to a given activity (say, competitive swimming or driving or paying taxes). Rules offer a measure of predictability, and therefore fairness, to human interaction. Simply put, they make civilization possible. The rest is up to us.

But even though simple adherence to rules does not make us good people, *violating* rules actually endangers us. Why? Because whenever we purposefully cheat—or even violate the spirit of a rule by being a bad sport—we tarnish our greatest trophy, our character. We have acted in a way that disadvantages and disrespects others—and we would *not* appreciate being treated similarly ourselves.

If we allow youngsters to see themselves as above or outside the rules, it should come as no surprise to us if they complain or even rebel when we can't (or don't) bend rules for them later on. Raising a child isn't easy, but it's important that we maintain both fairness and consistency when we establish rules during that time when our children so actively seek our approval. For Bruce Furniss, the memory of his parent's disappointment when he was once ejected from a high school water polo match (for cussing at an official) was more than enough to teach him what is important about citizenship and respect, two key aspects of what I would call a person of character. His relationship with others in his sport made him care about their opinion of him and reminded him to do the right thing.

To try to reach kids and athletes with the message that character really matters, I have become involved in the CHARACTER COUNTS! All Stars. These former and current champions from practically every major sport promote the nonpartisan values known as the six pillars of character: trustworthiness, respect, responsibility, fairness, caring, and citizenship. These values can provide meaningful guidance for our conduct as athletes, parents, wage earners, and citizens. These ethical principles should be as firm and unyielding as the marble columns used to build the ancient Olympic stadiums. Their measure should be as unchanging as the height of the basketball rim, the length between the pitcher's mound and home plate, the distance required to earn a first down. Upon these fundamentals we can build a better society, just as a strong house can be built on a strong foundation.

I honestly didn't think of all this back in 1973 when I chose disqualification over dishonor, but now I see how the character issues of trustworthiness (telling the truth), responsibility (being accountable for my actions), fairness (abiding by the rules), and citizenship (respect for authority) all came into play in that one instance. The right thing to do was obvious. I only wish that it had made it less painful.

## What We Can Do

People often talk about how sports "build character." Certainly, sports can foster habits of discipline that can be applied in other areas of our lives and thereby make us more reliable or responsible individuals. But good character is not developed through mere participation in sports. Sports provide challenges. Challenges provoke tough decisions. And it's the tough decisions that really test our character, for character is revealed when the price of doing the right thing is more than we want to pay.

Failing to test character is akin to enduring tough workouts but never going to a meet. Tests measure our skills and facilitate coaching and teaching. The presence of rules and the pressure of competition will test a child and allow a coach, teacher, parent, or mentor to fix problems early. By refusing to enforce rules, we deny the child the benefit of proper development and the exercise of good judgment.

As a society we must return to the truly valuable intention of recreational athletics: to prepare our young men and women for the real world that awaits them in adulthood. We should honor and reward those who demonstrate quality of character, even if it comes at the cost of our teams' win-loss records. And we should teach good character traits (such as trustworthiness, respect, responsibility, fairness, caring, and citizenship) rigorously in the early, formative years—in the home, at school, on the playing field, and in the church or synagogue.

When poorly chosen ends (winning, becoming rich and famous, and the like) justify such means as poor sportsmanship, trash talking, or performance-enhancing drugs, athletics will no longer prepare young people to be strong adults. The inescapable outcome will be totally selfish and unprincipled juveniles who have mastered a solitary, albeit lucrative skill, such as a smooth backswing or a quick jump shot.

Sports force us to keep score, and they usually force us to play by the rules. Children can talk about the character issues sports raise, usually with parents but often with coaches and teammates as well. By identifying problem areas early on, we can address them while the child is still in school, while the accidents are relatively innocent and the punishments usually benign. Accidentally breaking a rule is not in itself a character flaw. The challenge is whether we can be honest about the error and accountable for it. Even though the stakes are smaller in the early years, the decision-making process is pretty much the same. As someone once wisely said: our thoughts become words, our words become actions, our actions become habits, and our habits determine our character. We must help our children focus on building good character early on.

In sports as in life, the question we put to children—and to ourselves and all other adults—should always be: What is the right thing to do? Not the expeditious thing, not the selfish thing, not the attention-getting thing, but simply *the right thing*.

I can still remember that night twenty-five years ago and the long walk from the stadium to the parking lot where I had left my rental car. I could hear the public announcement of the winner's name for the 100-meter backstroke, the race I had gone there to win. I felt bad about the race, but I felt better about myself for making the decision I did. The loss of one race could never have compared with the loss of my self-esteem, my abiding belief that I was an OK guy. After all, was it really all that important that I prove myself able to swim quickly while on my back? Wasn't the more noble pursuit the one where we all (volunteers and coaches, officials and parents) could take pride in our sport—and ourselves? Now that I'm a father, I have an even stronger realization of the positive impact of my decision. How could I ever insist on honesty and respect from my daughter if I had made a different decision when I was her age? How could I teach her that it is better to be honorable than to be honored?

I hope that I can impress upon all the kids I work with that sports, when they have high and consistent standards applicable to all participants, not only produce champions on the field of play but also produce champions in life.*

---

*Although John Naber was denied a spot on the 1973 World Championship Team for the 100-meter backstroke, he did qualify for the 200-meter backstroke, where he won a bronze medal in Belgrade, Yugoslavia. Three years later, at the Olympic Games in Montreal, in addition to setting four world records and earning four gold medals, Naber won one silver medal behind his teammate and friend Bruce Furniss, who set a world record with his own gold medal performance in the 200-meter freestyle.

THE REVEREND ROBERT H. SCHULLER is founder and pastor of the Crystal Cathedral in Garden Grove, California. With a worldwide audience of more than twenty million, his weekly Hour of Power televised services reach more people than any other religious programming. His theology centers on self-esteem and what he calls "possibility thinking." He has counseled presidents, written thirty-one religious and personal-improvement books (five of them best-sellers), and sits on the boards of a dozen organizations, including the Horatio Alger Association of Distinguished Americans, the national Y.M.C.A., the Highpoint Cancer Education Center, and the Salvation Army. He is a member of the Guild of Architects of the American Institute of Architects. He is also the founder of New Hope, a twenty-four-hour telephone suicide prevention and crisis counseling center that has handled more than 1,255,000 calls in thirty years.

# 6

# The Essential Qualities of a Good Person

## *The Reverend Robert H. Schuller*

F OR MORE THAN A QUARTER of a century, I have been writing, lecturing, and listening, trying to discover humanity's unifying need. That search has brought me to a profound sense of appreciation of character and the role it plays in the lives of individuals and societies.

I have also come to appreciate the close relationship between good character and high self-esteem. I have found that in all cultures, civilizations, and ethnic groups, healthy character and high regard for the self are the bread of life. Self-esteem provides a rich soil for the growth of good character, and good character provides a constant source of affirmation and pride that supports and sustains high self-esteem.

When I first began to develop what some have called the Theology of Self-Esteem, I commissioned the Gallup Organization to survey the effect of self-esteem on human behavior. According to the poll, when people with a strong sense of self-esteem are compared to those with lower self-esteem, they demonstrate the following qualities:

- They have high moral and ethical sensitivity.
- They have a strong sense of family.
- They are far more successful in interpersonal relationships.
- They view success in terms of interpersonal relationships, not only in materialistic terms.
- They are far more productive on the job.
- They suffer far less from chemical addiction.
- They are more likely to get involved in social and political activities in the community.
- They are far more generous to charitable institutions and to relief causes.

Isn't it striking how people with high self-esteem have attitudes and behaviors—moral and ethical sensitivity, family commitment, a relationship orientation, a nonmaterialistic outlook, productivity, involvement, and generosity—that mirror the qualities we associate with good character?

That shouldn't be surprising. People with self-esteem recognize the significance of their inherent worth, their value to themselves and others, their place in the world. Every person has unique significance, simply because the precious and mysterious gift of life as a human being has been given. This is an inherent value that neither adversity nor adversary can take away.

A true and meaningful appreciation of our own worth and importance, however, must also be linked to an understanding of our moral duty to use our talents and power unselfishly. Each individual's sense of innate worth is reinforced when that person's unique abilities are recognized, developed, and used to enrich our society. The more our abilities are developed for the benefit of ourselves and others, the fuller our lives and the richer our world.

Self-esteem is a matter of belief and attitude; character is evidenced in action. Healthy self-esteem fosters such essential qualities of character as responsibility, integrity, honesty, compassion, discipline, industriousness, reverence, perseverance, devotion, forgiveness, kindness, courage, gratitude, and grace. People who are accountable—accepting responsibility for their own actions and for the consequences of their own behavior—value their own worth as capable people of good character.

## Developing Character

There is no fully adequate substitute for a loving family. That is the environment in which people best learn to appreciate their own worth and build strong character. Character is nurtured in the family that loves and accepts the child, thus affirming his or her worth and importance in the context of broader social obligations.

Unfortunately, not all people have the good fortune to be raised in such settings. Some people have to find other sources and models of good character. Schools, youth organizations, churches, and even workplaces can be nurturing communities that help build a person's integrity, character, and self-esteem.

Character is formed under a canopy of grace, the divine love and protection bestowed on us by God. Grace touches our emerging character with compassion, gratitude, patience, humility, and hope. The touch of grace is found in people who turn community and work relationships into places of creativity, accountability, and delight. Life without grace is drab; in this life, issues of ethics and character seem controlling and negative. But life becomes Technicolor with the touch of grace, and issues of ethics and character become life filled instead of life controlling.

With God's loving grace, we can turn our scars into stars. Consider the story of June Scobee Rodgers. June is the widow of Dick Scobee, commander of the ill-fated *Challenger* shuttle, which exploded before the world's horrified eyes in January 1986. Along with

Dick, several other crew members died, including Christa McAuliffe, who was to be the first teacher in space. June felt tremendous guilt over Christa's death, for as a fellow educator she had advocated putting a teacher on the shuttle. But after prayer, June got creative; with the family of other crew members she founded the Challenger Centers for Space Science Education. To date, more than 1 million children have visited one of the thirty centers. "I have touched the future," June says. "I teach." Now, *that's* character.

In addition to being open to the healing, transforming power of grace, June was true to herself. This is a mark of integrity—another sure sign of character. Living with integrity means living up to our best selves, and that can mean forgoing life's temptations—ranging from self-pity and despair to dishonoring inconvenient agreements. Consider the story of my dear friend Ted Mann. Some years back Ted struck a deal to sell his highly successful chain of movie theaters. Then he received a call. "Have you signed contracts?" he was asked. "No." "Are lawyers involved yet?" "No." "Then I'll offer you $20 million more—cash." "Oh, no," said Ted. "I've given my word." Ted Mann: a person of character.

Do *you* wish to be person of character? Then you will also aspire to be

- Poised instead of tense
- Confident instead of confused
- Bold instead of timid
- Enthusiastic instead of bored
- Successful instead of failing
- Energetic instead of fatigued
- Agreeable instead of cantankerous
- Positive instead of negative
- Self-forgiving instead of self-condemning
- Self-respecting instead of self-disgusting

*Humans Need Love, Love Needs Faith.* At the core of every human soul is the need to be loved. Faith in God activates God's power within us. We can then begin to learn to love ourselves and others without fear.

Belief helps us to take on the hard questions and find answers. It opens up an exciting reality of possibilities and adventures with the certainty that life has meaning.

Jesus Christ puts a divine skin on the mysticism of religion. He helps us understand the impassioned heart. People of belief, who understand and enjoy God's love, manifest a changed love for self and others that transforms their own conscience. This in turn transforms their behavior. Born of security and grounded in love, this right behavior empowers them to meet a variety of individual and community needs more effectively.

When we believe in God and know we belong to the family of God, we develop the healing, helpful, divine awareness of the redemptive power of self-worth and self-love. The dignity of all persons and all creation becomes our most important concern.

Believing brings a love that provides inner certainty and security. This transformation irreversibly and divinely changes our deepest character; our lives come to reflect beauty, glory, honor, and dignity. When we experience the Christ within us, we can understand our innermost potential for good, and we will persevere in our God-given possibilities. God's acceptance and unconditional love infiltrates the hardest of hearts and can permanently rebuild the most broken of lives.

When we realize God's love for us and we believe, we want to live as God would have us live. We find we are not distracted and never destroyed by the evil that surrounds us. Believing inspires our involvement in God-inspired projects. Our life has real worth when we believe we have been redeemed and we know we are part of God's family. We are ready to dream the great divine dream of building the kingdom of God in the world.

Thus, through God's love, not only are we transformed as individuals, we become agents of change and pioneers for justice. We want to see a fair and equitable society, and we want to help others experience the power, love, and grace of God; not for our sakes but for theirs. We find ourselves wanting to challenge the paradigms and power structures of a secularized world. Authentic love motivates us to get involved.

***We're Not Perfect.*** Faith in God is a marvelous reflection of spiritual and emotional intelligence. The results of such faith are creativity, commitment, compassion, caring, and other qualities of a healthy character. All of these human forces become spiritual drives, maximizing the creative potential in each person.

Still, we don't get it right all the time. We miss the mark even when we believe. We don't live up to our own expectations of ourselves, let alone the expectations of others. We often behave selfishly and self-indulgently. Believing in the God who believes in us means accepting His gift of unconditional love, forgiveness, and a chance to start again.

God offers to save us from guilt, shame, insecurity, fear, and boredom. He brings a life of security, serenity, and stimulation. The character born of this salvation glorifies God, for it glorifies His children. It lifts them and the world from hostility, doubt, and fear to a life of creativity, love, and peace.

We are constantly changing; sometimes for the better, sometimes for the worse. People of good character will change as they feed their minds and their bodies healthy food. In addition:

- People of character move forward with confidence, believing that good things are possible.
- People of character are people of enthusiasm and constructive thinking.
- People of character look for new horizons to open.
- People of character will find much to achieve.
- People of character like themselves in a normal, healthy way and create a likeable life for themselves.

- People of character are dynamic and creative; they are always searching for truths that can be meaningful in their own lives and that they, in turn, can communicate with others.

- People of character believe that when they are confronted with a problem, they can find a solution.

*Self-Love and the Character of Jesus.* Humanity's search for purpose and meaning is the driving force for philosophers, thinkers, and pilgrims of every society. Through Jesus Christ, God gives us a clear picture of who He is, and offers us the power to choose the path we will take. This choice needs to be made not only with the cerebral intelligence but also with the emotional and spiritual intelligence of the person who seeks to be whole—*fully human, fully alive*—involved in a transforming process with the God who loves and empowers.

I believe that self-love is a vital force in human existence and in human character and that anyone who lacks love of self can never truly live in harmony with the world. People without self-love either cannot truly realize their dreams and goals or cannot enjoy their triumphs.

The self-love that produces character is not a selfish or narcissistic love but the creation and realization of true beliefs and confidence in oneself as a real person.

People of character are able to inspire and influence many people. They will have a strong belief that they must think and act in positive terms in order to realize their goals and ambitions.

People of character learn lessons that can be applied in their own lives and also in the lives of their families, friends, and associates.

Jesus treated every person as if he or she were a beautiful gem of infinite worth and irreplaceable value. Whether He was speaking to a harlot, a thief, a crooked politician, or a saint, Jesus treated that person as a beautiful human being. By the very nature of His character He influenced people to see the good person they *could become.*

He urges us to treat one another with respect and dignity. He taught a spiritual ethic: do unto others as you would have them do unto you.

In the intellectual and ethical milieu of the Western world, we locate the emotions in the heart and the intellect in the head. However, character is not only a matter of intelligence; it is the most important emotional choice each of us can make. As we choose to believe in God, we are transformed. Our source of power for life and for change is immediately elevated. We are better able to communicate and establish relationships with others because we no longer live in fear.

People of character will become their own best friends, carrying themselves cheerfully when the going gets rough. Hope, faith, love, optimism, and cheerfulness will rise within them. Others will naturally like them. Strength will grow in them, and success will follow.

## Character Is the Staff of Life

Character is formed as a result of the discipline, the daring, and the delights of life. In 1988, Sue Cobb took an opportunity to be the first woman from the United States to attempt to reach the top of Mount Everest. Fifty years old at the time, Sue had trained for two years for her three-month ordeal. She knew that 10 percent of those who attempt to master the mountain's 29,028 feet die. After spending eight weeks above 20,000 feet, she and her thirty-five-member team were finally forced to retreat by bad weather—only 3,000 feet from the top. A bitter disappointment, yes, but Sue came down the mountain realizing that life is not really about the destination, the peak. It's about the journey. Living fully, living with character, means taking advantage of every opportunity. It means using every talent in the best way you can. Reaching out. Meeting challenges. Not giving way to disappointments. Now *that's* character.

My advice to you who would be people of character is this: take charge. Take control. Leadership is the force that selects your dreams and sets your goals. It is the force that propels you to success. Never surrender leadership of your life—except to faith. Let faith be in control of every decision you make and every action you take. You do that when you let the positive possibilities set your goals.

Look at your life and ask yourself, "Who's in charge? Who's in control? To whom have I surrendered leadership?" Surrender leadership to God. Let Him be in control of your life. Ask Him three questions: "God, who am I? Why am I here? Where am I headed?"

At the very least His answers may surprise you. They will open your eyes to the beautiful person that you are and will become and to the fantastic future that awaits you.

**RABBI JOSEPH TELUSHKIN** is the author of several works on
Jewish religion and culture: *Jewish Literacy: The Most Impor-
tant Things to Know About the Jewish Religion, Its People
and Its History,* a Book-of-the-Month Club selection; *Jewish
Humor;* and *Words That Hurt, Words That Heal: Using Words
Wisely and Well,* a book that inspired two U.S. senators to
sponsor a Speak No Evil Day. He is coauthor (with Dennis
Prager) of the seminal *Nine Questions People Ask About
Judaism* and *Why the Jews? The Reason for Anti-Semitism.*
He has also written novels and a screenplay. A leading activist
in the cause of Soviet Jewry, he was the first foreign Jew to
meet with Jewish activists in Siberia (in 1973); he also met
with Andrey Sakharov and has been a guest of the Vatican.
Rabbi Telushkin serves as spiritual leader of the Synagogue for
the Performing Arts in Los Angeles.

# 7

# The Power of Words

## *Rabbi Joseph Telushkin*

CHILDREN ARE TAUGHT to respond to taunts with, "Sticks and stones can break my bones, but names can never hurt me." Adults should know better. Unless you have been the victim of terrible physical violence, there's a good chance that the worst pains you have suffered have come from words used cruelly: ego-destroying criticism, excessive anger, sarcasm, public humiliation, hurtful nicknames, betrayal of secrets, and malicious gossip. Throughout history, names and words have motivated people to pick up sticks and stones and knives and guns to murder others. The medieval Crusaders didn't get up one morning and begin randomly killing Jews. Rather, they and their ancestors had been conditioned for centuries to think of Jews as "Christ-killers" and thus less than human. Once this verbal characterization took hold, it was easy to kill them.

---

Words can have a profound impact on others. Some words hurt, others heal. So the choices we make about the things we say are matters of ethics and character.

## Recognizing the Power of Our Words

There are two aspects to character: knowing what is right and doing it.

People who act cruelly or dishonestly often know that what they are doing is wrong, but they choose to do it anyway, or they have lost the ability to stop themselves. When it comes to the ethics of speech, however, the matter is more complicated. In addition to having problems of self-control, many people have never systematically (or even superficially, for that matter) thought through the moral significance of the things they say.

One of the most powerful and also problematic uses of words is name calling, the use of derogatory terms for individuals and groups. I've often wondered how otherwise decent white people in the American South could have bought, sold, and enslaved African Americans. But notice how many derogatory terms existed in American society for black people. These terms probably were created to dehumanize them; by defining African Americans with words that made them seem less than human, whites were able to go on treating them as less than human. Without the special, ugly words for African Americans, the whole system of slavery might well have collapsed much earlier. Similarly, in the late 1960s, when members of the radical Black Panther Party started calling policemen "pigs," they did not do so in order to hurt policemen's feelings but rather to establish in people's minds that policemen were not human beings but animals. Ultimately, then, when a person murdered a policeman, he was not murdering a human being but an animal.

Words are used to injure individuals as well as groups, and the damage they inflict can be irrevocable. This is the problem of gossip. A nineteenth-century Hasidic folktale tells of a man who for months went about slandering the rabbi of his village. When the High Holy Days approached, the man realized the enormous evil he had committed and, overcome with remorse, sought out the rabbi, confessed what he had done, and begged for forgiveness. The rabbi told the man that he would forgive him on one condition: that he go back to his house, cut up a feather pillow, scatter the feathers to the wind, and then return to the rabbi. The man raced home, followed the rabbi's instructions, then returned to the rabbi's residence: "Am I forgiven now?" he asked.

"One more thing," the rabbi answered. "Now I want you to go out and gather up all the feathers."

"But that's impossible," the man responded. "They're all scattered."

"Precisely," the rabbi said. "And although you truly wish to correct the evil you have done, it is as impossible to repair the damage done by your words as it is to recover the feathers."

The stunning insight in this story is that words have consequences and that people must have the moral imagination and the strength of character to foresee these consequences before they use words irresponsibly.

Consider this example. In 1980, when Democrat Tom Turnispeed ran for Congress, his Republican opponent unearthed and publicized evidence that Turnispeed once had suffered an episode of depression for which he had received electric shock treatment. When Turnispeed responded to the information's release with an anguished attack on his opponent's campaign ethics, Lee Atwater (later famous as director of George Bush's 1988 presidential campaign, but then directing the Republican campaign in South Carolina) responded that he had no intention of answering charges made by a person "hooked up to jumper cables."

What a grotesque violation of privacy and how cruel a public humiliation of another human being! Atwater put into voters' heads a graphic and vicious image with the potential to poison voter's perceptions not only of Turnispeed but of everyone who has had electric shock therapy.

Ten years later, Atwater, stricken with an inoperable brain tumor, found himself attached to all sorts of unpleasant hospital machinery. During the last months of his life, he wrote Turnispeed a letter asking forgiveness. I am profoundly moved by this action but find it sad that Atwater seemed to grasp the full enormity of the cruelty he had committed only when he found himself in a similarly painful situation. This lack of moral imagination is common, and one from which many of us suffer. That is why a real measure of our strength of character is our willingness to systematically think through the implications of our words before we say them; otherwise we will, time and again, inflict great suffering on others.

Verbal abuse inflicts horrors in the lives of private as well as public figures. Roberta, a woman I know, recalls a recurring and humiliating trauma from her teenage years. As a young child she had been her mother's favorite. But when she became an adolescent and gained twenty pounds, her mother's expressions of love turned to withering verbal attacks. Once, when her aunt was visiting, Roberta brought some food to the kitchen table, and as she walked away, her mother said to her aunt in a loud voice, "Do you see how big her behind is, how fat she's become? Doesn't it look disgusting?" The mother repeated this sentiment many times, often in the presence of others. During her high school years, Roberta would wait until every other student had left the room when a class ended; she didn't want people to see her from the back. Although she's now over fifty and her mother has long been dead, her miserable physical self-image remains perhaps the largest part of the legacy her mother bequeathed her.

## Avoiding Gossip Even When It's True

People are hurt by words in two ways: by what people say *to* them and by what they say *about* them. Jewish law denotes saying unkind things about another with the term *lashon ha-ra* (literally, "evil tongue"). Jewish ethics' innovative insight is that *lashon ha-ra* is not libel or slander; by definition it refers to statements that are true. Truth might be a defense for a person accused in court of libel or slander, but it is no defense under Jewish law.

The fact that something is true does not mean that it is anybody else's concern. Thus Jewish law forbids, as *lashon ha-ra*, relating any information or statement that will lower another person's status. (An exception can be made only if you are speaking to a person who needs the information: for example, if someone is thinking of hiring someone whom you know to be lazy and unreliable, you should relate the relevant facts, but only to the prospective employer, not to anyone else. In the case of public officials it is permitted to relay information relevant to their ability to perform their jobs; thus the dredging up of private life scandals would normally not be regarded as relevant.)

The fact that this standard for speech is fair doesn't mean that it's easy to observe. The Talmud itself concedes that virtually everyone speaks unfairly of others at least once a day. But that doesn't mean we should drop this standard. Similarly, few people systematically fulfill the biblical injunction to "love your neighbor as yourself." But that doesn't mean we should ignore it. Our awareness that the Bible demands this standard from us goads us to be better than we otherwise would be.

Does Jewish law place too great an emphasis on avoiding speaking ill of others? Certainly many people think so, but my own rabbinical counseling experience repeatedly suggests that unfair speech is a major, not a minor, issue in people's lives. At the workshops I conduct on ethical speech, I often ask listeners, "How many of you can think of at least one incident in your life which would embarrass you if it became known to everyone else here?" Invariably almost all the hands go up—except for those who've led very boring lives, have poor memories, or are lying. "What's perverse about human nature," I add, "is that while we don't want others to know about this event in our lives, almost all of us are curious to learn about the events that the other people here are so anxious to conceal."

Why don't we want other people to know about our highly embarrassing episodes? The deep secrets we conceal generally don't involve criminal acts. But we all intuit that if other people knew about
these personal incidents, these *scandals* would forever define us (just
as electric shock therapy became people's leading association with
the candidate in the congressional race).

What's most interesting about other people is usually what's not
so nice about them or what's unusual or embarrassing (saints such
as Mother Teresa excepted). Thus, if we ask a group of people to
spend twenty minutes talking about someone they all know, how
likely is it that they will spend the entire time saying, "Oh, you know
that story that shows how nice she is? I know an even *more* flattering
story!" Similarly, if you and I are talking about someone we both
know, and I comment, "I love that guy. He's great; there's only one
thing I can't stand about him," what do you think we'll spend the
next fifteen minutes talking about?

Isaac Bashevis Singer, the great Yiddish writer and Nobel Prize
winner, used to say, "Even good people don't like to read novels
about good people." For this reason, Jewish law passionately urges
people to observe the laws forbidding *lashon ha-ra* and asks them
not to repeat opinions and incidents that unfairly lower another person's status. With their own doctrines and traditions, other world religions also forbid our treating other people in ways we ourselves
would not appreciate.

We all know the Golden Rule: do unto others as you would have
them do unto you. There's probably no area of life in which more of
us systematically violate this essential rule than the realm of gossip.
If you were about to enter a room and heard the people inside talking about you, you undoubtedly would least like to hear them discussing your character flaws and the intimate details of your social
life. Yet what do we talk about when we gossip about other people?
Their character flaws and the intimate details of their social life. People of good character, whatever their religion, know that talking un-
necessarily about another's supposed character flaws is itself a major
character flaw. So they don't.

# Trying a Twenty-Four-Hour Experiment

Can you go for twenty-four hours without saying anything unkind *about* or *to* anyone? I often challenge workshop audiences to try to do so.

Invariably some people laugh nervously. They're sure they can't go a whole day without at the very least making an unkind reference about another person. "Then you have a serious problem," I tell them. "Because if I were to ask you whether you can go for twenty-four hours without drinking any alcohol and you said that you can't, that means that you're an alcoholic. And if you can't go for twenty-four hours without smoking a cigarette, that means you're addicted to nicotine. And if you can't go for twenty-four hours without speaking unkindly about or to another, that means you've lost control over your mouth. Regaining control will require vigilance. But such vigilance also will bring great blessings into the lives of those with whom you live."

If you are willing to carry out this experiment, check your watch. Resolve that until this time tomorrow, you won't say anything negative about another person. (The only exception will be the very rare instance where it's *necessary* to transmit such information: for example, you learn that a friend of yours is about to date a man who beat his ex-wife.)

Throughout the day, in relating to others you will constantly monitor how you speak, and you will keep your anger and judgmentalism under control. If you need to criticize, you will restrict your criticism to the incident that provoked your ire and not engage in a generalized attack on the person who angered you. If you enter into an argument, you will argue fairly, without allowing your disagreement to degenerate into name calling or other forms of verbal abuse. Throughout the day, you will not disseminate negative rumors. You will refrain from defaming groups as well as individuals.

In other words, for a full twenty-four hours you will follow the Golden Rule, speaking *about* and *to* others with the same kindness and fairness that you wish them to exercise when speaking about and to you. You will act as a person of good character, focused on helping people with your deeds and healing them with your words. At the least, you will not hurt people with your words.

A rabbi once told me this favorite expression of his grandmother: "It's not within everyone's power to be beautiful, but all of us can make sure that the words that come out of our mouths are." And Rabbi Harold Kushner has written, "Only God can give us credit for the angry words we do not speak."

I wish you twenty-four hours of beautiful, healing speech.

# part two

# CHARACTER ROLE MODELS

DAN RATHER is anchor and managing editor of the *CBS Evening News* and *48 Hours*. In a career spanning almost half a century, he has narrated defining moments ranging from the assassination of President Kennedy to the death of the Soviet empire. His books include *The Camera Never Blinks, The Camera Never Blinks Twice, I Remember,* and *The Palace Guard.* His most recent book is an abridgment of Mark Sullivan's *Our Times: America at the Dawn of the Twentieth Century.* An outspoken advocate for accurate news reporting, he has received every major honor in broadcast journalism, including numerous Emmy Awards, the Peabody Award, and citations from critical, scholarly, professional, and charitable organizations. His alma mater, Sam Houston State University, has named its journalism and communications building after him. He also writes a weekly newspaper column and contributes to CBS News Radio.

*8*

# Some Personal Favorites

*Dan Rather*

CHARACTER IS A WORD we use without thinking, a word like a color that defies definition: failing to find the words we need, we rely on repetition ("blue is blue") or negation ("blue is not yellow").

Thus I can tell you that character is character and that character is not yellow.

But, just as we know blue when we see it, we know character.

Character has much to do with reputation, but character and reputation are not the same thing. We may know ourselves to have truly terrible characters but be hailed by our communities as good. I feel confident that it's better to know your own character to be

---

*Note:* © 1998 Dan Rather.

good and to be reputed as a bad character by others than the other way around. (But I wouldn't tell you on which side of that formula lies my own experience.)

Character has much to do with conscience, the faculty that tells us right from wrong. But character and conscience are not the same thing. Character is what we have after we listen to our consciences. If we ignore our consciences, we are considered to have a bad character. If we heed our consciences, we are considered to have a good character. Our character can be improved—and the best experts agree on this point, thankfully.

## A Portrait of Complex Character

Ancient philosophers used to wrestle with moral issues by considering the careers of kings. For my part I've learned a great deal about character from a lifelong study of the career of Sam Houston.

Houston was what we call ornery, which is to say belligerent, stubborn, and egocentric. Although he got along pretty well with the Cherokee Nation, he was prejudiced toward many others. Chemical dependencies and amatory pursuits frequently brought him down. Yet he managed to overcome his flaws long enough to lead: he was governor and congressman from *two* states (Tennessee and Texas), ambassador and chief of the Cherokee Nation, general of the rebel Texas army, and first president of the Republic of Texas. He might have been president of the United States.

At the end of his life, he pleaded with his fellow Texans to stand fast while Southern states all around were seceding from the Union. He was voted down, humiliated, but he held to the belief that joining the Confederacy was a mistake. How, I have often wondered, when his character was so often lacking, did he manage to stick up for a principle that was so right? Sam Houston made so many bad bargains with his conscience, committed so many specific acts that were not moral or ethical according to anybody's philosophy, that you could hardly conclude Houston's character was fundamentally *good.*

What's most impressive about Houston is that, while his flaws were of epic proportions, so were his accomplishments. That's a balance few ever strike. Many people are possessed of characters less flawed than Sam Houston's; their actions are generally less violent, debauched, or cruel; and yet they've never touched the heights of leadership. They've often enough made smaller-scale moral compromises; they have not approached even a fraction of Houston's stature. A more profound or tricky thinker than I, such as Machiavelli, might posit a discrepancy between good character and good leadership or say that good character is irrelevant to good leadership—and yet in my shallowness I can't believe that's true. (At the very least, accepting that supposition would let too many would-be leaders off the hook, excusing too much of their bad behavior and denying any reason for them even to try to improve.) I insist that Houston would have been an even better leader if he'd possessed a better character. Yet I can't explain how he managed as well as he did. The question becomes a tangle, and I extricate myself from it clumsily, leaving the question for wiser heads than mine.

## Portraits of Good Character

I am a reporter, not a moralist. I've shared a conundrum of character with you to illustrate that character is rarely simple and can be disturbingly complex. I prefer, however, to show you good character, and I've been lucky enough to know some people with plenty of extraordinarily good character. Here are three portraits from which you may be able to draw your own conclusions.

*Integrity.* First, there's my wife, Jean, whose ability to keep our family together despite the wandering path of my working life rivals that of any pioneer heroine and whose love for me in spite of all my faults is everyday proof that she's a better person than I am. *I could never love anyone as I am; I can only thank heaven that *she* can love me.

Jean is an artist, so it's not only love that commands Jean's character; art also guides her, and she in turn serves her art. History is replete with examples of painters whose devotion to their art was so great that it overwhelmed their characters, but in Jean's case, art serves her character—and becomes a manifestation of her good character. Over the years of our life together, I have marveled at her ability to see, and to make others see, through her art. She is disciplined; she makes time for art. In an ostensibly free moment, when a lazy goof such as your narrator might be watching a ball game, Jean uses her time to sketch, to paint, to study. The demands of motherhood, which might likewise have been a distraction, instead only nourished Jean's art. Motherhood called forth a tenderness and a passion from the hand that holds the brush just as motherhood has called forth those same emotions from the hand that stills the fear or cools the fever. Jeannie doesn't paint because she expects praise or reward; she paints because she must paint. But that necessity doesn't inhibit her kindness, her courage, her generosity, her fiercely burning integrity: all those things are a part of her art, a part of her character, symbiotic and inseparable.

We live in an age of relativism, when it is no longer chic, and only barely acceptable, to say, "Great art does not justify bad behavior." We sometimes seem to hear a better music in the rock star who trashes his hotel room, and we find a poetic romance in the musician who is too stoned to perform; we too often disdain the singer who loves his family and says "please" and "thank you." Yet I suspect there may be fewer useful truths to be gleaned from the work of artists of bad character and more to be learned from the artists who are good both in their work and in their characters. I know I have learned from my Jeannie.

*Sacrifice for Others.* My parents struggled and sacrificed to get all three of their children a college education. My brother and sister and I were the first Rathers (except for one expeditionary aunt) to get within the same zip code as any institution of higher learning. In those days a college education was not the automatic expectation of every boy and girl in America, as predictable an accessory as a belly button. A college education was expensive, and very few people could afford to get one. My parents worked with their backs and their hands and their hearts, and I suppose that if they'd ever confessed their dream of sending their children to college, their listeners might have burst out laughing. It wasn't a realistic dream in that time and place; even if I'd been as good a student as my brother and sister, there was still the question of where we'd get the money. My father worked for the oil pipeline; we lost count of all the jobs my mother held outside the home, from dressmaking to waiting tables. It wouldn't have been unusual if they'd channeled most of their efforts (and the small income derived therefrom) toward their own present and future comforts. Instead, they worked toward the goal of securing *our* futures, giving us the tools we would need to improve ourselves and our lives.

My brother and sister actually put their educations to good use, becoming teachers themselves and thus improving the lives of other young people, in a line—no, a root system, as I like to see it—that begins with my mother and father and extends to the farthest reaches of humanity's future.

***Excellence and Stamina.*** I'd be kidding myself to think that I'd ever had such an effect on anyone through my work. Yet we in journalism aren't the moral reprobates we're sometimes supposed to be. We do care about good character, our own and other people's. Some few reporters have actually possessed good characters too. In my professional life, I've had the good fortune to know a few such people. The most impressive of these may have been Douglas Edwards.

Douglas Edwards was the first anchor of the *CBS Evening News* on television and thus the first network television news anchor

anywhere. Along with his colleagues Edward R. Murrow, Eric Se-
vareid, and Charles Collingwood, Doug held a lofty position in my
pantheon of journalistic heroes long before I ever came to work at
CBS. He was a pioneer, a radio reporter who'd had serious doubts
about working in television but was determined to make the best of
it. Many of the hallmarks of modern electronic journalism—going
beyond the headlines, digging deep, getting out of the studio, taking
people to the stories and helping them to understand, fighting to
maintain the highest standards of integrity and excellence—Doug
Edwards brought to the *CBS Evening News.*

In 1962, Doug found himself on the losing front of two battles:
one with the bottle and one with the network brass. Doug faced up
to both. He sought treatment for alcoholism, and triumphed. And
he went to the bosses and said, "OK, so you don't want me to anchor the *Evening News*—what *do* you want me to do?"

It takes courage to say such a thing. It also takes a lack of ego-
tism, for which network anchors, even the prototypes, are not usually known.

Doug stuck to his guns. The bosses gave him another anchoring
job. He became one of the best-loved members of the CBS News
team. By the end of his career, April 1, 1988, he was anchoring a
late-morning program called *Newsbreak,* just a roundup of the headlines, perhaps no big deal until you look at the record. He had been
a network television news anchor for forty years, the longest anybody had ever held such a title (a decade later, David Brinkley probably met or broke that record, but nobody else is ever likely to, even
in this era of youth-ism.)

Nothing grand or glorious about it. Just one guy who worked
hard, for a long time, and in spite of some pretty tough obstacles.
*That's* character.

At Doug's farewell party, you wanted to congratulate him, not
only on his work but on his character—*mostly* on his character. But
you sensed he'd find it awkward, that your admiration was not a
burden he wanted or would accept because it was not what he'd ever

sought. So you praised his work instead, and wished him well when he left anchoring for the first and last time, and wondered whether you'd ever do as well—not as an anchor, but as a person.

## Improvements in Our Own Character

In spite of the reassurance from philosophers that we can improve our characters, I sometimes wonder whether they meant to include my character. My conscience tells me to find the integrity of my wife, the self-sacrifice of my parents, the dedication of my colleague Doug Edwards. And yet too often I don't heed my conscience; or else, in searching for those good qualities, I come up short.

I could despair, I could throw myself on the mercy of my loved ones and my God. But really there's nothing to do—except to keep trying.

SENATOR MAX CLELAND is a Democrat from the state of Georgia. He went from being named outstanding senior in high school to Emory University to Vietnam, where he lost three limbs but not his purpose. Recipient of the Bronze Star for Meritorious Service and the Silver Star for Gallantry in Action, Cleland returned to Georgia, where he was elected to the state senate at the age of twenty-eight (that body's youngest member) and wrote the law making public facilities accessible to the handicapped. Later he became the first Vietnam veteran, and the youngest person ever, to head the Veterans Administration, and then Georgia's youngest-ever secretary of state. In 1996, he was elected to the U.S. Senate. "He is an authentic American hero," columnist David Broder has written, "an inspiration to people everywhere; a living, breathing testament to the power of the human spirit."

# 9

# Strong at the Broken Places

*Senator Max Cleland*

T HE HISTORIAN PLUTARCH termed it a "longstanding habit." Another ancient philosopher called it "perfectly educated will." And Goethe said it means simply, "In great and little things, carrying through what you feel able to do."

They all are talking about character, one of the great preoccupations of sages and educators—and all those concerned with the *real* quality of life. However it is described, character is an essential building block in each youngster's growth to become a responsible, moral adult. I believe it is critical to bring to the attention of our youth the importance of character building and the teachings of morality and citizenship.

An individual develops character by overcoming obstacles and temptations. The temptations can be as mundane as choosing laziness over diligence. The obstacles can be profound—something I know quite a bit about myself. After I was wounded in Vietnam and lost three of my limbs, recovery proved a difficult time for me. How could I face coming back home after what had happened to me? In time, I would see the wisdom of Ralph Waldo Emerson, who said, "What lies behind us and what lies before us are tiny matters compared to what lies within us."

## Vietnam

I left my hometown of Lithonia, Georgia, a strong young man heading to a foreign land to fight for my country. Vietnam—another world, unlike anything I had ever seen before. I remember standing on the edge of the bomb crater that had been my home for five days and five nights, stretching my six-foot, two-inch frame, and becoming caught up in excitement. The battle for Khe Sanh was over, and I had come out of it unhurt and alive! Five terrible days and nights were behind us. In spite of dire predictions, we had held Khe Sanh. I had scored a personal victory over myself and my fears. I had become a soldier and could really look the old sarge in the face. As Stephen Crane put it in his great book on war, *The Red Badge of Courage,* "I went to face the Great Death and found it was only the Great Death." My tour of duty in Vietnam was almost over. In another month I'd be going home. I smiled, thinking of the good times waiting stateside.

On April 8, 1968, I volunteered for one last mission. The helicopter moved in low. The troops jumped out with M16 rifles in hand as we crouched low to the ground to avoid the helicopter blades. Then I saw the grenade. It was where the chopper had lifted off. It must be mine, I thought. Grenades had fallen off my web gear before. Shifting the M16 to my left hand and holding it behind me, I bent down to pick up the grenade.

A blinding explosion threw me backwards.

# Recovery

In the early days of my recovery, my emotions were on a roller coaster. Within the same minute I could be exhilarated and depressed. Laughter and tears often welled up in me during the same sentence. What a hand to be dealt at the age of twenty-five! The only amputee I knew of was the town drunk back in Lithonia, whose life pretty much consisted of holding up the lamppost on the street corner. All I knew was I did not want to end up like that. I knew there must be bigger things out there for me, and eventually, I knew, I had to take the adversity I was facing and turn it into something positive. Life is how you find it—and what you make of it. One of the nation's great first ladies, Eleanor Roosevelt, once said, "You gain strength, courage and confidence by every experience in which you really stop to look fear in the face. . . . You must do the thing which you think you cannot do."

In search of purpose in *my* life, I turned to public service. I would express myself by helping others. Through it all, I would have as my constant support the inspirational thoughts and powerful examples of others. These have shaped my public service career—my life's work—just as surely as they have shaped my self-regard and regard for the world—my character. I like to think I successfully turned my "scars into stars," as my friend Robert Schuller says.

I believe Ernest Hemingway best describes my philosophy then and now: "The world breaks everyone and afterward many are strong at the broken places." I was fortunate enough to be able to take my physical and emotional scars and turn them into purpose in my life, my stars. Today, my public service is my purpose, and my strength. And now I feel I am strong at the broken places.

I am approached every day by people who identify with me because of adversity they have faced in their own lives. Perhaps they or a child served in Vietnam; perhaps they have lost a family member or close friend; perhaps they have gone through a divorce or are struggling to make ends meet financially. Perhaps, like me, they are wheelchair-bound and up against life's many staircases and six-inch curbs. They feel pain. I understand that.

What can I tell them? Henry Ford said, "Believe in your best, think your best, study your best, have a goal for your best, never be satisfied with less than your best, try your best—and in the long run, things will work out for the best." That works for me.

## Sources of Inspiration

When I first decided that public service was my calling, I spoke with my good friend and political mentor, Jim Mackay. I was involved in his campaign for Congress in 1964 and had followed him to Washington as his intern. He was a great help to my parents after they learned of my injuries in Vietnam. He too had suffered a loss as a result of this war: his daughter's fiancé was killed in the Tet offensive in 1968. I have the greatest admiration for Jim. He was an incredible role model and inspiration for me, and he has helped me and my family through some very rough patches.

Jim knew about winning and losing, and I knew he would give me insight on running for the Georgia state senate in 1970. I wanted to run a campaign that would ultimately end with a great victory but, more important, one that would make him proud. "I've got to tell you this," he said when I sought his advice, "Running for public office is like combat—you can get shot." (Winston Churchill was of the same mind, once remarking that "in war you can only be killed once, but in politics many times." How true!)

"It must be borne in mind that the tragedy in life doesn't lie in not reaching your goal—the tragedy lies in having no goal to reach," said Benjamin Mays, the great educator. Through his leadership example, advice, and guidance—and sometimes a friendly word of caution—Jim has influenced me greatly. By his wise and compassionate counsel as well as by his example, he is someone who shaped my definition of good character.

Another person that I have a tremendous admiration for is Franklin Delano Roosevelt: not just the president but the *whole man.* Our dedication to public service binds the two of us, but my tie to this great man goes much deeper. FDR spent time in Warm Springs, Georgia, rehabilitating his legs and was so impressed with the facility that he built and established the Georgia Warm Springs Foundation. We both began our political careers as state senators (oh, yes, I *did* win that race in 1970). And on a lighter note, the hand controls on my car were installed by the same Warm Springs brake shop that installed hand controls on Roosevelt's 1940 convertible (a gift from Henry Ford). Every time I visit Warm Springs, I sense the presence of Roosevelt—the character, the personality, *the man.*

The polio had weakened his legs but not his spirit. Roosevelt refused to think of himself as disabled. He vowed to find a way to build up his strength and carry on. He has inspired many, including myself, to continue with that spirit today in our mission to empower individuals with disabilities to achieve personal independence. Most important, he continues to inspire our dreams. Some of the landmark domestic programs that helped lead this country out of the Great Depression came from ideas developed in Warm Springs, including the Rural Electrification Administration, which brought electric power at affordable rates into rural homes across the country.

FDR also developed the Civilian Conservation Corps (CCC), which created employment and job training for a Depression-weary generation of young men, including my father. The CCC was instrumental in protecting and improving public lands. One of the most important fundraising campaigns in America, the March of Dimes, evolved from President Roosevelt's Birthday Balls, events established to raise funds for the Georgia Warm Springs Foundation, polio research, and aid for polio patients. His death in 1945 left the nation in mourning, especially in Georgia, where the people embraced him as one of their own.

To me, the wheelchair now depicted at the new FDR memorial in Washington, D.C., is a testament to FDR's ability to transcend disability and infirmity to become the leader of the free world. That is why I fought for a statue of FDR actually seated in his wheelchair. It adds a human dimension—beyond the world statesman, beyond the politician, beyond the Democratic Party leader, beyond the great speechmaker. It adds a personal dimension of triumph over adversity and disability. Far from a sign of weakness, it tells people precisely what helped make FDR a great example of character.

Aldous Huxley once said that "experience is not what happens to a man. It's what a man does with what happens to him." What happens to us in our lives and how we face each challenge is what builds our character. And the way we learn how to face our challenges and to turn our scars into stars is by learning from example.

Being a member of the U.S. Senate has truly been a dream come true for me. If it were not for my parents, friends, role models, and heroes, I would not be where I am today. I would not have had the motivation to pick up the pieces after Vietnam, dodge the bullets fired in a political race, and go for my dream. And I would not be able to face the challenges I face now in the U.S. Senate. General George S. Patton Jr. was right! "Success is how high you bounce after you hit bottom."

## Character: Now More Than Ever

A Times Mirror poll last year showed that American voters place a far greater importance on electing political leaders with strong character—ethical standards, compassion for the average citizen, and good judgment—than they did twenty years ago. I feel that this yearning that Americans have for leaders with strong character is the result of a general loss of faith, not only faith in our political system but faith in American society as a whole.

How many times have we heard that our children are "the future of our country"? How seriously do we take that? We must ensure that the youngsters of this country and all other countries start out on the right foot and that these children have the right values and beliefs instilled in them from the beginning. We must strengthen our schools and communities, fostering a stronger environment for learning for our nation's youth. We must teach our children to set high goals for their lives, to raise the bar even higher than before. And importantly, we must allow our children to dream.

During my first year in the U.S. Senate, I was an original cosponsor of the bill designating a National CHARACTER COUNTS! Week. The bill states: "Young people will be the stewards of our communities, nation and world in critical times, and the present and future well-being of our society requires an involved, caring citizenry with good character. . . . Although character development is, first and foremost, an obligation of families, the efforts of faith communities, schools, and youth, civic and human service organizations also play a very important role in supporting family efforts by fostering and promoting good character."

After defining the core elements of character as trustworthiness, respect, responsibility, fairness, caring, and citizenship—elements that transcend cultural, religious, and socioeconomic differences—the bill continues: "The character and conduct of our youth reflect the character and conduct of society; therefore, every adult has the responsibility to teach and model the core ethical values and every social institution has the responsibility to promote the development of good character." I believe this with every fiber of my being.

George Matthew Adams once said, "There is no such thing as a 'self-made' man. We are made up of thousands of others. Everyone who has ever done a kind deed for us, or spoken one word of encouragement to us, has entered into the make-up of our character and of our thoughts, as well as our success." This truth is why we must all work hard to instill character, values, and morality in our youngsters. In doing so, we can successfully restore faith in individuals and ultimately in our country. And we can build up ourselves.

MARIANNE WILLIAMSON is the spiritual leader at the Church of Today in Warren, Michigan, and an internationally acclaimed lecturer and author. Three of her books—*A Return to Love, A Woman's Worth,* and *Illuminata*—achieved number one best-seller status on the *New York Times* list; her newest book is *The Healing of America.* In addition, she is the author of a book for children, *Emma and Mommy Talk to God.* A hugely popular professional lecturer since 1983, she has also performed extensive charity work nationwide on behalf of critically ill people.

*10*

# A Father of Solid Oak

*Marianne Williamson*

WHEN I THINK about character, I think about my father. My father *was* a character. That's what was often said about him: "That Sam Williamson—what a character." The only thing more outrageous than his enormous personality was his profound compassion and his courage to express it.

Sam Williamson was one of those people about whom we hear it said, "They just don't make 'em like that anymore." My father was like an old oak tree: he had seen so much and weathered so much that every plane of his being was like a testament to the triumph of time.

His character, though, did not stem from what he had been through so much as from what he chose to *do* with what he had been through. My father had suffered deeply in his life, having experienced poverty, violence, and all manner of hardship. What made him a man of character was that he had taken these things into his heart, where they had alchemized into something beautiful: a genuinely noble person. My father had seen the meaninglessness of the world, and it made him commit to meaning. My father had seen the chaos of the world, and it led him to a lifelong search for some higher order. My father had seen the heartlessness of the world, and his broken heart then became a vessel for a huge and committed universal love. His hatred of injustice, his willingness to fight for the right as he perceived it, his love for those crushed beneath the weight of unfair dominion, his awesome sense of right and wrong, his unbelievable bravery in stating his convictions without fear of ridicule or rejection—this was the stuff of his character.

My father grew up in poverty in a Russian immigrant family in an immigrant community in Illinois. When he was still a young boy, his parents and their immigrant friends would come to him for help in filling out this or that form or dealing with this or that problem in the English which only he could speak and write. Early in his life he was helping people in a way that only he could do, the anxiety and gratitude of the beneficiaries of his kindness weighing upon him then and inspiring him forever. The immigrant was to my father a most sacred responsibility of American society, the personification of the search for the American dream. He took very seriously the notion that this was a land where people could come, having fled the most vicious tortures of body and soul, to find freedom and dignity and opportunity and hope. This was not theory or abstraction to my father: it was a reality he saw reflected in the eyes of thousands of men and women and children who graced his path, as he graced theirs, for decades. He saw the pain in people's pasts, their hopes for their futures, and their desperate fears of being deported. In adulthood he became an immigration lawyer, that he might continue and expand his efforts to give aid and succor to the immigrant. From his reading and writing while still in the third grade—"Sam, what does this say?" "Sam, will you write my name for me?"—to his death at the age of eighty-five, my father lived his life in service to the strangers among us.

No immigrant will ever have a more passionate, creative champion. My father had a prophet's sense of moral outrage at the forces, whether here or abroad, that would deny people their God-given rights to opportunity and freedom. He instilled in each of his children that same sense of outrage, born not of anger but of love, and that same gut-level determination to do whatever we could to make our corner of the world somehow more fair, more just, more tender.

There are, fortunately for my father's children and grandchildren, many written examples of his spirit.

To the Honorable Immigration Judge:

I saw it with my own eyes, from my hotel balcony in Darjeeling, India, some years ago. This obviously high-class Indian woman with a manservant at her side holding a box of coins. They are walking down the hotel driveway, beggars all lined up alongside the pavement, and the servant hands each a coin, one or more. At the very end of the line of beggars lay a quadruple amputee, whom I had seen daily while staying at the hotel. He begged with his eyes alone, and one didn't know where to put a proffered coin. I saw this high-class Indian woman step over this quadruple amputee like he wasn't there.

The Government's opposition to our Motion to Reopen recalled this incident to me.

RESPECTFULLY SUBMITTED,
SAM WILLIAMSON

To Each Member of Congress:

Some of the laws which have recently issued from Congress are wrong, in that your counseling has been, at least in part, a con-job by a FAIR-disposed INS Commissioner.*

We were taught, years before any of us went to law school, never to humiliate a person, never to press a person's back to the wall, never to vex the stranger among us. In IRCA we have done all these, so that now we

---

*INS, Immigration and Naturalization Service; FAIR; IRCA, Immigration Reform and Control Act.

bear the shame of denying authorization to gainful employment to those whom INS despite their deport-ability, suffers or permits to reside among us, directly producing profound trauma among a large percentage of our people, both sufferers and onlookers, which you must agree ought not to be part of our national experience.

*SAM WILLIAMSON*

My father could not be bought. His life was simply not driven by external things. It was driven by values and principles and deeply held convictions. He was wrong at times and stubborn at times, but every day of my life I have a greater understanding of the rock on which he stood. That rock was neither money nor ambition nor pride. It was an almost spiritual fervor for the idea that the world could be better, and a most tenacious refusal to abandon those most vulnerable to the evils of the world.

Most people I know—myself included—have not known poverty, as my father did. We have not seen its ravages firsthand, as my father did. We have not fought in a righteous war, as my father did. And as a consequence we are not giants, as my father was. But perhaps we are simply not giants *yet.* Perhaps the fact that we are reading and writing books like this, that we are looking at these issues, that we so feel something missing in ourselves and in our culture, means that something deep inside us is yearning to be more.

It's not as though there are no longer sufferers among us. They are all around us. We need courage in American culture today, not only to help those less fortunate than we but also to stand up to the political tides of obfuscation that would have us either deny the existence of the sufferer or the meaning of his suffering.

I didn't have my father's hardships to teach me, but I had my father's example. We have to find our own ways to inner peace and strength and character; they cannot be bequeathed to us by those who came before. The issue isn't ultimately whether others stood up for what they believed. How often our parents' efforts to shield us from the pain they knew delay or even obstruct our journey toward our own character. Even though people before us have developed character, now each of us must develop his or her own.

We all know what character is, not because we can define it exactly but because we know when we have seen it. We know when we have exercised character; at those times we feel clean. And we know when we compromised character; at those times we feel dirty. Character is a glue that holds this world together; without it there is no counter to the forces of chaos and disruption. It is our beacon of light in a darkened world.

My father's eyes will always be a beacon for me. I see them in my mind's eye, and I always will. They are still full of fire and laughter and love. He was crusty at times and could be as ornery as he was entertaining and inspiring. But the lesser things have faded away, while his character never will. It remains in the universe, and I hope that in some mysterious way it remains a part of me.

Susan Estrich is the Robert Kingsley Professor of Law and Political Science at the University of Southern California Law School, where she focuses on criminal law, gender discrimination, and politics. She is a syndicated columnist, political television commentator, and contributing editor to the *Los Angeles Times* Opinion section. A former radio talk show host and columnist for *USA Today*, she was a senior policy adviser for the Mondale-Ferraro campaign in 1984 and national campaign manager for Michael Dukakis in 1988. Her numerous books include *Making the Case for Yourself: A Diet Book for Smart Women*; *Getting Away With Murder: How Politics Is Destroying the Criminal Justice System*; *Real Rape*; and *Dangerous Offenders*. She serves or has served on the boards of the Center for Early Education, the Virginia Women's Leadership Institute, Planned Parenthood, and Common Cause.

# 11

# A Modest Giant Who Changed the World

*Susan Estrich*

H E WAS THE MOST MODEST giant I have ever met, a slight man who believed in justice, drove a Pinto, and changed the world. You want to know about character? Let me tell you about J. Skelly Wright, a great judge because he was a great man. Integrity, fairness, and courage marked his whole career.

He was a Catholic boy from New Orleans who went to law school at night while teaching high school. And then, as he once told me, he crossed a line and never turned back. Four years before *Brown* v. *Board of Education* (the U.S. Supreme Court case that mandated forced integration of schools), he ordered the integration of the Louisiana State University Law School. It was not what people expected from the local boy who was at the time the youngest federal judge in America. Before the doctrine of separate but equal was declared by the Supreme Court to be inherently unequal, he integrated the bus system in New Orleans. Then he integrated the first grade.

Last year the Walt Disney Company made a television movie about the first black girl to attend a white elementary school in New Orleans, the teacher who befriended her, and the professor who counseled her. Heroes all, certainly, but none would have been there were it not for the courage of Judge Wright, who declared forty separate state statutes unconstitutional while the crosses burned on his front lawn. "We are, all of us, freeborn Americans, with a right to make our way, unfettered by sanctions imposed by man because of the work of God," he said. He entered injunctions against Louisiana's governor, state legislators, and attorney general as well as against the New Orleans school board and the superintendent of schools. His rulings were appealed to the U.S. Supreme Court eleven times; U.S. marshals at times guarded his family twenty-four hours a day. "Let me speak to that dirty nigger-loving Communist," a caller from the White Citizens Council once demanded of Wright's thirteen-year-old son, Jim, in the midst of the battle. "He's not at home," Jim told him.

But he was there for those who needed him. "I guess I am an activist, but I want to do what's right," he said, as captured in a tribute issue of the *George Washington University Law Review*. "When I get a case . . . the first thing I think of automatically is what's right, what should be done—and then you look at the law to see whether or not you can do it. That might invert the process of how you should arrive at a decision, of whether you should look at the law first, but with me it developed through making decisions, which involves resolving problems. And I am less patient than other judges with law that won't permit what I conceive to be fair."

That's not exactly how they taught us to do it in law school. We learned about the legal process—about applying precedent, writing footnotes, and following the logic of the law—and about the tricks of the trade that allow political judgments to command respect under the rule of law.

"Now there's a legitimate criticism of [my approach]," Judge Wright acknowledged, "because what's fair and just to X may not be fair and just to Y—in perfect good faith on both sides. But if you don't take it to extremes, I think that it's good to come out with a fair and just result." As a person of good character, Judge Wright was typically focused not just on what a person had the right to do (the law) but on what was right to do (morality and ethics). He focused on the good. For instance, he would have never declared separate to be equal, regardless of legal precedent. He believed contracts could be so one-sided that courts should not enforce them, a radical notion at the time he first articulated it. He also stated, in the court of appeals, that freedom of the press protected the publication of the Pentagon Papers.

What gave him the right to decide such things? In an era of moral relativism, Judge Wright understood that the legal process was a mode of judging, not a substitute for judging. Long before the critical legal studies crowd deconstructed judicial decision making to lay bare, as their realist predecessors had before them, the inevitability of value judgments even in the supposedly neutral application of precedent, Judge Wright understood that there was no escaping the mandate to judge and that the fact that political judgments must be made along a "slippery slope" doesn't eliminate the need to make them. The relativity of moral judgments does not rend them all equivalent.

That isn't to say that judges, even self-described activists like Judge Wright, operate without constraints. They must, first of all, win the support of their colleagues. After leaving Louisiana, Judge Wright served on the U.S. Court of Appeals of the District of Columbia between 1962 and his death in 1988. (He would have gone further, but certain Southern senators made it clear that they would block him from the Fifth Circuit, the appeals court reviewing the implementation of *Brown* v. *Board of Education* in the South, and from the U.S. Supreme Court, where he truly belonged.) Decisions in appeals court cases are usually made by panels of three judges (drawn from the nine judges who make up the court), although in the most important cases they are made by the court as a whole. Like most great judges, Judge Wright was one part politician, with a crafty ability to get things done. Competence, too, is a measure of character.

His strategic skills were awesomely demonstrated in the way he handled an appeals court case that came before him while I was serving as his clerk (a recent graduate of law school assigned to do research and draft opinions). The case involved review of a judicially imposed requirement that the testimony of an alleged rape victim be corroborated by independent evidence. It was the first and only time I ever wrote a bench memo to Judge Wright, and it was a doozie. I remember the facts clearly twenty years later. The defendant had been found guilty of rape, based on the testimony of the alleged victim. The jury had believed the victim's story that the defendant had attacked her as she was leaving a beauty parlor and getting into her car and that he had forced her to drive into the woods and have sex on the ground. On appeal he was claiming that she had consented and that her testimony was insufficient to support the conviction because there was no corroborating witness, nothing but the twigs in her newly coiffed hair to support her account.

I had very strong feelings about this case for logical and personal reasons: three years earlier I had been raped by a man who caught me getting into my car. I wrote about my story for the first time in my memo to Judge Wright. A woman had a right to tell her story and have it believed by a jury, I argued, just as I should have had if the man who had attacked me had been found. Besides, I demanded in my memo, what woman has sex on the ground with a perfect stranger after having her hair done?

Moved by the logic and emotion of my memo, Judge Wright focused his attention on overturning the corroboration precedent of the law. "We'll do it," he told me, and then he told me how. It would require skill and diplomacy. The appeal would be heard by a panel of three judges, one of whom was the court's chief judge, David Bazelon—who, it so happened, had written the original corroboration requirement in rape cases (for a different case) in Washington, D.C. Therefore we would convince the other eight judges first, and then Chief Judge Bazelon would have to come along. ("No need to humiliate him," as Judge Wright thoughtfully put it.) But how would we garner the support of judges who weren't even impaneled to hear the case, so that our determination to change the law would become a fait accompli?

Here's how. The appeal for the defense was being handled pro bono (for free) by a fancy law firm. The lawyer was a former beau of mine, a man I'd been crazy about—until he went back to his wife. Should that disqualify me, I asked Judge Wright? No, he said, he was deciding the case, not me—but this old relationship might provide us an excellent opportunity. My fellow law clerks, of course, knew the story of my traumatic breakup with this defense lawyer and would be very interested, to put it mildly, in checking him out. Normally clerks have no time for hearing arguments in cases that their bosses aren't assigned to, but they would make an exception for this case. The clerks would then report what had happened in court to their bosses, the six judges not assigned to the case. These six judges could then be persuaded to join my footnote to the decision, stating their opposition to the traditional corroboration requirement.

The defense counsel stood up to argue, basing his case on the Bazelon decision that in Washington, D.C., corroboration was required to support a rape conviction. Before he could finish his first sentence, Judge Wright broke in. "Counsel," he asked, "why should we continue to enforce a requirement that treats women who have been raped as inherently less reliable than all other victims of every other crime?" The judge smiled at me.

"This one's for you," he said to me afterward, letting me write the opinion. I wrote a footnote that said that even though only three judges had heard the case, we had nine votes to get rid of the corroboration requirement. It was done.

Later, I wrote a law review article and a book about being a rape victim. I found my voice, clear and strong. How could I not? When

I went to work for Judge Wright, I was a mess. My father, my hero, had recently died. I could barely remember why I had gone to law school. Judge Wright reminded me. Through the law I could make a difference. Judge Wright showed me how with courage and creativity the law could be shaped to reflect justice, compassion, and common sense.

Politics was not the only constraint on Judge Wright. There was also the law. "I grew up around the federal courts and had respect for them, and I tried to carry on the tradition," he told me. "But I think the key in all of this is doing justice within the law. You have to stay within the law, but you can press against the law in all directions to do what you perceive to be justice."

Judge Wright pushed the law to do what was right. He understood the fearsome reality: law is a guide, not an answer; it is a route to creativity for those who dare to embrace it. Judge Wright dared. He pressed. He changed the world. He is my hero, still.

Not long ago my daughter came home from school to tell me the story of Ruby Jones, the little girl who integrated the first grade in New Orleans some thirty-seven years ago. I tell her the story of J. Skelly Wright, the man who issued forty court orders so Ruby could go to school. When my daughter tells her teacher of Judge Wright, she is asked if she would like to share this amazing story with the class. Well, I would like to share it with the world.

I was lucky to work for a great man. I even knew it at the time. I sat at my desk, halfway between the Capitol and the White House, and knew that it was the best job I would ever have. Character? Let me tell you about Judge J. Skelly Wright. May he rest in peace. He not only changed the world, he changed my life. Such is the power of character.

*part three*

# FAMILY
# MATTERS

STEPHEN R. COVEY is the author of *The 7 Habits of Highly Effective People,* which has sold more than twelve million copies and is the *New York Times* number one international nonfiction best-seller. He has also written *First Things First, The 7 Habits of Highly Effective Families,* and *Principle-Centered Leadership.* One of the "25 most influential Americans" according to *Time* magazine, he is the recipient of the Thomas More College Medallion for continuing service to humanity, the 1994 International Entrepreneur of the Year Award, *Inc.* magazine's Services Entrepreneur of the Year Award, and the 1996 National Entrepreneur of the Year Lifetime Achievement Award. He founded the Covey Leadership Center, now called the Franklin Covey Co. He also serves on the board of the Points of Light Foundation, a volunteer coordination organization.

## 12

# Growing Great Children

*Stephen R. Covey*

I HAVE A DEAR FRIEND who once shared with me his deep concern over a son he described as "rebellious," "disturbing," and "an ingrate."

"Stephen, I don't know what to do," he said. "It's gotten to the point where if I come into the room to watch television with my son, he turns it off and walks out. I've tried my best to reach him, but it's just beyond me."

At the time I was teaching some university classes around *The 7 Habits of Highly Effective People*. I said, "Why don't you come with me to my class right now? We're going to be talking about Habit 5— how to listen empathically to another person before you attempt to explain yourself. My guess is that your son may not feel understood."

*Note:* © 1998 Franklin Covey Co.

"I already understand him," he replied. "And I can see problems he's going to have if he doesn't listen to me."

"Let me suggest that you assume you know nothing about your son," I said. "Just start with a clean slate. Listen to him without any moral evaluation or judgment. Come to class and learn how to do this and how to listen within his frame of reference."

So my friend came. Thinking he understood after just one class, he went to his son and said, "I need to listen to you. I probably don't understand you, and I want to."

His son replied, "You have never understood me—ever!" And with that, he walked out.

The following day my friend said, "Stephen, it didn't work. I made such an effort, and this is how he treated me! I felt like saying, 'You idiot! Don't you realize what I've done and what I'm trying to do now?' I really don't know if there's any hope."

I said, "He's testing your sincerity. And what did he find out? He found out you don't really want to understand him. You want him to shape up."

"He should, the little whippersnapper!" he replied. "He knows full well what he's doing to mess things up."

I told him, "Look at the spirit inside you now. You're angry and frustrated and full of judgments. Do you think you can use some surface-level listening technique with your son and get him to open up? Do you think it's possible for you to talk to him or even look at him without somehow communicating all those negative things you're feeling deep inside? You've got to do much more private work inside your own mind and heart. You'll eventually learn to love him unconditionally, just the way he is, rather than withholding your love until he shapes up. On the way, you'll learn to listen within his frame of reference and, if necessary, apologize for your judgments and past mistakes or do whatever it takes."

My friend caught the message. He could see that he had been trying to practice the technique at the surface instead of learning how to produce the power to practice the technique sincerely and consistently, regardless of the outcome.

So he returned to class for more learning and began to work on his feelings and motives. He soon started to sense a new attitude within himself. His feelings about his son turned more tender and sensitive and open.

He finally said, "I'm ready. I'm going to try it again."

I said, "He'll test your sincerity again."

"It's all right, Stephen," he replied. "At this point I feel as if he could reject every overture I make, and it would be all right. I would just keep making them because it's the right thing to do and he's worth it."

That night he sat down with his son and said, "I know you feel as though I haven't tried to understand you, but I want you to know that I am trying and will continue to try."

Again, the boy coldly replied, "You have never understood me." He stood up and started to walk out, but just as he reached the door, my friend said to him, "Before you leave, I want to say that I'm really sorry for the way I embarrassed you in front of your friends the other night."

His son whipped around and said, "You have no idea how much that embarrassed me!" His eyes began to fill with tears.

"Stephen," my friend said to me later, "all the training and encouragement you gave me did not even begin to have the impact of that moment when I saw my son begin to tear up. I had no idea that he even cared, that he was that vulnerable. For the first time I *really* wanted to listen."

And he did. The boy gradually began to open up. They talked until midnight, and when my friend's wife came in and said, "It's time for bed," his son quickly replied, "We want to talk, don't we, Dad?" They continued to talk into the early morning hours.

The next day in the hallway of my office building, my friend, with tears in his eyes, said, "Stephen, I found my son again."

What a powerful illustration of the different things that happen when we try to develop or use a skill to address a challenge in our lives without working on or possessing the underlying character strength that makes that skill effective! It demonstrates the difference between what I call *primary greatness* and *secondary greatness*.

Primary greatness is character. Secondary greatness is made up of positive personality traits, talents, and skills.

## Secondary Greatness: Skills and Personality

The world's value system is primarily focused on secondary greatness. It rewards and makes heroes out of incredibly strong and agile athletes, talented musicians and artists, gifted and persuasive speakers, powerful and wealthy business executives. But even though success may require the talents and skills that make up secondary greatness, long-term sustainable results and impact always come from primary greatness first—from tapping into the natural laws or principles that produce those results.

If we consistently use only personality techniques and skills to enhance our social interactions, we may cut off the vital character base for those techniques. We simply cannot have the fruits without the roots. Private victory precedes public victory. Self-mastery and self-discipline are the roots of good relationships with others.

If we use human influence strategies and tactics to get other people to do what we want, we may succeed in the short term, but over time our duplicity and insincerity will breed distrust. Everything we do will be perceived as manipulative. We may have the "right" rhetoric, style, and even intention, but without trust we won't achieve primary greatness or lasting success.

I once heard General Norman Schwarzkopf claim that 95 percent of all leadership failures in the last century were failures of character. That's quite profound. You see, many people with secondary greatness—that is, with social status, position, fame, wealth, or talent—lack primary greatness or goodness of character. And this void is evident in every long-term relationship they have, whether it is with a business associate, a spouse, a friend, or a teenage child. It is character that communicates most eloquently. As Emerson once said, "What you are shouts so loud in my ears, I cannot hear what you say."

## Primary Greatness: Character

Character, or primary greatness, is basically what a person is. It is reflected in three areas:

*Integrity.* When you have integrity, you integrate your whole life around a set of principles. It goes beyond just being honest. It means that you have gone through a process of identifying the principles and relationships that you value most—that are most important to you—and that you prioritize your everyday life and decision making around those principles. Integrity is making and keeping promises to yourself and to others. This private victory produces an inner core of security, guidance, wisdom, and power that becomes a wellspring of strength for every area of your life.

*Maturity.* I define maturity as balancing and bringing together courage and kindness. If we can express our feelings and convictions with courage balanced with kindness and respect for the feelings and convictions of another person, we are mature. If we lack internal maturity and ethical strength, we might try to borrow strength from our position, power, credentials, seniority, affiliations, wealth, or possessions. While courage may focus on getting things done and achieving bottom-line results, kindness and respectful openness work at building relationships and synergies that in turn build sustainable, long-term results.

*Abundance mentality.* This is the belief and deep mind-set that there is plenty out there for everyone. The abundance mentality flows out of a deep sense of personal worth and security. It results in sharing recognition, profits, and responsibility. It leads us to celebrate and feel genuine satisfaction in the strengths, talents, and accomplishments of others. It breeds generosity and opens up new options and alternatives. It turns personal joy and fulfillment outward. It recognizes and seeks to bring out not only our own unlimited possibilities for positive interaction, growth, and development, but recognizes and seeks to help bring out the unseen potential of others.

Most people are deeply scripted in the scarcity mentality. They see life as a finite pie: if another person gets a big piece of the pie, it means less for them and for everyone else. They have a zero-sum attitude toward life. The scarcity mentality has been fostered in most of us from infancy and childhood through adulthood. As children we are compared to siblings and other children: "Why can't you be more obedient like your older sister?" "You're so lazy! Why don't you do your homework and practicing like your friend Jimmy?" We're graded in school on normal distribution curves: your A means I get a C. Competitive sports, while beneficial in so many areas, also send scarcity messages: because you make the team, I don't. There are only winners and losers: if you win this game, I'm a loser. In competing for a new job or promotion, we see others' successes as lost opportunities for *us*.

People with a scarcity mentality have a hard time sharing recognition, credit, power, or profit. They also have a tough time being genuinely happy for the success of other people—even, and sometime especially, members of their own families or close friends and associates. It's as if something were being taken from them when someone else receives special recognition or achieves success.

Ultimately, we have to go back to integrity as the wellspring of all other character growth. Integrity creates the inner strength that enables us to be both courageous and kind in working through tough issues with others. Integrity develops the security and intrinsic sense of worth as a human being that fosters abundant thinking in us.

A character high in integrity, maturity, and the abundance mentality has a genuineness that goes far beyond technique. Your character is constantly radiating, communicating. From it, people come to trust or distrust you. If your life runs hot and cold, if you're both caustic and kind, if your private performance doesn't square with your public performance, people won't open up to you, even if they want and need your love or help. They won't feel safe enough to expose their opinions and tender feelings.

# The Roots of Primary Greatness: The Home

Although there are many powerful threats to the development of primary greatness today—including the unraveling of the family in America and across the world; the overwhelming bias in the broader culture, media, and entertainment world toward recognizing and rewarding mostly secondary greatness; and the sense of hopelessness that is the fruit of the first two threats—there is also a great deal we can do. And my greatest hope lies in the children. Though storms may rage in the schools, in the streets, and in the theaters around the world, parents still have opportunities for even greater primary influence in the family rooms and at the dinner tables of their own homes. The home is the true farm wherein character is sown in a human being.

Let me offer just a few suggestions to parents or loved ones who desire to foster primary greatness in their children:

- Help your children develop a sense of who they are and of their intrinsic worth. Avoid comparing them to brothers or sisters or to other children. Help them develop a vision of their possibilities and the kind of unique, meaningful contributions they can make to the world. Affirm and believe in them.

- Teach them by your own example that to have character means to live outside yourself, to help and serve other people.

- Help them grow up with a vision of education as the tool of their influence and their contribution to the world.

- Encourage their involvement in team sports or school bands or orchestras. These pursuits teach interdependence—and it is interdependence not independence that is the essence of life.

- Teach and model for them the supreme importance of the private victory—of taking responsibility for one's life and one's choice, of developing a sense of vision for one's life and what is most important, and then of living with integrity to that vision.

It all starts with and ends with the family. And each of us can say, "In my family it all begins with me." In other words, each of us can become a model, mentor, and teacher to a child. We can become agents of change in our families—stopping our weaknesses and the weaknesses of our parents and ancestors from passing on to the next generation. Just as my friend who found his son again first learned his own underlying character strength, so too can we, through our effort, humility, and patience, develop the primary greatness necessary to sustain and empower our deep need to have secondary greatness victories. In the words of Gandhi, "Let us become the change we seek in the world."

VARTAN GREGORIAN is the president of the Carnegie Corporation of New York and a leading American educator. The former president of Brown University and the New York Public
Library, he also advises such major philanthropists as Walter
Annenberg and Ted Turner. He is an author and the recipient
of numerous fellowships and awards, including citations
from the Urban League, the League of Women Voters, PEN-
American Center, and Literacy Volunteers of New York; the
cities of New York and San Francisco; and the states of New
York, Massachusetts, Texas, and Rhode Island. He serves on
the boards of the Institute for Advanced Study at Princeton,
the Gates Library Foundation, the Aga Khan University, the
J. Paul Getty Trust, and the Museum of Modern Art. He is a
fellow of the American Philosophical Society and of the American Academy of Arts and Sciences.

*13*

# Our Moral DNA

## *Vartan Gregorian*

WHEN I WAS a boy in Tabriz, Iran, I learned very early about two Armenian words (and their Persian and Turkish counterparts): the first was *chakatagir* (what was written on your forehead, namely fate); the second was *nekaragir* (your picture, what is imprinted in you, namely character). Over the first, I was told, I had no control. Over the latter, however, I definitely had some responsibility. *Nekaragir* is the embodiment of one's own uniqueness as an individual: it embraces one's dignity, honor, and independence and one's commitment to a corpus of moral and social values that forge ties among individuals, families, ancestors, generations, and society and that affirm our common humanity on the one hand and our uniqueness on the other.

In sum, character is one's commitment to a value system that transcends individual limitations and universalizes us. It pays tribute to our ancestors and serves as a witness and as a moral link to future generations.

We are told that our character is shaped from the moment we are conceived until, as Shakespeare says, we pay "all debts" by dying. I believe character is developed through nurture, experience, and education, and in the following pages I offer some examples of how and what I have learned.

## Nurture and Experience

Psychologists are right when they assert that to grow up well we must have the reliable, loving attention of at least one guardian, whether parent, grandparent, or another person. There are many who have been blessed with a family and its loving critical care and nurture, but many others have been deprived of their childhood and have not received the love and guidance of a caring adult.

I was very fortunate, in the aftermath of the premature death of my mother, to be loved and guided by my maternal grandmother. She raised me, and she was in a sense my first teacher. She instructed me in the moral lessons of life and the "right way" through her sheer character, stoic tenacity, formidable dignity, self-reliant individuality, and utter integrity. She was, for me, the best example of what good character meant. In spite of much adversity (she lost all seven of her children), wartime ravages, poverty, scarcity, and deprivation, she never became a cynic, never abandoned her values, and never compromised her integrity. Even though she was illiterate, she was a wise teacher who believed fervently in education as a redeeming, liberating, and enlightening force. She was, for me, a living book of ethics and good conduct. By her example, she shaped the foundations of my character.

Among the many things my grandmother taught me was that earthly belongings are ephemeral; so are, unfortunately, vigor and beauty. What endure, she told me, are good deeds and reputation:

one's name, one's dignity. For her, dignity was not a social construct but rather a living reality; it embodied the true character of the individual. It was not love of the self; it was appreciation of one's true values, the essence of one's humanity, one's enduring qualities and values. She admonished me to properly guard my dignity and my honor, for they are not negotiable. They are part of our moral DNA.

She also taught me not to envy, because envy tends to deform character. "You must not have a hole in your eye," she used to say, because that hole would be bottomless; it would never be filled. Human envy is insatiable and will always tend to diminish one. Instead of envying individuals for what material possessions they have or high positions they hold, one must always respect them for what they are, what values they possess, and what good they do. She insisted that one must do good because it was the right thing, not for the anticipation of reward.

These teachings and musings of my grandmother were not original. Indeed, as a choirboy and altar boy I heard some of them during church services and later at school. What was unique about my grandmother was that she practiced what she taught. She had character.

My grandmother was not the only adult whose guidance I benefited from. Like many extended families of that time, we had three generations in our household—my mother, my father, my sister, myself, and two grandparents—living together in what was then the Armenian quarter of Tabriz. Then there were the church and the broader community, including the merchants of our quarter. Witnessing the interactions of all the individuals in question, I had a living laboratory to observe values and actions and learn about character.

## Education

The next forum that helped shape my identity, and hence my character, was school, at first parochial, then secular. In the latter, my Persian literature teacher had a strong impact on me. He translated everything profound into didactic lessons, and one set of these lessons in particular has left an enduring impression on me. He instructed us to make the following distinctions: "If you see a donkey carrying gold, remember it is not a golden donkey; it is only a donkey carrying gold. If you see a donkey carrying a diploma, remember it is not an educated donkey but only a donkey carrying a diploma. Lastly, if you see a donkey in a holy city, don't say it is a holy donkey; it is only a donkey in a holy city." This admonition has served me well in distinguishing means and ends, form and substance, style and character.

The school was not a place for aphorisms alone. It, along with its small and exquisite library, provided me an opportunity to read world literature, to read didactic fables, inspirational novels, short stories, history, and poetry. In this literature, I discovered universal norms and values; I discovered authenticity, dignity, freedom, integrity, and honor. I found that all of us have responsibilities toward past generations and we in turn have to earn the right to be good ancestors.

I read avidly of King Arthur and the knights of the Round Table and all the adventure books of Alexandre Dumas, *père* and *fils*. I was especially moved by Victor Hugo's *Les Misérables* and the character of the protagonist, Jean Valjean. From this novel, I learned many things about the power of forgiveness and the possibility of personal redemption: that one can make restitution for one's mistakes and cleanse the soul of error through a transcendent act, that it is impossible to protect one's character in the midst of social turmoil.

Reading stimulated my thinking, my imagination, my aspirations; it later helped determine my choice of career as a historian, and it enriched my understanding of the human soul in all its complexity and contradictions. Literature reinforced in me the notion that all the things we have of this world are mere possessions. They are products of civilization and culture, but they are not the inner part of us. Possessions may be instruments for the achievement of welfare or power, for our destruction or our health, for our good or our evil, but the only constant value is our sense of inner worth, which is intangible. To paraphrase the Gospels, we may possess the world but lose our souls. We do have to make compromises in life, but not to the detriment of our inner integrity.

Children's advocate Marian Wright Edelman expresses something of the kind in her little book of life's lessons, *The Measure of Our Success: A Letter to My Children and Yours* (1992). In it, she counsels her three sons to

> Affirm who you are inside regardless of the world's judgments: God's and my very precious children who are loved unconditionally, not for what you do, look like or own, but simply because you are a gift of a loving God. As parents we often forget to convey this, and I have been as guilty as any. . . . Many young people feel, as you have, so much pressure to achieve, to get top grades, high test scores and good jobs and to perform well in nonacademic ventures—all of which are important for acquiring the self-discipline needed to improve your life choices. But it is important of us overly perfectionist parents to make clear that you are far more than your SATs, good grades and trophies. However desirable these achievements are and however proud we are of them, they have no bearing on your intrinsic value or on our love for and acceptance of you as a person.

In times of travail, it is sometimes tempting to lose sight of who one really is *au fond,* as the French say, at bottom. Whenever I have been beset, I have found comfort in the meditations of the Roman emperor Marcus Aurelius, who lived from A.D. 121 to 180. A follower of the Greek Stoic philosophers, Marcus Aurelius spent many lonely, somewhat melancholy years posted on the frontiers of the empire, where he consoled himself by writing his reflections.

He embraced a few simple precepts for pursuing the path of rectitude: for example, never to implicate oneself in what is degrading, to love truth and justice (including toleration)—and never for a moment to leave reason out of sight. A realist as well as a philosopher, Aurelius had an answer for those of us who strive unsuccessfully to meet such a high standard. "Do not be distressed, do not despond or give up in despair if now and again practice falls short of precept.

Return to the attack after each failure, and be thankful if on the whole you can acquit yourself in the majority of cases as a man should."

These teachings have fortified me in dark moments. Indeed, how does one saying go? "Character is what you are in the dark."

But admirable personal character is not enough to help us solve the many ethical quandaries that are apt to confront us in real life today, especially in an age of rapid advances in the medical, biological, and behavioral sciences. Whose profession is free of cruel moral choices? A secret source gives a journalist valuable information about a criminal case before a jury. Should the journalist cooperate with the authorities or protect the source and go to jail for contempt of court? A businessman is troubled by evidence of illegal practices by his superiors. Should he report this to government investigators, possibly at the cost of his job and career, or stay mum at the price of his self-respect and possibly the company's bottom line?

The code of the American Bar Association enjoins lawyers to exercise zeal in the pursuit of justice. But does zeal permit a lawyer to take any case and make any argument—in effect to become a hired gun for the highest bidder? In practice, under the pressure of conflicting interests, our ideals and principles are often put to the test and found wanting. Periodically, revelations of professional, corporate, and political misbehavior contribute to our sense of natural unease about the state of public and private virtue in America. We are in such a time now, as we were twenty-five years ago during the Watergate hearings. Then one question that invariably arises is whether ethical or moral reasoning and decision making be taught in venues other than the home or church.

Some people believe that they can, and courses have mushroomed in schools and on college and university campuses and are offered by independent organizations, like the Josephson Institute of Ethics. Other people, however, believe "you either have morals or you don't." Learning to reason more carefully about ethical problems certainly will not guarantee that young people will behave morally in the future. But there is also no guarantee that a person will ever pick up a novel or read a history book once out of college, either. That doesn't make literature or history classes any the less worth taking. What courses on ethics and character can do, perhaps, is leave students with the understanding that they are moral agents, that they have moral responsibilities, that there are methods for evaluating and defending their own positions on a moral question, and, finally, "after all the beautiful drifts away" (in Yeats's words), that there is a higher purpose to living than self-interest alone.

RICHARD M. EYRE AND LINDA EYRE have produced six best-selling books, among them *Teaching Your Children Joy; Teaching Your Children Responsibility;* and *Teaching Your Children Values*, the first parenting book since Dr. Spock's to reach the top of the *New York Times* best-seller list. More important, they have produced the raw material that gives them their credentials: nine children. On programs like *Oprah* and *Today,* they emphasize the importance of strong families and balanced lifestyles. A management consultant and former candidate for Utah governor, Richard serves on the board of governors of the Josephson Institute of Ethics. Linda wrote *I Didn't Plan to Be a Witch,* the story of a harried 1990s mom. They also host a national cable television show, are the founders of Homebase, a parents' cooperative, and were named by Ronald Reagan to direct the White House Conference on Children and Parents in the 1980s.

*14*

# How to Raise a Kid with Character

*Richard M. Eyre*

*Linda Eyre*

AS PARENTS, we all live for compliments about our kids. ("Your boy had a great game last night; what a ballplayer!") Our hopes and our efforts are so centered on our children that any recognition they get feels like a reward. ("Your daughter has really worked hard this term in my class. She's pulled her grade up from a B to an A.") Maybe it's partly our own egos, but it's mostly our love and happiness for *them* that is boosted. ("Congratulations, your son got the part he auditioned for in the play.")

Personally, we value one particular compliment, a simple one, more than any other that we could receive about any of our children. Let us present it through a recent experience. We had been at a Christmas party with a lot of young children. Noah, our seventeen-year-old, was with us although there were other more exciting places he'd probably rather have been that night. Because there were no other kids his age, he spent most of the evening entertaining toddlers and preschoolers. As we were walking to our car afterwards, a good friend remarked, "You know what I like most about your Noah . . . is just that he's such a good kid."

Now this friend knew Noah pretty well, knew that he was president of his class, star of the basketball team, honor roll student, and that was our friend's point: all those other things are fine, they bring plenty of compliments and recognition to Noah and to us, but they are actually far less important than a much more basic and simple thing—Noah is a *good* kid. This friend had observed Noah playing with smaller kids, taking delight in making them happy, caring more about them than about himself. His compliment wasn't about Noah's physical appearance or about his skills or abilities or about his personality or social skills or about his accomplishments or achievements; it was about Noah's character. He is a good kid—he cares, he loves, he gives.

The timing and wording of our friend's compliment to Noah was interesting because just the day before someone else had used the same words in a different context regarding one of our other children. This child was having some academic struggles, and his teacher had said, "But you know, he's a good kid. I appreciate having him in my class, and he'll improve."

Does being a good kid transcend other accomplishments and supersede and compensate for other failures? Is being a good kid more important than being a smart kid, or a talented kid, or a successful kid? Is character ultimately more important than ability? Is the teaching of values a higher parental challenge than the teaching of skills?

Simple answer: Yes!

As any parent would testify, parenting is complex and multifaceted, and we all want to give our children all that we can. We want to give them tools and capacities and opportunities. We want to give them insight and understanding. We want them to be accomplished; we want them to be successful. Most of all, we want them to be happy.

And here's the bottom line: happiness is more dependent on character than on anything else.

As we pointed out in our book *Teaching Your Children Values,* parental stewardship over children involves two important responsibilities beyond meeting their physical and emotional needs for food, shelter, clothing, and basic security:

- Teach them values (that is, build character within them).

- Give them educational and experiential opportunities.

The education and experience can be, to some extent, "subcontracted" to schools, organizations, coaches, tutors, music teachers, scout troops, clubs, teams, camps, and other entities. Some of these, along with churches, can also be helpful in teaching values. But when it comes to teaching character, about ninety-five cents of the buck stops with parents.

## Six Things You Can Do With Your Kids

How does a parent go about the challenges of teaching character, of instilling values? Not as experts but as fellow strugglers, we suggest a half-dozen things that work with children of any age. (The earlier you start with a child, the better; but it is never too late.)

1. Personally commit yourself to a clear and particular set of values or qualities of character and commit yourself without apology, caveat, compromise, or equivocation to teach them to your child.

On *Donahue,* we were once faced by a fellow guest who argued that parents are presumptuous when they decide what values their children should be taught, that kids deserve the "freedom and autonomy" of growing up and choosing their own values. Linda answered by saying that was analogous to putting children in a boat without paddle, engine, or rudder and yelling, "I hope you make it," as they drift toward Niagara Falls.

Regardless of your religious persuasion (or lack thereof), regardless of your politics, religion, race, or other classification, you will recognize that there *are* universal and fundamental values: honesty, courage, peaceability, self-discipline and moderation, self-reliance and potential, loyalty and dependability, fidelity and chastity, love, kindness and friendliness, unselfishness and sensitivity, respect, and justice and mercy. These twelve values may be known to you by different names, of course. For example, CHARACTER COUNTS! presents them as trustworthiness, respect, responsibility, fairness, caring, and citizenship.

2. Talk with your child about the values or character traits you've chosen. List them on a chart. Make them prominent topics in your family. Use everything from TV shows to situations at school or with friends as springboards or catalysts to talk about how each particular value applies to daily life. Always connect values to happiness. Point out that over the long term, good character contributes more to people's happiness and the happiness of those around them than any other factor.

3. Commit yourself to being an example of the values you choose. Once you have consciously chosen the character traits you want to teach, your most powerful tool will be your example. You have to walk your talk. You can't talk about honesty and then say, "Billy, tell the insurance man mommy's not at home."

4. Focus on one particular value or character trait each month. Help your child make a poster on the value of the month. Talk about it, think about it, and be especially aware of applying the featured value all month.

5. Set up a family infrastructure that teaches values continually. This infrastructure should include three things.

A *family legal system*. This consists of a set of family rules that are simple, few in number, and consistently applied.

A *family economy*. This requires a simple list of household responsibilities for each child, a way (a star chart or pegboard, for example) for each child to keep track of what he or she has done, and (in place of an allowance) a Saturday "pay day," where children receive money commensurate with how well they have done their household jobs.

*A set of family traditions* (for holidays, birthdays, and other special times). The traditions should be designed to underscore certain values, such as making a list of things you are grateful for on Thanksgiving.

These three elements of family infrastructure will be ongoing reminders and reinforcers of values like self-reliance, honesty, self-discipline, respect, fairness, loyalty, unselfishness, and initiative.

6. Rank values and character traits *above* everything else in your family and give more praise and recognition for the exercise of values than for anything else. *Attention* is the key to encouraging behavior. Kids invariably do what they get attention for—positive or negative. For example, small children act up if it gets them more attention than being good. As children grow, they gravitate toward the things they get recognition for.

In this competitive, ego-centered world, parents are often so intensely interested in their kids' grades and auditions and teams that their kids can easily get the impression that these things matter more than anything else. Therefore it's important to develop a family lexicon and communication pattern in which character is more highly prized than anything else. In our own family, we have attempted to do this in a very open and straightforward way by categorizing the pursuits of all family members (adults and children) according to three prioritized levels:

1. Character, values, or spirituality

2. Academics or work

3. Extracurricular (sports, music, hobbies, and so forth)

This simple three-tiered mental framework affects daily conversations in our family. When Noah comes home from school, we might want to ask, "How did basketball practice go?" but first we ask, "Who did you help today?" and "How were your classes?" When we pick up daughter Charity from her flute lesson, before we ask, "How did you do on the piece you've been practicing?" we try to remember to ask, "Did you treat your teacher with respect?" and "How did your math test go earlier this afternoon?"

At the start of each school year, we help our children formulate individual goals in each category.

Over the years this simple, constant categorizing of goals and ranking of character ideals above all else has had a noticeable influence on our children (although they're still not perfect!). We're convinced that our attempts to teach and promote character have been our best and most effective efforts as parents—our best-spent parenting time.

## What Our Kids Have to Say

Here are some of our children's thoughts about values and character:

CHARITY (AGE ELEVEN)

I think that if you have values and character in your life, your life will be better. I think it is more important to have these qualities than academic or athletic skills because they leave you and everyone around you happy.

ELI (AGE FOURTEEN)

I really like the categories we have in our family. They help me to realize how to treat each aspect of life and which ones to concentrate or spend the most time on. Basketball and school, which are categories 3 and 2, are really important to me. I have, mainly this year, taught myself to start with category 1 and work up from there. Then I end up doing better on 2 and 3!

NOAH (AGE SEVENTEEN)

Everyone is born with a certain potential and certain capabilities, but in order for each to fulfill this God-given potential to the fullest, values are key. Once a foundation is built with these values, the building up that follows can be large and stable, influencing others for the better.

Because of the values I've been brought up with, I feel like I can do some good things with my life. The examples and strong character of others have helped so much. Each individual has a unique spirit, with a strong potential for good and happiness.

Shawni (Age Twenty-Five)

If you grow up valuing honesty, self-reliance, beauty, respect, and courage, these values are woven into your inner tapestry, your *character*. If you grow up valuing somewhat more worldly things—popularity, wealth, personal possessions— these values too are woven into your character, although with a much different result.

Sometimes I feel like the world gets so into not stepping on toes that we forget that the values taught to children will directly influence the future. We let a little lie slide by or ignore a person in need, we expose ourselves to violent movies and justify premarital sex or unfaithfulness.

I am so thankful for the strong values I was taught in my family. I'm so thankful for the time when I was little my mom helped me return the extra change I received in error at the store. I'm so thankful for the time my dad pushed me to get out of my comfort zone and run for school office. I'm so thankful my parents praised me when I saw another child in need and had the sensitivity to stand up for them. I'm so thankful they cared when I came home at night—had long talks with me about my goals and needs. I'm so thankful they taught me to stand up for what I believe—*always*—even in difficult situations.

Now that I'm a mother I'm even more thankful for *values* that can develop strong character. I hope I can instill good values in my children—to stand up for what they believe in a world that sometimes makes it difficult. To have the *character* they need to help others and give joy—and to have joy.

SAREN (AGE TWENTY-SEVEN)

We talked about values around the dinner table and nominated each other for such awards as the Self-Starter Award, the Leader-for-the-Right Award, the What-Would-Jesus-Do Award. We learned about honesty and love and kindness in formal lessons and discussions at church and at home. But more than these formal methods for teaching values and building character, I think I developed the list of values I hold dear and live by based on the example set for me by my parents and the simple constant reinforcement I received on a daily basis as values were woven into discussion on any topic. Deciding whether to take a challenging new class or try out for something that interested me led to discussions on courage and potential. Complaining about having to go to yet another family event led to discussions on loyalty and love and sensitivity and respect. Commenting on friends' actions led to discussions on kindness and friendliness and honesty.

Having a set of values simplifies so much in my life. Among other things, my current job involves working with elementary school–aged children. As I've come to know these children and their families well, I've seen so clearly the difference it makes when a child has a sense of *who* he or she is as defined by his or her values. I work with a lot of children with behavioral problems. The ones I really worry about are those who seem unable to connect their actions with any sense of values. I'm so grateful for the way I was brought up.

# Making a Start

Values and character are their own reward and thus become self-motivating and self-perpetuating. As children practice a value or begin to develop a positive character trait, they feel good—about themselves and about the results they begin to perceive in their lives and in the lives of those around them. Parents may find that just like pushing a heavy car it is hard to get started teaching values, but once some momentum is achieved, once there are opportunities for praise and recognition, values will begin to become part of your child's character.

**RABBI STEVEN CARR REUBEN** of Kehillat Israel congregation in Los Angeles has worked and taught in the field of moral education for more than twenty years. He is the founding editor of *Compass* magazine for teachers and was national associate director of education for the Union of American Hebrew Congregations, the largest publisher of Jewish educational material in the world. A frequent lecturer around the country on education and teacher training, he is the recipient of numerous community awards, including the Micah Award for founding the largest full-service homeless shelter in Los Angeles. He has a monthly column in *Children* magazine and is the author of several books, including *Children of Character* (1997), *Raising Ethical Children* (1994), and *Making Interfaith Marriage Work* (1994).

*15*

# Help! How Do I Teach Character When I'm Still Questioning My Own?

*Rabbi Steven Carr Reuben*

THERE I AM, driving in my car on a beautiful Sunday afternoon in Southern California, with my wife, Didi, in the passenger seat and my daughter, Gable, in the back. We're on our way to a local shopping mall. It's a picture-perfect day as we chat about what we are going to buy, where we might go for lunch later, and the gift Gable needs for a birthday party. As we stop for a red light, I see out of the corner of my eye a man with a hand-painted sign that says, "Veteran—hungry and need work." He's walking up to my window with a somewhat challenging, somewhat expectant, yet questioning look. I pretend I don't notice him and continue talking to Didi and Gable. When the light turns green, I drive on (with a mild sense of relief) to our family day at the shopping mall as if nothing happened.

The problem is, something *did* happen—and no amount of ignoring it will make it go away. A moral lesson was taught. A moral lesson was learned. In fact, probably several lessons were passed on to my young daughter in that brief moment that day, lessons I may or may not have intended to teach but that she learned nonetheless. I often think that the most difficult part of character education is to be attentive to all the things we do that convey messages about our values and to have the courage to admit how often we fall short of living out the ideals we are so anxious to pass on to our children.

For example, in that brief moment in the car, what did I teach about honesty? (Wasn't I trying to deceive everyone by pretending I actually didn't know the homeless man was standing outside my window?) What did I teach about compassion? (Why didn't I just open the window and give the man a dollar?) What did I teach about respect? (Did Gable learn that it's OK simply to ignore another human being when he is standing right beside you?) What did I teach about responsibility? (Don't I want my child to grow up feeling that she has a responsibility to help those less fortunate and help make the world a better place?) What did I teach about citizenship? (Don't I think part of being a good citizen is taking care of those most vulnerable in the society?)

The most daunting part of being a parent is the realization that everything you do matters. Everything teaches something, whether you intend it or not. It was the great American novelist James Baldwin who once wrote, "Children have never been good at listening to their elders but they have never failed to imitate them." With these prophetic words, Baldwin captured the essence of the parenting challenge—to understand that as a parent you are *always* the primary moral model for your children.

That's why being a parent is both exhilarating and terrifying. And because we have an enormous impact on the dreams and hopes, sense of self-esteem, and personal values of our children, the best rule we can have for raising children of character is what I like to call the Golden Rule of parenting—*be the kind of adult you want your child to grow up to be.*

When I remind myself of the qualities and attributes I want to see in my daughter—things like the six pillars of character: trustworthiness, respect, responsibility, fairness, caring, and citizenship—I become more aware of my own behavior and of all the opportunities I have to teach and model good character. Parenting is the most difficult job in the world precisely because it is a never-ending challenge. It is the day-in and day-out experience of doing our best to act as we would like our children to act, being willing to recognize when we fall short of our own ideals, and then doing our best to correct our own behavior so that our children's behavior will be positively affected as well.

## Modeling Character and Values

Parenting is a heavy responsibility, and our challenge is to act each day as if what we do that day will determine the kind of adult our child will become. But as we all know, that is a lot easier said than done. Ignoring the homeless man on the street, gossiping about the parents of our children's friends in front of them, telling our children not to drink alcohol yet being drinkers ourselves, preaching about the health hazards of smoking even though we are still addicted to the habit—the list of do-as-I-say-not-as-I-do sins of the parent goes on and on.

It is important to know that children have always and will always see their parents as their primary models for how to be an adult, a friend, a colleague, a spouse, and a parent. This knowledge should be a catalyst for us, raising the level of our awareness of how we act and the model we set in each of these areas. The more aware we are of how we act, the better we are able to both modify our behavior when necessary and possible and confront our own failings and mistakes and deal with them openly, honestly, and constructively with our children.

Unfortunately you can't tell your kids, "Watch what I do on Monday, but don't pay any attention to my behavior on Tuesday." Every day is a modeling day, filled with *teachable moments*, ethical mini-lessons, endless character studies for your children and yourself. These lessons take place when you are shopping in the supermarket (how do you react when you are undercharged for an item?), picking your child up from school (do you cut into the car pool line or have the child ignore school rules and meet you at the corner?), walking through a shopping mall (do you ignore the Salvation Army lady?), or raking leaves in your front yard (where do you put the leaves when you are done?).

Perhaps the most frustrating aspect of character education for us as parents is remembering that many, if not most, of the valuable moral lessons we learned from our parents were not consciously taught at all. They were learned in the midst of casual moments of real life, just as our children's real lessons come from being, living, and interacting with us in a hundred different ways we could never predict in advance. That is why the first step to coping with the impact of our own moral missteps is to recognize the teachable moments as they occur, those moments in which our children develop their sense of ethics and character.

## Recognizing When We Fall Short

So how do we teach our children character and good moral values even as we ourselves keep making moral mistakes? Do we have to be perfect ourselves before we can attempt to develop good character in others? If we do, very few of us will qualify. It takes character to teach character, but it also takes character to admit when you are wrong. Admitting mistakes is perhaps the single most difficult skill for parents to learn. In all my years of working with parents throughout the country, the greatest resistance I have experienced from parents of all ages, races, religions, and socioeconomic backgrounds is in their unwillingness to admit their mistakes to their own children. Parents will seemingly go to almost any lengths to rationalize their own behavior, justify the punishments they mete out to their children, and defend their own choices even when they know that something they did was exactly the opposite of the example they want to teach their child.

My story about the hungry veteran is a case in point. Had I had the presence of mind to think about it at the time, I certainly would have known that the negative lessons about honesty, responsibility, compassion, and other important values that Gable might have learned from the incident were not the kind of character lessons I had in mind for my daughter. But I didn't think about it, and by doing and saying nothing, I may have sent the message that compassion and respect are matters of convenience.

## Correcting Our Behavior

In my parenting workshops I tell people that the good news is it is never too late to correct the situation. Indeed, perhaps the most important lesson to learn about our personal character failures and mistakes is that they can be turned into positive character lessons. In fact, the lesson is all the more powerful when we also model for our children the ability to reflect on our own behavior and the willingness to admit a shortcoming.

The key to turning moral mistakes into positive moral lessons is to take the time to replay the experience with your child. I could have sat with Gable at any time later in the day and created my own instant replay of the incident at the red light. I would first have needed to admit my mistake—to tell her that it didn't feel good to ignore that poor, hungry man when he came up to the car, that it was the wrong thing to do, and that sometimes I don't feel like helping others, even when I know that it's the right thing to do.

I might have asked her what she thought I could have done differently. How could I have helped this man? What would have happened if I had looked at him? Or talked with him? Or given him some financial help? I believe that one of the most powerful lessons you can teach your children is that it's OK to make mistakes in life; it's OK to mess up; it's OK not to be perfect. What isn't OK is being unwilling to admit when you are wrong and feeling that you always have to be right, that you always have to defend every move you make, that somehow you are less valuable and good as a person if you admit your mistakes.

After all, we demonstrate a mature sense of responsibility when we are accountable enough to admit we are wrong and to take action to prevent similar moral errors in the future. And one of our greatest blessings as parents is the knowledge that we can fix almost any mistake if we acknowledge it and deal with it sincerely. Our children *want* us to be right. They want us to be the example and model that they can follow, because they look up to us anyway. They will not only forgive us but respect us more for our human frailties, especially if we are willing to admit them honestly.

What if we don't think we made a mistake, but we are concerned that we sent an unclear message? For example, what if I had ignored the hungry veteran out of fear and concern for my family? He was unkempt and dirty. He might have been unstable and desperate. Would it have been wise to roll down the window and expose myself and my family to a possible danger?

There's nothing wrong with teaching our children caution, personal safety, and family protection—those are important aspects of responsibility and caring as well. But we can teach those values best by discussing our fears and doubts directly and honestly. Concern for safety is a very different justification than callousness. We should even be willing to discuss the reasonableness of the fear and whether it was real or based on a prejudice or sense of discomfort. Then we can come up with a plan to deal with similar situations in the future and, possibly, to help the homeless, hungry, and vulnerable in a way that keeps both our dignity and theirs intact. This type of discussion will reinforce the positive character values that we want to teach without compromising personal and family safety.

My goal is for us to exercise moral authority over our children in a way that respects them and that models the respect we want them to have for others. We do this best when we set the example, honestly confronting moral dilemmas, explaining why we made the choices we made, and openly discussing whether those choices were consistent with our highest values. As we do this, we also teach them by example that they should be accountable for thinking through their own moral choices in terms of their values.

## Setting Parenting Goals

Sadly, most people spend more time planning a two-week vacation than how they will raise their children. If we want our children to grow up to be people of character, we must take the time to identify the specific values we want to teach. These will be our ethical parenting goals. Mine are pretty basic. In addition to the six pillars of character, I want to teach my child that what she does and who she is really matter. I often think of a story told about Abraham Lincoln's mother. As she was dying, she called her small son to her bedside and whispered, "Be somebody, Abe." I want my daughter to be somebody, not in the sense of fame or power but in the quality of her character (in Yiddish, we call such a person a *mensch*). I want my daughter to treasure her integrity and to know that at the end of the day, the most important source of approval or disapproval in her life will be her own face in the mirror. I want her to have faith in herself and the conviction that she can be whatever she chooses to be and that she can triumph over every adversity. I want her to have faith that in spite of all its pains and frustrations, life has meaning and purpose.

How are we going to convey these values? We should develop a realistic strategy based on the fact that the key to translating values into the reality of a child's everyday life is to make ethical behavior a family affair. We should understand that teachable moments arise not only from positive events in our lives, not only from the occasions when we returned too much change in the market or the neighbors' sunglasses that were left on the porch, brought a meal to the local homeless shelter, or volunteered for a community-wide cleanup day. Our mistakes, moral failings, and missteps can teach valuable lessons as well if we just own up to them. If we show our children the courage and integrity to confront our own weaknesses as a human beings, we will teach some of the most important lessons about true character.

I know it takes a bit of arrogance (if not *chutzpah*) to give parenting advice to others. Although I travel the country doing just that, I am always mindful of the young schoolgirl's essay on ancient Greece that said, "Socrates was a Greek philosopher who went around giving people good advice. They poisoned him." It always reminds me that perhaps the best advice of all is to remember that there are no magic answers. All you can do is the best that you can do, and ultimately the best advice I can give is simply this—be the kind of adult you want your child to grow up to be. And the rest will take care of itself.

SYLVESTER MONROE is South bureau chief for *Time* magazine. He also reported for *Newsweek* for fifteen years, focusing on urban affairs, national politics, and the White House. Long interested in ethnic, racial, cultural, and educational issues, he is best known for his 1987 award-winning cover story "Brothers," which chronicled the lives of eleven of his boyhood friends from a Chicago housing project and later became a best-selling book. He has also won journalism awards for such cover stories as "Why Johnny Can't Write," "American Innovation," and "Why Public Schools Are Flunking." A graduate not just of the inner city but also of Harvard and Stanford, he is an alumnus of A Better Chance, Inc., a thirty-four-year-old outreach program that sends minority kids to elite secondary schools. A frequent public speaker at schools, he is now working on *The Class of '73*, a book about his graduating class at Harvard.

*16*

# My Mother's Gift to Me

*Sylvester Monroe*

H ᴇʏ, ᴍᴀ, which one should I be when I grow up, a scientist or a jet pilot?" I often asked my mother when I was about eight.

"Which one do you want to be?" she would reply.

"I don't know," I would shoot back. "I kinda want to be a scientist. But I think I want to be a jet pilot, too. Which one do you want me to be?"

"Whatever you want to be will be all right with me," she'd answer, "as long as whatever it is, you're the best you can be."

"You mean you don't care if I'm a bum?" I'd counter.

"I didn't say that," she'd respond, refusing to take the bait. "But if a bum is what you want to be, then as long as you are the best bum you can be, that's all I ask."

Note: © 1998 Sylvester Monroe.

My mother never told me what she wanted me to be. There was a time when I suspected she'd have liked to see me become a minister, though she never verbalized it. And I did not become a scientist or a jet pilot. But I also did not become a bum or a thug or succumb to any of the other pitfalls too often associated with poor black kids who grow up in low-income housing projects. A major part of the reason I didn't was because from an early age my mother instilled in me and my brother and sisters the value of being the best person each of us could be, no matter what we chose to do for a living.

When I was eight, I could never have imagined that I would become a journalist. I didn't know any reporters or writers, and no one in the South Side Chicago tenement where we lived had ever aspired to being a journalist. But thanks to my mother, when the ambition did sprout, there were no obstacles either in my family or, more important, in my mind. For though she never pushed me toward one career or another, she never pushed me away from any either.

In twenty-five years as a professional journalist, the question I have been asked most often is why I didn't turn out like a lot of my friends who grew up in that same South Side ghetto. In the past I deeply resented that question because what I heard being asked was why I was better. As I've gotten older, I've come to realize that there was something different about me. But it wasn't that I was better. It was that I had something my friends did not. And that was a very special gift I received from my mother.

Indeed, after life and an unconditional love, my mother gave me two things that I have always cherished. The first was the capacity to dream, to see beyond the meager probabilities of life as a child of poverty and into the boundless realm of possibility that is the haven of all dreamers. The second was a deeply rooted conviction that being born black and poor is no excuse for not being the best person I can be.

Being black and poor, my mother used to say, is no excuse for lying, cheating, and stealing. And it certainly doesn't give anyone the right to rob or kill. In other words, just because I was black and poor didn't mean I couldn't and shouldn't rise above my circumstances.

She never used the word *character*, but years later I understood that was what she was talking about. She was saying that character counts even in the ghetto. In fact, for many African American parents like my mother, born in the rural South and raised in the values of the Baptist church, character was especially important.

Black people must work twice as hard and be twice as good just to get the same opportunities as whites, she said. But she'd always temper that hard admonition with the encouraging note that if I did work hard and get the best education possible, I could do whatever I wanted in life or be anything I wanted to be. Of course she knew that the world wasn't that open to a black boy (or girl) living in Chicago's Robert Taylor Homes housing project in the 1960s. But she also understood that if my brother and five sisters and I were to have a chance of making it at all, we had to have something to reach for, something to hope for. Indeed, she had to give us a reason to get up every morning and run the gauntlet of gangs and violence that confronted us going to and from school every day.

Her regular dose of hopefulness was especially important in that it helped to counter the negative reality of black life I soaked up regularly from my often-bitter Mississippi-born grandfather and uncles, who often talked in my presence about the discouraging limitations placed on black ambition and accomplishment. A black man can't do this or that or will never be this or that, I heard them say, feeling the frustration and anger in their voices. Beneath the anger, I also heard and felt the fear that even if a black man did achieve a certain level or position in society, "the white man" would kill him if he got too big, too rich, or too powerful.

As a boy, I never quite understood the source of this anger, fear, and frustration, other than the message that white people never meant black people any good. Nor did I understand the tremendous sadness that engulfed my maternal grandfather like an ever-present cloud all the years that I knew him. Only after his death and the advent of my own adulthood did I learn its source.

The head of a family of Mississippi sharecroppers, my grandfather had once owned a large parcel of land in the Mississippi delta town of Leland, where I was born. The white family for whom we had worked as sharecroppers had left it to him. But his claim on that land was immediately challenged by other whites, who threatened his life and the lives of his family if he resisted. Barely able to read and write and recognizing the real danger for a black man making such a challenge to whites in early 1940s Mississippi, my grandfather relinquished his claim on the land.

My uncles—my mother's five brothers—not much better educated but younger, stronger, and much more reckless—vehemently disagreed with my grandfather's decision and vowed to fight to the death rather than be pushed off the land. As head of the family and knowing what could happen, my grandfather prevailed. But he was never the same after that and lived the remainder of his life plagued by chronic poor health. He died in 1977 at the age of seventy-nine, a sad, broken shadow of the man he had once been.

But he too gave me something that I have always cherished. And that was an understanding and appreciation of the value of education. Indeed, as far back as I can remember, he constantly drummed it into me that education is the key to black people's salvation. From the time I was old enough to understand the meaning of the word, my grandfather taught me that in this world, education would be my greatest asset, the one weapon I could always count on in a world often hostile to black people and to black males in particular. "It's the one thing nobody can take from you," he'd say.

One of the great joys of my life is that my grandfather lived long enough to see me graduate from Harvard College, one of the most prestigious plots of land in America. That happened only because of the character-building values I received from my family. How easy it would have been to give up and turn my back on a world that had treated nearly everyone I knew and loved so unfairly just because of the color of their skin. How easy it would have been to explode on crime and violence or implode on alcohol and drugs, as many of my friends did. But strength of character kept me off that path and on the straight and narrow, at least most of the time.

Lest anyone should think that I was some sort of goody-two-shoes as a boy, I was not. I cannot say that I never lied or stole or did things I knew weren't right. I did and I was punished for them. Like the time in sixth grade or so when a girl kicked me in the privates and I decked her. I had always been taught that it was wrong for a man to hit a woman, but I figured I had cause under the circumstances. "No," said my mother. "I don't care what she did. There is never any reason for a man to hit a woman." There it was again. Character.

Many of the values I learned as a child, which could be boiled down to one simple phrase—doing the right thing—have shaped the kind of man I've become. Education and training helped me become a reporter, but character determines what kind of reporter I am. For many of my journalistic colleagues, getting the story is paramount to everything else. But there have been times when getting the story just wasn't the right thing to do because it would have hurt someone.

Once, while reporting a story on a then new and successful drug abuse treatment program, I learned that one of the patients was the brother of a famous Hollywood celebrity. It was just the kind of scoop that would give my story that little something extra that editors love. But when the director of the program learned that I had discovered who the patient was, he asked me not to reveal it because it would cause great pain for the patient's family. Since there had been no rule or agreement up front that I could not use any information that I uncovered in my reporting, I had every journalistic right to publish the patient's name.

But the question was not whether it was legal but whether it was right. I could hear my mother's voice saying, "What would you want the reporter to do if the roles were reversed and it was your brother in that program?" I decided not to publish the patient's name. I lost the scoop, but I felt better about myself because I hadn't selfishly hurt other people just to get a story. As my mother would have said, I had done the right thing. That time the choice was relatively easy. There have been other times when it was much more difficult to choose the right course, and I have not always done the thing I knew to be right. But I have always understood the difference and tried to place character before expedience. And most of the time, thanks to the values instilled in me from an early age by my family, I've been able to make the right choice.

In some ways, having to overcome poverty and racism have developed my character as nothing else could. "Adversity," it is said, "builds character; character builds faith, and in the end, faith will not disappoint." I was an adult before I realized that was exactly the lesson my mother had always tried to teach me. I was even older before it sunk in that the linchpin of that statement, often quoted by the Reverend Jesse Jackson and others, is the role of character.

So, when I think back on that old recurring question, Why didn't I turn out like so many of my childhood friends? the answer is really simple. I was blessed to have the kind of mother they didn't.

It wasn't that their mothers didn't love them as much as mine loved me. It was that my mother taught me that while life is often not fair, the key to making the most of it is playing the very best game you can with the hand you're dealt. My grandmother called it understanding the difference between a glass that's half empty and one that's half full. I call it the gift of character.

Though I never became a jet pilot or a scientist, and whether I ever become the journalist I still aspire to be, the one thing I truly hope to be is half as good at teaching character to my children as my mother has been at teaching it to me.

# part four

# CHARACTER
## *at*
# WORK

WARREN BENNIS is distinguished professor of Business Administration and founding chairman of the Leadership Institute
at the University of Southern California. He is the author or
editor of more than twenty-five books on leadership, change
management, and creative collaboration. More than one million copies of his books are currently in print. He consults
with global corporations, as well as political leaders. His book
*Leaders* was named one of the fifty best business books of all
time by *Financial Times*. *Forbes* magazine has called Bennis
the "Dean of Leadership Gurus." His latest book, *Organizing
Genius: The Secrets of Creative Collaboration*, explores one of
Bennis's abiding interests—how leaders can create the social
architecture that generates intellectual capital.

*17*

# The Character
# of Leadership

*Warren Bennis*

S UCCESSFUL LEADERSHIP is not about being tough or
soft, assertive or sensitive. It is about having a particular set of attributes—which all leaders, male and female, seem to
share. And chief among these attributes is character.

E. B. White once said, "I wake up every morning determined
both to change the world and have one hell of a good time. Sometimes this makes planning the day a little difficult." Every leader
today shares a similar wake-up call and charge—both to change the
world and to have a good time doing it. But I would add an important footnote: the noble mission of the leader can't be used to justify
the means. In the leadership arena, character counts. I am not saying this casually. My convictions about character-based leadership

---

come from years of studies, observations, and interviews with leaders and with the people near them.

Most organizations evaluate their executives and managers using these seven criteria: technical competence or business literacy (knowledge of the territory), people skills (capacity to motivate people), conceptual skills (ability to put things together), results (track record), taste (capacity to choose terrific people most of the time), judgment (ability to make wise decisions in a fog of reality and uncertainty), and character (integrity to walk the talk).

Of all these, we know the least about judgment and character, including how to teach them. That's a shame, because I've never seen a person derailed from positions for lack of technical competence. But I've seen lots of people derailed for lack of judgment and character. The stakes are high for the individual, the organization, and the country, so it's worth knowing more about the character component of successful leadership.

Character isn't a superficial style. The word comes from an ancient Greek verb meaning "to engrave" and its related noun meaning "mark" or "distinctive quality." Character is who we essentially are. I also believe, however, that our character is continuously evolving. Unlike some of the Freudians, I don't think character is fixed at age six. I think we continue to grow and to develop. The corollary of this is that the process of *becoming* a leader, to me, is much the same process as becoming an integrated human being. I see a real connection between what it takes to be a leader and the process of character growth.

Leaders have vision and a strongly defined sense of purpose, they inspire trust, and they work for change. Thus one way to define leadership is as character in action.

## Vision

Leaders create a vision *with meaning*—one with significance, one that puts the players at the center of things rather than at the periphery. If organizations have a vision that is meaningful to people,

nothing will stop them from being successful. Not just any old vision will do, however; it must be a shared vision with meaning and
significance.

A vision can be shared only if it has meaning for the people involved in it. You can't be the only one making decisions. You can't
be the only leader. Rather you have to create an environment in
which people at all levels are empowered to be leaders, to subscribe
to your vision, and to make effective decisions.

To communicate a vision, you need more than words, speeches,
memos, and laminated plaques. You need to live a vision, day in, day
out—embodying it and empowering every other person to execute
that vision in everything he or she does, anchoring it in realities so
that it becomes a template for decision making. Actions do speak
louder than words.

## Purpose

I can't exaggerate the significance of a strong determination to achieve
a goal—a conviction, a passion, even a skewed distortion of reality
that focuses on a particular point of view. And the leader has to express that determination, or purpose, in various ways. There can be
many different purposes. Michael Eisner once told me that Disney
didn't have a "vision statement," but rather a strong "point of view"
about the Disney culture. When making big decisions, Eisner says,
"The strongest point of view almost always wins the argument."

Max De Pree, the former CEO of Herman Miller, once said,
"The first task of a leader is to help define reality." That's another
way of talking about purpose. Without a sense of alignment behind
a purpose the organization will be in trouble, because the opposite
of having purpose is drifting aimlessly. And it can't be any old purpose if it is to galvanize and energize and enthrall people. It has to
have meaning and resonance.

There's no reason why a persuasive point of view can't be an ethical one. Do you want a more ethical organization and society? Then

show leadership when decisions are being made, and be a *forceful, committed* advocate for ethics. Your deeply held point of view may carry the day.

But there is also a danger in presenting a strong point of view: it can intimidate others and shut down communication, and that's deadly for character and for effective leadership.

A leader needs candor to operate effectively. Unfortunately my studies show that seven out of ten people in organizations don't speak up if they think their point of view will vary from the conventional wisdom or their boss's point of view—even if they believe their boss is going to make an error. What a leader needs to cultivate are firm-minded subordinates with the wisdom and courage to say no. That means the leader needs to be trusted as a fair and honest person of integrity, someone who does not kill the messenger who tells the truth.

## Trust

Real leaders, and people of strong character, generate and sustain trust. I can't overemphasize the importance of encouraging openness, even dissent. An executive once wrote to me that his organization had "thousands of folks, union workers, who want the world to be the way it used to be, and they are very unwilling to accept any alternative forecast of the future." The problem was that there was no trust in that organization. This executive was an old-fashioned control-and-command type who never could regenerate trust among the key stakeholders. The union members were not the problem in this case.

Leaders must be candid in their communications and *show* that they care. They have to be seen to be trustworthy. Most communication has to be done eyeball to eyeball rather than in newsletters, on videos, or via satellite. One of the best ways to build trust is by deep listening. People's feeling that they're being heard is the most powerful dynamic of human interaction. Listening doesn't mean agreeing, but it does mean having the empathic reach to understand another.

To trust others, to have confidence in them, people of course also need to see evidence of competence. Yet another indispensable aspect of character, and leadership, is constancy. One of the things you hear about the least effective leaders is that they do whatever the last person they spoke to recommended or that they plunge forward with the latest good idea that pops into their heads. Before they can trust a leader, followers have to know what to expect. So sometimes leaders have to put off their grand ideas or glorious opportunities until they have had a chance to convince their allies of the ideas' value. In business, as in politics, the effectiveness of a decision is the quality of the decision multiplied by the acceptance of it.

What all these behaviors and skills surrounding trust add up to is integrity, and that means character. A leader with drive but not competence and integrity is a demagogue. One with competence but not integrity and drive is a technocrat. One with ambition and competence but not integrity is a destructive achiever.

## Action

What employees want most from their leaders is direction and meaning, trust and hope. Every good leader I have spoken with has had a willful determination to achieve a set of goals, a set of convictions, about what he or she wanted the organization to achieve. Every leader had a purpose. Remember what hockey great Wayne Gretzky says, "It's not where the puck is that counts. It's where the puck *will be*." Character counts because, in the leader, character is having the vision to see things not just the way they are but the way they should be—and doing something to make them that way.

Leaders have a bias toward action. They have the capacity to convert purpose and vision into action. It just isn't enough to have the great vision people can trust. It has to be manifest in some external products and results. Most leaders are pragmatic dreamers or practical idealists (even though those descriptions may seem like oxymorons). They step up and take their shots every day, perhaps knowing that "you miss 100 percent of the shots you don't take," to borrow another line from ice-rink philosopher Gretzky.

"Strike hard and try everything," wrote Henry James. You're never going to get anywhere unless you risk and try and then learn from each experience. Leaders have to play even when it means making mistakes. And they have to learn from those mistakes.

Companies are the direct reflection of their leaders. All the leaders I know have a strongly defined sense of purpose. And when you have an organization where the people are aligned behind a clearly defined vision and purpose, you get a powerful organization. Effective leaders are all about creative collaboration, about creating a shared sense of purpose. People need meaningful purpose. That's why we live. With a shared purpose we can achieve anything. And that's why a central task for the leader is the development of other leaders, creating conditions that enhance the ability of all employees to make decisions and create change. The leader must actively help his or her followers to reach their full leadership potential. As Max De Pree once put it: "The signs of outstanding leadership appear primarily among the followers."

We need more leaders, not managers. Leaders are people who do the right things. Managers are people who do things right. There's a profound difference. When you think about doing the right things, your mind immediately goes toward thinking about the future, thinking about dreams, missions, visions, strategic intents, purposes. When you think about doing things right, you think about control mechanisms. You think about how-to. Leaders ask the what and why questions, not the how questions. Leaders think about empowerment, not control. And the best definition of empowerment is not stealing responsibility from people. Grace Hopper, a management expert who was the first woman admiral in the U.S. Navy, has said, "You manage *things,* but you lead *people.*"

How do you go about becoming a good leader? Figure out what you're good at. Hire only good people who care, and treat them the way you want to be treated. Identify your one or two key objectives or directions and ask your coworkers how to get there. Listen hard and get out of their way. Cheer them. Switch from macho to maestro. Count the gains. Start right now.

RALPH S. LARSEN is chairman and chief executive of Johnson & Johnson, one of the world's largest corporations. Hired as a manufacturing trainee in 1962, he rose through the ranks of this highly respected health-care giant, known for its commitment to ethics, customers, employees, and communities. At a time when the commitment of many companies to their ethics codes and mission statements is being questioned, Johnson & Johnson made headlines by adhering to the company Credo and acting promptly to recall all its Tylenol products after tampering was discovered. The company lost millions of dollars but secured once again the trust and admiration of the country. Larsen is also a board member of Xerox and AT&T and a member of the Business Council and the Policy Committee of the Business Roundtable.

*18*

# Creating Corporate Character

*Ralph S. Larsen*

WHAT DO WE MEAN when we say that a person has character? Context aside, we mean that the person has *good values* and the integrity to live up to them. Where do these values come from? Given the powerful influence of family life and school, it is natural to assume that a person's character is formed long before that person becomes an adult and enters the workforce. It is easy to accept the common prejudice that, if anything, the influence of the workplace on character is *negative,* that work brings out the competitive worst in people.

Yet it is my experience that the modern workplace can be an extraordinarily powerful character-building institution. Indeed, in a fast-moving, competitive global culture and marketplace, I feel character

---

is a corporation's most valuable resource and product. A successful corporation's, that is.

At Johnson & Johnson (a $24-billion-in-sales consumer products and pharmaceutical concern) we expect our executives to demonstrate a number of exceptional qualities. They must be intelligent, innovative, and diligent. They have to master complexity, work well with other divisions, and be able to develop the people who report to them. But no matter how clever or competent they are, they must also have sound values and a powerful sense of integrity. In a world where corporate reputations built over decades can be destroyed overnight, it is absolutely essential that we employ and are represented by people of character.

At Johnson & Johnson we are terribly conscious of the need for leaders with the character to safeguard our reputation as a values-driven company at the same time as they press hard to produce outstanding business results in domestic and international markets. Our present growth rate of $2 to $3 billion per year creates exponentially increasing demands to hire, train, and retain leaders who can effectively deal with opportunities and challenges arising from new products and technologies. The problem becomes both more urgent and complex as we acquire companies whose employees have operated under different corporate cultures.

Of course we make every effort to hire people of exceptional character. But we don't rely entirely on their existing values. We also train our managers to make decisions according to our core values. We do this not only because we think it is morally right but also because we are essentially in the trust business. People of character are trusted people, and that gives us a significant competitive advantage.

For example, Johnson & Johnson consists of 180 companies located all over the world, and these companies conduct business in some countries where bribery and corruption are more common than in the United States. Under these circumstances in particular, competition tests our values—and provides continual opportunities to demonstrate integrity. With thousands of managers exercising significant responsibility, we know there is always a risk that some people will lack the moral fortitude—the character—to resist the temptation to elevate expediency over ethics. However, this simply intensifies our commitment to inculcate the core ethical values that form the bedrock of our corporate character—the Johnson & Johnson Credo.

## Mr. Johnson and His Credo

Ralph Waldo Emerson said that an institution is the lengthened shadow of one man. Robert Wood Johnson was chairman of our company from 1932 to 1963, and the influence of his character pervades our corporate culture to this day.

In the 1930s, during the Depression, Johnson wrote "Try Reality," a pamphlet that asked business to adopt "a new industrial philosophy." He said, "industry only has the right to succeed where it performs a real economic service and is a true social asset. . . . It is to the enlightened self-interest of modern industry to realize that its service to its customers comes first, its service to its employees and management second and its service to its stockholders last."

This was an unorthodox view at the time, and the business community was largely unresponsive. Yet Johnson was undaunted. A few years later he wrote the Johnson & Johnson Credo, a comprehensive statement of the company's obligations to its primary stakeholders: customers, employees, suppliers, communities, and shareholders.

He was not about to allow this document to be a meaningless wall hanging. He vigorously set about ensuring that the Credo became the bedrock of the company's management principles. While the Credo was not the first document of its kind in American business, it gained recognition as an innovative way to run a company and became a model for business. From its declaration of the primacy of our responsibility to the people who use our products to its articulation of our organization's duty to be a good citizen, the Credo has become the moral backbone of our worldwide operations.

It is truly wonderful to have a worthy doctrine that simply and eloquently defines the heritage of our organization. But how do we sustain that heritage as the years go by? How do we keep it vital and relevant in a changing world? These are the most critical questions we contend with, for we are convinced that the success of our organization is rooted in its special character. And we work very hard at sustaining and strengthening that character.

One of the great advantages we have is that so many of the people who work at Johnson & Johnson came here with personal values that are fully compatible with the Credo. Thus the Credo *reflects* the kind of individuals you find at Johnson & Johnson. People do not necessarily become Credo-ized after they join our company. They join us because some of the fundamental ways we think and act make sense to them.

The operative word here is *fundamental*. All of us at Johnson & Johnson start from a common set of beliefs, but we are anything but automatons. "Everyone must be considered as an individual," the Credo boldly declares, and respect for people courses through its every provision. We know the Credo is not self-enforcing. It must be interpreted and applied by individuals. Without people of character the Credo would become a hollow pledge.

The Credo has served us well even as we have grown larger and more diverse because it is a democratic, and therefore resilient, document. It provides a transcending set of principles that appeal to the ethical aspirations of people from many different cultural, ethnic, religious, and educational backgrounds. *That* is its magic.

We have discovered that the basic character of our organization—with its emphasis on responsibility to our customers, employees, and shareholders—strikes a chord with people whether they are from Cincinnati, São Paulo, Madrid, Bombay, Tokyo, or Sydney.

Although the CEO has always borne the ultimate responsibility for the Credo's vibrancy and perpetuation, it is a responsibility shared by every member of the Johnson & Johnson family of companies worldwide. That is the only way the Credo can remain a living document.

## The Credo in Practice

How does this play out in the everyday world? Here are three tests to our individual and group character, events that have the potential to result in great accomplishment—or disheartening setback.

*A test of ethics.* Like people everywhere, we at Johnson & Johnson face moral choices every day. When there is a clear choice between doing right or wrong, the decision is obvious. But we are often faced with moral dilemmas that present no easy answer, no clear ethical choice. The Credo cannot possibly be a formula that gives us the answer for every issue that comes up. However, it does give us an ethical framework for decision making. It helps good people be the best they can be. In this sense, it is a character builder. It leaves no doubt that we expect our employees to pursue the highest standards of integrity and ethics.

For example, say we enter a new business in a country where some customs run counter to our practices. While we will certainly always be honest, respectful, and law abiding, the answers to all questions may still not be obvious. We have to work our way through them. If we simply push ahead and insist on doing things our usual way, we may offend and possibly alienate well-intentioned people who simply do not see things the way we do. Individual decisions requiring patience, sensitivity, and good judgment must be made. Perhaps we would choose to talk the issue out in a way in which both sides gain understanding. This might take time, and we might give up some competitive advantage or lose an immediate business opportunity. Yet, if we were to compromise our integrity in this situation, what sort of message would that send the next time a moral or ethical decision had to be made? Because our corporate character is paramount, we will not betray the traditions or sully the reputation of our company for short-term gain.

Over the long term, principled action is not only the moral thing, it is the correct business decision.

Sometimes the moral challenges we face as individuals are less dramatic, seemingly trivial—yet equally telling. Take the scenario in which people from different departments are working as a team on creating a new, very promising product. A senior executive hears of the effort and is of the impression it's largely the work of one person, whom he commends. It may not be immoral for this team member to say thanks and walk off with a glow of satisfaction and heightened career expectations; but within a community where people have a strong sense of responsibility to each other, people expect more. They will see this as an opportunity to share earned credit with their colleagues. I would suggest that a duty to share credit is rooted in the ethical principles of respect and fairness and is a matter of character that speaks volumes about an individual. Though this is a simple example, its importance cannot be overstated. It has been my experience that people who can be counted on to make the ethically correct decisions on the big things—when the crisis hits and the pressure is on—are most often those who have made it a habit to work at making the correct ethical decision in the countless small choices each individual faces in life.

Are we perfect at Johnson & Johnson? Of course not. Do we misstep at times? Absolutely. What matters most is that we continue to strive to live up the moral standards we set for ourselves, to own up to our mistakes and to learn from them. From our view, that's character at its best.

*A test of leadership.* The twenty-first century promises an ever more dizzying pace of change. That means tougher competition. Heavier cost pressures. Greater needs for innovation. Continued technological challenges. And on and on.

What qualities will leaders need to be successful in this tumultuous world? They will have to be extremely responsive and adaptive to change. They will have to be able to embrace ambiguity and uncertainty, to look at change as a source of new opportunities to compete and grow. They will have to have the will, the energy, the determination, the fire, and the courage to take ever more vigorous, creative action. They will have to be entrepreneurially spirited, encouraging and rewarding individual effort and risk taking, but they will also need to be team oriented, to be able to break down dysfunctional, organizational, and geographic barriers to sharing the best ideas and taking action. And they will need to be able to do all these things in a way that reflects sound ethical and moral values.

It's one thing to identify the characteristics needed for leaders in the next century. It's quite another for a company to take the steps necessary to ensure that such leaders flourish, to provide an environment in which leaders can come forward with the ideas, the skills, and the initiative to take charge of change. At Johnson & Johnson, as one way to encourage leaders, we have created a program called FrameworkS.

The FrameworkS process flowed from our belief in the centrality of the individual and from our sense of our responsibility to treat each person with respect and dignity. It is built on the assumption that the people of our company have a great amount to contribute, have extraordinary pride in Johnson & Johnson, and want to be involved in keeping our company great.

FrameworkS is simple in concept, but it requires a very big commitment of time, energy, skill, and enthusiasm. Teams (representing members of our executive committee, operating company management at all levels, and corporate staff) address issues of great importance to Johnson & Johnson's future. Through a global process of intense research and no-holds-barred discussion and debate, FrameworkS enables the best ideas, talent, and experience at Johnson & Johnson to be directed toward mastering the challenges of change. Never before has such a broad-based group of people been invited to be central, active participants in matters of substantial corporate significance outside their own direct responsibilities.

Bringing this diverse talent and enthusiasm into the process of changing our corporation has had a remarkable impact. We are finding that Johnson & Johnson is more responsive and adaptive than ever before. We've started new businesses and entered new markets. We've set up global programs that are harvesting great returns for us in critical areas such as leadership development and innovation.

Perhaps more than any other single step we have taken, FrameworkS is helping to ensure that the special character of our firm is not only preserved but strengthened and kept vital and relevant.

We leave no room for doubt that we expect all our managers to live up to the highest standards of integrity. The senior management team of every Johnson & Johnson company attends a five-day leadership seminar in which nearly one full day is dedicated to an extensive discussion of how our Credo values apply to very specific and challenging hypothetical questions. This portion of the program is extremely powerful because the discussion is led by one of the nine most senior officers from Johnson & Johnson's international headquarters.

*A test of innovativeness.* Our Credo states that our first responsibility is to meet the needs of "the doctors, nurses and patients . . . mothers and fathers and all others who use our products and services." That means we must constantly be improving products and services. But as we see it, innovation in business is not simply the invention of a new product, service, process, business system, or management method. These things are the end result of innovation. For us, to be truly innovative goes to the heart of individual character.

Let's imagine somebody who develops, makes, or markets health-care products sitting in an office pondering how to come up with something really new. The usual approach is to look at the existing marketplace, scientific data, or manufacturing processes with the hope of identifying a need or operating efficiency that has yet to be tapped. This is fine. But we look for something more. And the search starts by looking within. We ask ourselves, what assumptions, biases, or habits might we have that could limit the scope of our ability to see with complete openness and clarity? What limits in skill, knowledge, risk taking, and self-initiative do we bring to the creative process that could diminish the potential for results? Whom should we reach out to with our ideas—and how do we work most effectively with such people?

Each time we answer these questions, we take ourselves into a broader dimension of thinking, creating, and acting. As we seek to see through others' eyes and to serve others' needs, we engage in a terrifically valuable character-building exercise.

What does such a way of looking at innovation mean to a company like Johnson & Johnson? The answer once again can be found in our respect for the individual and our belief in the capacity of every individual employee to make a contribution to our organization. It means that we view creativity and personal leadership as something every single person is capable of. It means that within every person can be found the knowledge, skill, motivation, and zeal to make something special happen.

By unleashing the incredible capacity of each individual to make a difference and by applauding good values, integrity, and fairness, we make the workplace an extraordinarily vibrant and enriching place of character building. This is the spirit in which the shared beliefs and values of Johnson & Johnson have evolved.

**B. David Brooks,** a pioneer in the character education field, is an international education consultant and president of the Jefferson Center for Character Education. A former teacher at all school levels and a principal at two Los Angeles area high schools, he is a member of the Character Counts! Coalition Advisory Council and of the Character Education Partnership. He has trained over four thousand teachers in his Lessons in Character curriculum (adopted by the L.A. Unified School District), and his STAR program to teach common core values systematically has reached over three million students. He is coauthor of *The Case for Character Education* (1983) and has also written books and articles about parent education, self-esteem, and preventing gang violence. Often serving as an expert in character education for the national media, he has appeared on numerous radio and TV talk shows.

*19*

# The Bottom Line
# on Character

*B. David Brooks*

D OES HAVING A WORKPLACE full of trustworthy, respectful, responsible, fair, caring, civic-minded employees make for a better workplace? Does it make for a more profitable business?

Consider the following story. A large bank in northern California started a program to train unemployed people as bank tellers. These individuals were hired and trained with full pay and benefits and were treated as regular employees. After only one year the bank terminated this uniquely worthwhile program, but not because of the inability of the participants to learn banking skills and not because of a lack of funding or participant interest. The reason the bank gave for ending the program was the participants' lack of "character."

Bank officials and trainers reported that they could teach banking skills, and the participants demonstrated that they could learn these skills. But too many of the participants were unreliable, failed to show up for training, arrived late, failed to call in when they were not going to be at work, could not take constructive criticism, and lacked initiative; in some cases they were dishonest.

These kinds of problems are no secret within the business community; yet when questioned about them, employers frequently shrug their shoulders in dismay and reply that they do the best they can given the type of worker they are getting. They bemoan the fact that they have no strategies to alleviate the problem. One employer said, "I don't have the time or the skills to teach my employees values and character. I just have to keep an eye on them, and if I catch them doing something wrong, I document it, and when I get enough, I let them go." My question to her was, "How much of your time and profits are you sacrificing while you are keeping your eye on your employees?" Her response was, "I think quite a bit."

This is an issue not only for the huge corporations that spot the business landscape but for all employers, from small companies with a few employees to those with several hundred or several thousand. When employees behave unethically, everyone suffers: the consumer, the vendor, the owner, the stockholders, and the other employees. Conversely, when a company's employees act ethically, there are many winners.

During the past several years, business and professional communities have begun to look at the issue of employee character and how it affects the bottom line—in other words, profit. Evidence of this growth of interest in values and ethics in the workplace is being underscored by the growth of the Ethics Officer Association (EOA), a national organization dedicated to promoting ethical business practices. The Ethics Officer Association was formed in 1992 with 12 members. At the end of 1997, it had a growing membership of 476 members. During 1997 alone, the membership nearly doubled.

In 1997, the EOA, along with the American Society of Chartered Life Underwriters and Chartered Financial Consultants, released the landmark study *Sources and Consequences of Workplace Pressure: Increasing the Risk of Unethical and Illegal Business Practices.* Study results showed that 16 percent of the employees who responded cut corners on quality control, 14 percent covered up incidents, and 11 percent abused or lied about sick days. These are but a few of the unethical behaviors reported, and each of them has an impact on the bottom-line issues of profitability, customer relations, and internal morale.

## The Character Education Movement

The heightened interest in character and values in the workplace has expressed itself as well in the swelling character education movement in schools. In 1983, Frank Goble and I wrote *The Case For Character Education,* the first book calling for a national discussion about returning to the systematic teaching of values and character in our nation's schools. In the fifteen years since then, there has been a phenomenal rise, especially among educators, in awareness of the importance of teaching the habits of good character in the same purposeful manner that we teach academics. It is apparent that educators have rediscovered the point made by Theodore Roosevelt when he said, "To educate a person in mind but not in morals is to educate a menace to society."

The character education movement has spawned a number of books, curricula, and organizations, and it has not been without its doubters and debates. Nonetheless, the need for character education is moving into the mainstream thinking of educators and is being supported by research studies that demonstrate the positive outcomes of systematic character education.

The students of today are the employees and executives of tomorrow. So it is natural for businesses, communities, and schools to work together to make ethics prevail in the classroom and in the office. They are coming to understand that as Esther Schaeffer, executive director of the Character Education Partnership, points out: "A person is not truly educated if her/his academic or technical knowledge is used or applied in a way that is inconsistent with high moral principles and practices. . . . Employees who are technical 'whizzes' can do much to improve a company. But without an ethical underpinning they can be highly destructive."

## What Can Be Done?

Let us assume for the sake of discussion that many people entering the workplace or already employed in it lack character. They may not be the majority perhaps, but they are certainly enough to cause a negative effect on the bottom line. What can an employer do?

- Understand that ethical leadership begins at the top. This is the first and perhaps most important principle. If management does not behave in a manner that models good character, then the rank and file cannot be expected to perform ethically.

- Make character training a part of the work experience. Simply acting with good character, though essential, is not enough. Leaders cannot expect those who follow them to adopt the habits of good character by osmosis. Like other skills training in the workplace, character training must be formalized.

- Act to support character education in the communities in which the business operates.

- Do not entertain the logical fallacy of thinking that ethics is *always* good business. Sometimes acting ethically—acting with character—will cost us more than we truly want to pay. We may lose an account or lose a job by being decent and honest. Nevertheless, immediate bottom-line considerations cannot drive all our decisions.

Current public attitudes are encouraging. The EOA 1997 study states: "When asked if they believed that 'ethical dilemmas are an unavoidable consequence of business and cannot be reduced' only 15 percent agreed. A substantial majority (60 percent) disagreed. This finding indicates a significant shift in public opinion." The report goes on to state: "In the 1970s and 1980s the pervasive view was that 'business ethics' was an oxymoron, or contradiction in terms. It has been assumed that this view has continued to be popularly held. This survey however indicates that today, a majority of workers believe that business and ethics can mix, and that ethical dilemmas can be reduced."

## How One Company Upholds Good Character

Today, major corporations are working hard to incorporate values and ethics into the mainstream thinking of their employees. Among these companies are Johnson & Johnson, 3M, Levi-Strauss, Sears Roebuck, Santa Barbara Research Center/Hughes Aircraft, Sprint, and Sun Microsystems.

One company at the forefront of this movement is Lancaster Laboratories in Pennsylvania. Earl Hess, the company's founder and CEO, realized that if his company was to grow and prosper, it was imperative that his employees practice the values he knew were vital. In the corporate mission statement, he crafted a statement of not only *"what* we do" but also *"how* we are committed doing it."

LANCASTER LABORATORIES' MISSION STATEMENT AND PRINCIPLES
We will provide quality, independent laboratory services in the chemical and biological sciences by:

fully understanding and always meeting the requirements of those we serve;

relating to our clients, coworkers, suppliers and community in a fair and ethical manner;

managing our growth and financial resources so we can serve our clients well, preserve independence and maintain our meaningful and enriching workplace.

Lancaster Labs then set up a committee, which became known as the ethics committee, to

> encourage and maintain commitment among employees to our core ethical values;
>
> act as a think tank in developing a "total ethics process" for orienting new employees and maintaining a high level of awareness and commitment of all within our organization;
>
> serve as a monitoring/oversight group for that purpose.

The next step Hess took was to institute a values training program. Its purpose was, first, to "develop a sense of urgency for the issue not only in our workplace but in society in general" and, second, to develop a statement of values shared by all employees.

LANCASTER LABORATORIES' STATEMENT OF VALUES
Lancaster Laboratories' heritage has as its core the ethical treatment of everyone involved with our business. As a corporate community, we embrace our heritage of integrity and strive to live by the following principles:

> Fairness and honesty in all our relationships;
>
> Mutual trust;
>
> A respect for ourselves and others;
>
> A sense of caring that leads us to act responsibly toward each other in society, now and in the future;
>
> Loyalty to our clients and one another;
>
> A spirit of open-mindedness as we deal with all;
>
> Dedication to serve;
>
> Good stewardship of our resources;
>
> A commitment to flexibility and continuous improvement.

We each take personal responsibility to live these values in all our dealings, knowing full well our pledge may involve difficult choices, hard work, and courage.

## The Community Example

Trying to improve the ethical climate just in one organization can be daunting. One way to make it easier, ironically, is to take on the world. Consider, for example, the huge and diverse city of Albuquerque, New Mexico. The city is an active member of the education movement CHARACTER COUNTS! As members of a CHARACTER COUNTS! Community, the city's institutional superstructure (consisting of the schools, government, and business and professional community) has embraced the six pillars of character: trustworthiness, respect, responsibility, fairness, caring, and citizenship. Not only are schoolchildren taught these nonpolitical, nonreligious (and therefore, nondivisive) values in the schools, but businesses are working to put these values in front of their employees. Initially the plan calls for a few local businesses to volunteer as *pilots*. Following this initial effort others will be invited to become involved. While it is too early to assess the effort's impact, the need for such an effort was verified by the fact that more companies requested to be pilots than the Albuquerque CHARACTER COUNTS! in the Workplace Leadership Council could handle.

The council has stated that character matters in the workplace because

> All workplaces have "customers," the organizations who receive the results of "employees" and "vendors." These are our work, our fellow workers, and those who provide to us. Customers who have confidence and faith in us return to buy our products and services, over and over again. Treating customers with respect and dignity enhances customer service. Listening and caring means more satisfied customers—and more profits.
>
> Fair and open communication and caring about our employees result in increased productivity, better morale and less turnover. Honest and ethical behavior means fewer business losses. Citizenship and responsibility promote teamwork and a sense of pride in job performance.

The workplace effort includes employee training in many areas in an effort to link the six pillars of character to various aspects of the working environment. Seminars focus on both awareness and implementation. The design is to have all workers develop the habits of good character. Training covers the following elements:

The Josephson Institute Decision Making Model, which states:

1. All decisions must take into account and reflect a concern for the interests and well-being of all stakeholders.

2. Ethical values and principles always take precedence over nonethical ones.

3. It is ethically proper to violate an ethical principle only when it is *clearly necessary* to advance another *true ethical principle* which, according to the decision maker's conscience, will produce the greatest balance of good *in the long run*.

Instruction in how to use the company's vision or mission statement to define character in the workplace.

Instruction in relating the six pillars of character to product creation, sales, customer services, invoicing, delivery, interviewing, hiring, and performance review processes.

## Recommendations

- Develop a code of ethics, regardless of the size of your company.

- Create ownership in the code of ethics by asking all levels of employee to participate in creating the code.

- Keep the code of ethics alive by making it part of the language and culture of the company.

- Make values and ethics an integral part of your interview, orientation, and review procedures.

- Ensure that ethical leadership starts at the top. Ethics must be a central belief and practice of management.

- Institute ongoing training in ethics and values.
- Institutionalize the notion that ethical dilemmas can be reduced through communication, awareness, discussions, training, and practice.
- Support character education in the schools.
- Recognize and reward ethical behavior. Ethical practices do have an impact on the bottom line!

ADMIRAL CHARLES R. LARSON was superintendent of the
U.S. Naval Academy from 1994 to 1998. Prior to that, he
served as commander in chief of the U.S. Pacific Command
(CINCPAC), the senior U.S. military officer in an area cover-
ing more than half the earth's surface. After first serving as
superintendent of the Naval Academy for three years in the
1980s, Larson, now a retired four-star admiral, was brought
back to the academy in 1994 to restore the elite institution's
reputation and reform its teaching of ethics after a highly publicized cheating scandal. His decorations include the Defense
Distinguished Service Medal, six Navy Distinguished Service
Medals, three Legion of Merit Medals, the Bronze Star Medal,
the Navy Commendation Medal, and the Navy Achievement
Medal. He has also been decorated by the governments of
Japan, Thailand, France, and Korea.

*20*

# Training Leaders

*Admiral Charles R. Larson*

J UST OUT OF the Naval Academy and flight school,
I was assigned the job of training officer at my first
squadron. I discovered that many of our people hadn't completed
required classes and that a major inspection was on the horizon. My
department head, the man whose performance evaluations would
affect my career, then informed me of the "standard" way these
things were handled. "Go ahead and make up phony records," he
said. "Take two or three different colored pens; put your X's on
there; smudge up the marks a bit so the records look old; and it'll
look real."

I had no idea the ethical and leadership principles I had just been
taught at the academy would be tested so soon! I wasn't anxious to

start my military career by antagonizing my superior officer, but sacrificing my integrity wasn't an option. I pledged to do a great job of getting everything up-to-date, but I said I wasn't going to fabricate the records. "If you want that done," I said, "you'll have to put someone else on the job." Fortunately the officer backed off. We did take a hit on the inspection, but it wasn't serious. I learned the valuable lesson that one could live up to high principles and survive.

This was just one experience that taught me that officers—and for that matter all people with responsibilities—face continual temptation to subordinate principle to expediency. Now, as Superintendent of the United States Naval Academy, I am responsible for ensuring that we instill in the next generation of leaders the moral courage to live up to the highest ethical values. I take that responsibility very seriously. Underlying every aspect of our training is the belief that one of the most essential attributes of a good officer is a sense of ethics, a quality often referred to as character.

## Why We Teach Ethics

I believe that moral integrity is the most important asset and duty of a military professional. If integrity fails, all else fails. There is no feeling of outrage equal to that of a public shocked by scandal when members of the military fall short of the high standards expected of them. In incidents as diverse as civilian casualties on the battlefield and sexual misconduct, we have seen the consequences to the military when individuals stray from strict adherence to ethical values like honesty, respect, and simple law-abidance. At the Naval Academy, we have taken great strides to overcome the impact of a major cheating incident that occurred several years ago.

As we approach the task of training leaders, we are keenly aware of the social forces that bear upon the values and character of the pool of young people from which the academy draws its students. We are concerned with mounting evidence that America is losing its moral bearings. We are especially concerned with a growing gap between the standards of ethics and integrity that seem prevalent in society as a whole and those that are indispensable to a military environment. We have thought a great deal about the erosion of values among young people and its potential impact in the armed forces, and as a result, we have intensified our efforts to instill values and build character.

We are, of course, not the only branch of the military concerned with ethics and character. Each branch has a statement of core values that serves as the basis of leadership training and evaluation. The Army singles out the values of loyalty, duty, integrity, and selfless service. The Air Force lists integrity, service before self, and excellence. At the Naval Academy, we build on the Navy and Marine Corps's three core values: honor, courage, and commitment. These sorts of values, however, cannot simply be imposed from the outside. The challenge is to get students to understand, appreciate, and assimilate them so they translate into daily habits and thus prepare students to take on one of the primary responsibilities of leadership—to teach and model values by word and example.

Good leaders are accountable for organizational standards through what they say and don't say and through what they do and don't do. As they prepare their units for inspections, exercises, and actual missions, leaders send unmistakable signals about values. They communicate messages about what is desired and expected by the way they handle subordinates who tell them things they don't want to hear. Subordinates analyze virtually everything a leader says or does. Consequently everything leaders do either bolsters or undermines the ethical foundation of their organization.

No one wants to go to untrained doctors or fly with untrained pilots, yet for some reason many people believe that most anyone can be a good person or an ethical leader without any formal training in what it means to be *good* in real-world settings. This is not our belief. At the academy we stress two different aspects of ethical behavior. First, we seek to instill values and principles that will help our students know what is right. Second, we seek to strengthen their moral will power, the courage to do what is right even when it may be costly or risky.

## How to Make Ethics Practical

We do not overemphasize moral quandaries, those knotty unsolvable ethical dilemmas that tend to generate more heat than light and reinforce the false idea that all matters of ethics are just matters of opinion. Instead, we stress real-world ethical issues, the kinds of everyday challenges officers are likely to face: giving honest readiness reports even if they could result in negative performance appraisals; dealing fairly and respectfully with subordinates; avoiding fraternization and sexual harassment; and so forth. While the weighty moral issues of launching a nuclear attack or targeting civilians in wartime make for fascinating discussions, we realize that very few, if any, of our graduates will ever have to deal with such issues.

During my career in the Navy I have seen extraordinary demonstrations of character and moral leadership. The best leaders comply with laws and policies not because they worry about getting caught but because their conscience, their moral fiber, forbids them from doing what is wrong. The exemplary leaders we want to produce honor promises as a matter of *principle,* not prudence. They play by the rules; respect the rights, claims, and possessions of others; and work diligently, even when the boss isn't looking, not simply out of self-interest but as a matter of personal honor.

At the academy, I like to hold up the example of Admiral Red Ramage. As a lieutenant commander he put his career at risk when he persisted in telling the full truth about the design failures of magnetic torpedoes. As a result he was relieved of the command of the submarine U.S.S. *Trout.* His integrity, however, won the day, and a year later, in 1944, he commanded another submarine that singlehandedly decimated a heavily escorted Japanese convoy. For this, Congress awarded him the Medal of Honor.

Sometimes moral courage does not result in awards or adulation, but one always earns pride and self-respect through uncompromising integrity. At the same time, we don't want to discourage individuals' personal ambition and a healthy regard for their careers. The key is finding the golden mean between "I" and "we" and always being able to answer this question affirmatively: Would I be proud to tell my family what I did today?

## How to Understand Loyalty

We also devote special attention to the particularly troublesome issue of loyalty. I have found it helps to think of two types: loyalty to the unit and loyalty to the institution.

Loyalty to the unit—a better phrase may be *esprit de corps*—is essential for small-unit success in combat and in the preparation for war. This is the loyalty that causes young men and women to make unbelievable sacrifices, possibly including their own lives. However, there is a dark side to this personal aspect of loyalty; it is the side we experienced at the academy during our cheating incident. The idea of protecting your buddy at all costs is loyalty gone awry when your buddy has done something wrong—like cheat on a test. The idea of being more loyal to one's comrades or shipmates than one is to one's unit, service, nation, or constitution is unacceptable to me because it puts the interests of individuals over the interests of the whole institution. Every officer must ultimately face the fact that personal loyalty must have its limits, that one's higher loyalty is to the institution and the nation.

## How We Teach Ethics

My number one goal as superintendent is to develop the character of the academy's young men and women. We tell midshipmen that we will give them the opportunity to exercise and strengthen their moral muscles because ethical fitness is essential to our mission and integral to their overall development. We have linked our character development program in a practical way to things people will experience in the naval service throughout their careers. By stressing integrity without compromise and excellence without arrogance, we intend to produce graduates who will become leaders both in the fleet and society.

We want our character development and leadership programs to be the benchmarks by which other military and civilian programs measure their effectiveness. Toward that end we have created a fully integrated, four-year character development program that runs across the curriculum. As soon as freshmen arrive for plebe summer, before their first fall term, they are introduced to the concept of honor and responsibility. They come to be familiar with the backbone of the Naval Academy's value system, "The Honor Concept of the Brigade of Midshipmen," which states: "Midshipmen are persons of integrity: They stand for that which is right. They tell the truth and ensure that the full truth is known. They do not lie. They embrace fairness in all actions. They ensure that work submitted is their own, and that assistance received from any source is authorized and properly documented. They do not cheat. They respect the property of others and ensure that others are able to benefit from the use of their own property. They do not steal."

We encourage midshipmen to think about and discuss the honor concept so they can fully commit themselves to it as a matter of principle. We try to instill the idea that the demands of military leadership far transcend the simple precepts of not lying, cheating, and stealing. These precepts are absolute bare minimum standards for the professional soldier, sailor, airman, or marine.

In any organization, first impressions are so important that the indoctrination period is critical. That is why we immediately begin to shape the attitudes of incoming midshipmen in plebe summer. It's unlikely that they will ever again be so consciously focused on the values and expectations that the academy communicates to them. We discuss loyalty extensively in our honor education program during that pivotal first summer and climax the training with a trip to the Holocaust Museum in Washington, D.C. Here, midshipmen can see firsthand what can happen when misplaced loyalty, blind obedience, and a lack of concern for human dignity are taken to the extreme.

In saying that midshipmen "stand for that which is right," we are not trying to promote legalistic thinking; we are not differentiating between what is *legally* right and what is *morally* right. It's not enough that a leader doesn't break the law, and we unequivocally reject the idea that "it's OK as long as you don't get caught." We also are careful not to encourage or reward the kind of cleverness that looks for legal loopholes or manipulates the system for personal advantage. In our emphasis on doing what is right and honorable rather than what is legal, we hope we are a constructive counterculture force in society.

Recently we introduced a core course entitled Ethics and Moral Reasoning for the Naval Leader. It combines the talents of accomplished philosophers and experienced senior naval officers to give midshipmen a sound foundation in both theoretical and applied ethics, as these relate to the military profession. And during each of the four years the midshipmen will spend with us they will participate in Integrity Development Seminars—ninety-minute monthly forums that address case studies that pose ethics and integrity issues in realistic situations. The discussions give students a chance to look within themselves—to define and clarify their basic moral values, to share their thoughts with others, and to see why ethical attributes are important and how they relate to our profession. We offer these courses to prepare our midshipmen to tackle the tough ethical challenges they may face both at the academy and in their careers in the fleet.

But we know we can't accomplish our character-building goals through classroom courses alone. Though formal study of ethics and integrity can heighten the student's ability to perceive and deal with tough ethical issues, we go much further. We consciously infuse our values and concern for character development into every aspect of the academy experience. We expect our officers, teachers, and students not simply to talk about character but to live it. It is a matter of the overall spirit and atmosphere of the organization.

We have also incorporated ethics across the curriculum, ensuring that our core courses—English, history, political science, and naval leadership—contain strong ethical components. Many of our majors' courses have added ethical segments. For example, in 1997, all computer science majors received a minimum of twelve hours of ethics instruction in their computer science courses.

Additionally, our advanced foreign language courses debate ethical issues in their particular languages. This academywide effort is to impress upon the midshipmen that there are no areas where ethics does not in some way come into play. We know that before people can properly address an ethical issue, they must realize that the decision they confront is an ethical one or at least has a moral component.

Because of the authority and responsibility entrusted to a military officer, we have a special concern for teaching midshipmen how to deal fairly and respectfully with other people. Often it comes down to what is referred to as the Golden Rule, as it was first described by Confucius: treat other people the way you would like to be treated, and treat every person with dignity and respect. To this end we supplement our character development program with a four-year human relations education plan that emphasizes human dignity and mutual respect. The most serious challenges we can see for military ethics as we enter the twenty-first century lie in these areas. Minority issues, gender issues, and fair and equitable treatment of all service personnel should be of major ethical concern to all commanders and leaders.

Why do I feel so strongly about the academy's efforts at this time? The fact that the United States is the only remaining superpower has, in my opinion, profound ethical implications for those of us in the military and the government. We are normally quite good at analyzing problems in terms of the enemy, economic factors, technological issues, political considerations, and so forth. However, we also need to look at the options in the light of what is the *right* thing to do. And we must be clear about the stakes. As Jonathan Shay argues in *Achilles in Vietnam: Combat Trauma and the Undoing of Character,* leaders who violate basic accepted moral values in times of great stress can *permanently* destroy the character of individuals under their command.

At its best, education has to do with examining and instilling values. At the academy, we know one cannot become ethical and develop good character simply by reading a book or listening to a lecture. Developing good character means developing good habits, implanted with wise and rigorous training. People have good judgment because they work at it. Although it may be impossible to *teach* character, we believe it can be *learned* by a committed student who is encouraged by the example of leaders. And true leaders know that character is not about never failing; it is about never quitting the effort to be ethical, to do the right thing regardless of the cost.

RUSHWORTH M. KIDDER is the founder and president of the Institute for Global Ethics in Camden, Maine, and a former senior columnist and editor at the *Christian Science Monitor.* A prolific author, his writings include *Heartland Ethics; How Good People Make Tough Choices: Resolving the Dilemmas of Ethical Living;* and *Shared Values for a Troubled World: Conversations with Men and Women of Conscience.* An English professor for ten years at Wichita State University, Kidder has won numerous awards, including the Explicator Literary Foundation Award for his book on the poetry of e. e. cummings. His *Monitor* essays have also appeared in the American Society of Newspapers Editors' collections of the best in newspaper writing. He is a trustee of the Charles Stewart Mott Foundation and of Principia College.

*21*

# The Eagle and the Knapsack

## *Rushworth M. Kidder*

CHARACTER, WE'VE BEEN TOLD, is what you are in the dark, when no one's looking.

The test of character, by this definition, lies in how you behave when public approval and overt reward are stripped away. When you can get away with anything—because nothing's at stake except your own conscience—what do you do?

No question about it: character *does* get tested that way. But in the hurly-burly of today's world, such moments are few. Far more common are tests of character that happen when everyone's watching—and when the rewards are significant. Character is indeed private and personal. But it's also public and social.

That at least was how it played out for Floyd, who shared his experience in a seminar several years ago. Floyd (not his real name) was

---

a senior executive at a leading advertising agency. One of his top clients was preparing a line of lightweight knapsacks for the Christmas season and wanted to launch it with a major TV ad campaign. So Floyd's creative staff, after days of huddling, came up with an idea everyone thought was a winner. Here sits the knapsack on a rock in the wilderness, with snowcapped peaks in the background. Down swoops an eagle, grasps the knapsack in its talons, and carries it away. The imagery is terrific: lightness, strength, beauty, flight, and the great outdoors all rolled into one.

Terrific concept, says the client. So Floyd contacts an animal trainer in California to prepare an eagle. He nails down a Rocky Mountain site for the shoot. And he lines up the details—writers, producers, cameras, lighting, travel, housing, and all the rest. It will take a day on location to shoot the footage, which he budgets in the six-figure range. The client signs off and promises to send a representative along for the trip.

Several weeks later the trainer calls with good news: the eagle knows how to pick up the knapsack. Floyd arranges the date, sends the team off, and turns his attention to other matters. A few days later, he gets the videotape—a glorious sequence, with the bird soaring in, grabbing the knapsack, and flying away. The client loves it.

But one afternoon, just as Floyd is preparing to schedule advertising space on national television, two of his staff slip into his office, shut the door behind them, and ask if they can talk.

They were on location in Colorado, they tell him, and it was time to film the eagle. Everything was set. The cameras were rolling. The bird swooped down on command and grabbed the knapsack—and couldn't lift it. The crew tried the sequence again. Same thing. Then it dawned on the trainer that the bird, trained at sea level, couldn't get enough air under its wings at ten thousand feet. So with time running out, and the client's representative watching, the crew members tied some almost-invisible monofilament fishing line to the knapsack. Then two of them, holding the line and standing just out of camera range, gave it a jerk just as the eagle grabbed the knapsack—and up it went. The client's representative, new to advertising production, registered no complaint—perhaps because she mistakenly thought such practices were standard. Back in the studio, the crew used a computer to erase the faint images of the hair-thin line. Result: a visually flawless commercial, which only a handful of people would ever know was partly fabricated.

Floyd listened, astonished and dismayed. All kinds of things ran through his head. On the one hand, he knew the public doesn't always expect TV ads to be true to life. After all, how many housewives, cleaning their kitchen floors, have had a white-robed genie suddenly spin through the window and offer them a better bottle of wax? Yet nothing else in this ad announced it as a fabrication. Given its realistic appearance, wouldn't the viewer reasonably expect it to reflect a real situation? After all, what about the recent outcry in the press when a foreign carmaker made an apparently realistic ad to promote its products—and was later found to have rigged the filming? Yet this was different, Floyd reasoned. There was no attempt to deceive. The eagle could indeed pick up the knapsack—at sea level. It just couldn't do it at ten thousand feet.

Floyd knew that, in today's video culture, audiences are seasoned viewers of special effects. Some viewers would write off the entire ad as a studio creation, despite the fact that it really had been filmed on location. They wouldn't care about the fishing line.

Floyd also knew he could reshoot at a lower altitude—for another day's costs, which his company would have to swallow, and with serious consequences for the client's schedule, which was already running perilously close to the Christmas deadlines. Miss those deadlines, and the new product could be dead in the water.

He knew, too, that he could paste the word "simulation" onto the screen in the current ad—but that the client, having paid for the real thing, would be pretty upset with that solution.

Finally, he knew he had a stark choice before him. He could tell the client. Or he could let the ad run as it was.

His colleagues were waiting for him to make the call.

## The Two Components of Character

In fact, what his colleagues were waiting to see was an expression of character. In that context, they were not thinking of character in its commonplace meaning (almost synonymous with personality)—a set of individual attributes or qualities by which someone is known. They were thinking of character in its moral sense, the capacity to express integrity, virtue, goodness. They were waiting to see how Floyd's outward behavior—phoning the media buyers or phoning the client to break the bad news—would manifest an inner set of moral values.

Character, then, has two components: values and behavior. We reserve our highest sense of the word *character* for actions where the values and the behavior come together seamlessly. Individuals who lack character, we say, are those who can't bring themselves to do what's right—either because they lack moral courage or because their values are so flaccid and impoverished that any action based on them is also morally anemic. Individuals of character, in contrast, are those who walk their talk, keep their promises, do what's right. There's no daylight visible between the standards they profess and the ways they act. The one perfectly reflects the other.

Is there, then, a set of shared moral values upon which most people construct their character? That's a question I asked in interviewing twenty-four individuals from sixteen countries for my book *Shared Values for a Troubled World: Conversations with Men and Women of Conscience.* They represented a wide variety of cultural, political, and religious backgrounds, and each was a moral exemplar within his or her culture. Among other things, I asked them, "If you could construct a global code of ethics for the twenty-first century, what would be on it?" Out of their answers came a set of eight values so widely shared and so cross-cultural that they seemed truly global: love, truth, freedom, fairness, unity, tolerance, responsibility, and respect for life.

More recently, a report from the Institute for Global Ethics detailed the results of an October 1996 survey the institute conducted at the annual meeting of the State of the World Forum in San Francisco. The 272 survey participants represented forty countries and more than fifty different faith communities. Despite their differences, they came together strongly around a shared set of moral values that elevated truth, compassion, and responsibility to the top ranks. Nor did the survey find any differences in values correlated to such characteristics as nationality, sex, religion, age, or social status. The participants' values were apparently uninfluenced by such demographic characteristics.

In the institute's seminars—which have brought together more than five thousand people in small teams that discuss and determine their shared values—five values almost always stand out: honesty, compassion, fairness, responsibility, and respect. These values, in fact, square well with those of various codes already in existence: the Rotary Four-Way Test; the Boy Scout Law; the six pillars of character developed by the CHARACTER COUNTS! Coalition and the Josephson Institute; the ten rules identified by American philosopher Bernard Gert in his book *The Moral Rules: A New Foundation for Morality*; the "five basic commands to human beings" adumbrated by German philosopher Hans Kung in *Global Responsibility: In Search of a New World Ethic*; the seven "terminal values" identified by Milton Rokeach and Sandra Ball-Rokeach in their groundbreaking values research; the Universal Declaration of Human Rights; and the hundreds of corporate, professional, governmental, and educational codes of values.

What is the bottom line? A minimalist set of core shared values seems to be part and parcel of the human experience—not because we are Buddhists or Moslems, Jews or Christians, left-wing or right-wing, rich or poor, male or female, but because we are human.

That set of shared values is half of what we mean when we talk about character. If these core values are missing in any serious way—if someone is, say, compassionate and fair but an inveterate liar—we're hard pressed to describe him or her as someone of character. And if the moral boundary within which these values operate is so wizened and narrow as to apply to only a few other people—if individuals are compassionate only toward members of their own family, tribe, or race and treat everyone else with cold disdain or venomous hatred—there, too, we say that something is lacking in character. Character, then, roots itself in the core moral values.

But it doesn't stop there. True character arises in the *practice* of sound values. Now and then we encounter individuals with a finely turned moral conscience but a wholesale incapacity to act on their beliefs. Perhaps they feel above the world, dismissing it with contempt and refusing to act for its betterment. Perhaps they shrink into timidity every time they are called upon to take a stand. Perhaps they are consumed with desire for wealth, fame, or power—the three great drivers of unethical behavior—and cannot bring themselves to make any sacrifice, however small, for the sake of integrity.

Whatever the reason, a failure to align action with values—even when the values are splendid—leads to the perception that character is lacking. Usually, it seems, the fault lies in a lack of moral courage. My 1926 *Webster's* defines "courage" as "mental or moral strength enabling one to venture, persevere, and withstand danger, fear or difficulty firmly and resolutely." To illustrate, it quotes General William T. Sherman, who defined "true courage" as "a perfect sensibility of the measure of danger and a mental willingness to endure it." If you don't know there's danger—if you're sleepwalking on the ridgepole—you can't be said to have courage. Nor do you have it if you sense the danger and aren't willing to endure it. Sherman, of course, was talking about physical courage. Its moral counterpart arises when the measure of danger comes from taking the moral high ground.

Character? Think of it as the product of core values and moral courage.

## The Support for Values and Courage

What about Floyd's character? That's what his colleagues were asking. Would he bull on forward with the ad, trusting that it wouldn't make waves but willing to justify it if something broke? Or would he disappoint one of his lead clients—and cost the firm a bundle—by sticking to standards that many viewers might see as needlessly narrow?

It was not, Floyd recalled, an easy decision—not so much because of the cost as because of the deadline. In the end, however, he called the client, pulled the video, and offered to reshoot. The client was so disappointed that it opted for a wholly different ad campaign, abandoning the eagle entirely.

"You never saw that ad," Floyd reported to the seminar, "because it never ran."

Run a check on Floyd's values, and you'll find them very much like most people's. Truth was there, telling him to be honest and upfront about the experience. Responsibility was there, telling him that if his firm made a mistake they had to make it good, regardless of cost. Respect was there, telling him that his audiences deserved better than to be deceived, even modestly. Fairness was there, telling him that he had to make no special deals with one client that he was unwilling to make with every client, present or future. And compassion was there, telling him that his two colleagues deserved to be honored for speaking up—and to see proof that they were right in expressing moral qualms.

But all that could have been in place, and still Floyd could have lacked the courage to act. What helped him, he told the seminar, was his company's own moral standards. His firm, he felt, had a long tradition of ethical behavior. When he found himself staring down the barrel of this decision, he knew he had to do what would be in the best long-term interests of his firm. He knew he risked a lot of money. He knew he could lose a client. But that, for him, was less important than the possible loss of the firm's reputation for ethical business. And he knew, deep down, that many of his fellow executives would back him up. He knew that the culture of the firm was such that ethics would ultimately be rewarded—however much they all had to tighten their belts and admit mistakes in the meantime.

What made the difference here? It's easy to take the narrow view and say, "Floyd's character, because he had the guts to make the tough moral call." And that's certainly true. But there's more. At least three other things mattered:

- Floyd was the kind of person you could talk to about moral issues. Otherwise his colleagues would never have approached him with their concerns.

- He was surrounded by people who recognized a moral qualm when they saw one—and were willing to be publicly worried about it.

- His corporate culture supported ethics, and that culture had been well enough articulated that Floyd could feel its presence when he most needed it.

Too often the study of moral character misses these last three vital points. Yes, character is what you are in the dark. But it's more. It has a social as well as a personal aspect. First, it's what you let others know you to be—the way you communicate to others an openness to ethical concern, a willingness to engage tough moral issues, an invitation to openly challenge your actions by your values.

Second, character doesn't exist in a personal vacuum. Show me the person of solid character who doesn't have a single ethical colleague, and I'll show you a person who is either so inspired as to be a saint or so out of touch with reality as to be delusional. Like coals in a fireplace, we keep our sense of character warm by contact with each other. Set any one of us alone on the moral hearth, and we'll pretty quickly turn to a cold, dark cinder.

Third, character benefits mightily from an organizational culture. The most open and moral thinker, with the finest of friends, can get beaten into submission by a crass and immoral culture—unless (and this is more likely) he or she bails out altogether and finds another workplace. Conversely, those willing to learn more about their own characters—and we're all learning how best to square our values with our actions—will find it far easier to be ethical if, at every turn, the institution applauds and rewards such behavior.

If there's a lesson here, it's that organizations as well as individuals need to think about character as never before. Why? Because, as we move into the twenty-first century, the moral intensity is rising. Increasingly our new technologies are leveraging our ethics, so that single unethical decisions can now have worldwide consequences in ways impossible to imagine just a few years ago. Yet when a Chernobyl melts down, a Barings Bank goes belly up, a *Challenger* explodes, an Exxon *Valdez* goes aground—or when an ad gets made in a potentially deceptive manner—the fault lies not with new technologies. It lies with a collapse of character, a failure in ethical decision making by the actors who drive the technologies.

If character matters, it is not because a few impassioned thinkers know it's important. It is because we won't survive the twenty-first century without it.

Brigadier General Malham M. Wakin is William Lyon
Professor of Professional Ethics emeritus at the U.S. Air Force
Academy, where over the course of forty years he achieved
renown as a teacher, administrator, and authority of the subject
of ethics. He was featured as one of twelve "great professors"
by *People* magazine in the 1970s and profiled by *Newsweek* in
the 1980s. He was national chairman of the Joint Services Conference on Professional Ethics from 1979 to 1992 and is a member of the Ethics Oversight Committee for the U.S. Olympic
Committee. He is the author of several articles and books on
ethics, leadership, and the military profession, including *War,
Morality and the Military Profession; Introduction to Symbolic
Logic;* and *The Teaching of Ethics in the Military.* His military
decorations include the Distinguished Service Medal, the Legion
of Merit, and the Air Force Commendation Medal.

# 22

# Personal and Professional Ethics

## *Brigadier General Malham M. Wakin*

SOME YEARS AGO a student in my medical ethics class approached me after he got a B on a research paper (it was worth 40 percent of the grade in the course). This student had worked hard during the course and on his twenty-page paper, and there was tragic disappointment on his face. "I need an A on this paper," he said. "Please, you must raise my paper grade or you'll jeopardize my chance to be admitted to med school."

Now, I wanted to help this student get into medical school because I believed he had the potential to be an excellent physician, and I had said as much in the strong letter of reference I had written for him. But raise his grade on the basis of his request? My immediate response was, "I can't do that." It wasn't that I didn't have the power or even the authority to change the grade, and I wasn't worried about getting caught. I couldn't do it because it would be wrong.

An understanding of human character is often bound up with that answer—"I can't do that." Our personal moral values establish limits of what we permit ourselves to do—what we *can* and *can't* do. Our character is defined by these values and how well we live up to them.

Changing the grade to give a mark that was not earned was something I *could* not do because it would be wrong. It would be unfair to other students and dishonest to my true evaluation of the paper. Thus refusing the request was a matter of integrity. My *personal* integrity, my self-respect, my view of my moral character, my ability to live with myself if I knowingly chose to do what I believed to be morally wrong were at stake.

Moral integrity is the condition of being whole, undivided in values and conduct. A person with integrity steadfastly adheres to a moral code of conduct about what is right and what is wrong. Personal integrity, then, is about living up to one's own personal values.

But as a doctor, teacher, and Air Force officer, I've come to realize that there is also such a thing as *professional* integrity, a concept arising from the special duties and values of one's profession. There are, for example, a number of specific values associated with the teaching profession that place role-specific constraints on teachers' conduct. Among these values are the obligation to be competent in the subject matter and in teaching techniques; to be prepared; to demonstrate special concern for each student's intellectual and, yes, character development; and to fairly evaluate student work on its merits. Teachers also must be conscious of the example they set for students. Finally, teachers have special responsibilities to the institution, to their colleagues, and to the community they serve. My role-related professional values impose an additional set of obligations on me. They constitute an important part of who I am—they help identify my character.

## Relating Personal to Professional Ethics

How are personal character and professional integrity related? Some people believe that it is possible to compartmentalize integrity and character into separate spheres. They believe it is possible to live up to high standards of competence and ethics in one's professional role—at the hospital, in the school, at the military base—but live an entirely different kind of moral life in private. Thus they can choose to live to high standards of honesty and ethics at work but cheat on their spouses and taxes at home. Or they can be scrupulously ethical in their personal relationships and private dealings and be deceitful, unfair, or unaccountable on the job. Many people seem to believe in a double standard of ethics, feeling they can do certain things in their roles as professionals that they would never do in their private lives. Certainly there are pressures and customary practices that support this view. People in sales and marketing may be less scrupulous about absolute truth in their professional lives; journalists may believe it is their job, a professional necessity, to invade others' privacy; lawyers may knowingly discredit honest witnesses in the name of zealous advocacy; and military people may be expected to follow orders without questioning their wisdom or moral propriety. Quite simply, some jobs expect and even require conduct that would be clearly wrong in a different setting. But is an act ethical simply because it is customary in particular professions?

Despite the occasional clashes between the seeming requirements of professional and personal ethics, I believe that they are generally compatible and interdependent. Since professions exist to serve society's vital needs (education, health, justice, security, and so forth), the means used to provide those valued services and results should be morally decent means, and the persons in the professions who provide them should be morally decent persons. Wherever possible, disparities between private and professional values ought to be eliminated. Put in more direct terms, good teachers ought to be good persons, good doctors ought to be good persons, good lawyers ought to be good persons, and good military professionals ought to be good persons. That means that professional practices must always be constrained by basic moral principles.

At the Air Force Academy we want leaders who will do the right thing in a crisis. We believe the best way to ensure this is to put people of decent moral character in command. We believe that a superior officer can carry out professional duties with a clear conscience.

Consider a complicated case from the medical profession. Assume I am a general practitioner who has just received the results of the blood tests on a twenty-three-year-old male patient who turns out to be HIV-positive. He is also engaged to be married. I point out to him his responsibility to inform his fiancée, because she has a right to know about the danger to her and to any future children they might have. He reacts very emotionally to my suggestion because he believes she will refuse to marry him if she learns he has the AIDS virus. He says to me, "You must keep my condition a secret from her and from everyone. You're bound by the principle of patient confidentiality." The moral principles that guide me as a medical professional are ambiguous in this matter. On the one hand the obligation to respect patient autonomy and the duty to maintain patient confidentiality are very important professional principles. On the other hand I cannot ignore accountability if I allow him to endanger his fiancée, if I remain silent. In the end, I could not subordinate what I believe to be my moral obligations as a person to what some might construe to be my special obligations as a doctor. Although it is a tough decision that might subject me to professional criticism or discipline, I would tell my patient, "I can't do that."

Here is another example of the tension between personal and professional integrity, with even higher stakes. It's the spring of 1968, and I'm a young sergeant in a combat infantry company in South Vietnam. My platoon has captured an entire village of suspected Viet Cong sympathizers: four hundred people—women, old people, children, and babies. We find no weapons in the village. My lieutenant orders us to herd the villagers to a roadside ditch and shoot them. I say to him, "I can't do that." What I mean is, *we* can't do that—no one can do that. I know that I have a duty to obey the orders of my superiors (a mark of professional integrity), but I know that this order is in direct conflict with both my country's laws and with the fundamental moral law against harming the innocent. Several years earlier, General Douglas MacArthur had said: "The soldier, be he friend or foe, is charged with the protection of the weak and unarmed. It is the very essence and reason of his being. When he violates this sacred trust, he not only profanes his entire cult but threatens the fabric of international society." In this case of conflicting duties, my professional integrity tells me that my higher duty is to avoid harming the innocent, and when I'm ordered to kill babies— I can't do that.

## Defining Integrity

When we use the word integrity in a moral context, we refer to the whole moral character of a person, and we most frequently allude to living up to one's personal values. When we say to someone, "don't compromise your integrity," we usually mean, "act in accordance with your moral principles within your value system. Be consistent." There is a real sense in which integrity encompasses our personal identity. As Polonius has it, "to thine own self be true."

But we must be very careful here. Consistency between personal values and conduct is not all there is to integrity. There is little merit in being consistent with your principles if "thine own self" is egoistic, treacherous, criminal, or abusive. When we use integrity in the moral context and as a description of character, we are talking about strict adherence to ethical principles like honesty, respect, responsibility, fairness, and compassion. And *subscribing* to decent moral principles is not enough. A person of integrity must *act* on decent principles— consistently. As others have noted, integrity is the bridge between character and conduct.

Integrity is the modern name we use to describe the qualities possessed by people who consistently act according to a firmly established character pattern—people who do the right thing. We especially stress the concepts of integrity when there is temptation to diverge from what good character demands. People of integrity act in accordance with strong moral principle even when it is not expedient or personally advantageous to do so. People of integrity act like the ideal people they are trying to be. This is perhaps what the ancient Taoist had in mind when he said, "The way to do is to be." Thus the wholeness of the good person, the total identity, is what we mean when we refer to his or her integrity. When we say, "don't sacrifice your integrity," we really mean, "don't stop being who you ought to be."

If I'm a member of one of the professions, then who I ought to be must also involve my social role as a practicing professional. My professional integrity must surely be viewed as a component of my overall character. I stress here the social aspect of professional integrity because the community is involved at every stage of professional development. Members of the public professions are educated and supported by the society for the critical services they provide. Teachers in public institutions and military professionals are supported from the public coffers during their entire careers. Clearly, some of their role-specific obligations are based on this relationship and on their authority to act on behalf of the entire society. With the authority to act goes the public trust, and violations of that trust are serious breaches of professional integrity.

Professional integrity derives its substance from the fundamental goals or mission of the profession. For the military profession, that mission might be broadly described as the preservation and protection of a way of life deemed worth preserving. Just as performing unneeded surgical procedures for profit would violate a physician's professional integrity, so too would engaging in operations that are not militarily necessary in order to reflect glory on the commander be a breach.

## Understanding the Role of Competence

In the military, as in all of the professions, the issue of competence is directly relevant to professional integrity. Because human life, national security, and expenditures from the national treasury are so frequently at issue when the military act, the obligation to be competent is not merely prudential. In ethical terms, there is a moral duty, a responsibility, to develop, maintain, and employ the high level of skills and knowledge necessary for excellent performance of assigned tasks. Incompetence here is clearly a violation of professional integrity. A B52 pilot who engages in unsafe practices such as forbidden flying maneuvers, endangering the lives of other crew members and people on the ground, violates the mandates of professional integrity—and so do colleagues and superior officers who know of the conduct and take no action to prevent it from reoccurring.

Thus it isn't enough to conform one's own conduct to professional standards. There is also a social aspect to professional integrity that imposes on all members of a profession a responsibility to ensure that their colleagues live up to these standards as well. When surgeons bury the mistakes of their incompetent colleagues rather than expose them, when they protect each other by a code of silence rather than seek to remove the licenses of dangerous doctors, they fall short of their responsibilities to the profession—they sin against professional integrity.

The same is true in military service. Officers who spot dereliction of duty, failures of leadership, incompetence, or any form of corruption among their fellow officers have a duty to take corrective action. The wing commanders who know of repeated safety violations by that reckless B52 pilot yet who don't ground him before he kills himself and others fail in their responsibilities. They violate their professional integrity.

Often the obligations of professional integrity may be pitted against personal loyalties or friendships. Even then there should be no doubt how the conflict must be resolved. The highest loyalty is to the profession itself, and invariably that requires individuals to place their public duties above their personal relationships. The military profession has many codes, regulations, mottoes, and traditions that combine to form a military ethic on which professional integrity is based. At the Air Force Academy we have our honor code, our honor oath, and our specific list of core values (now identical with the official list of core values of the U.S. Air Force). Our core values are integrity first, service before self, *and* excellence in all that we do. It is no accident that we say, "integrity first." We are not training leaders to be blindly, unquestionably obedient. We agree with the observation of General Charles Krulak, commandant of the U.S. Marine Corps, that the military has "traditionally enjoyed its greatest success when its members concentrated on doing the right things instead of doing things right."

The essential nature of the military profession is to serve its parent society. We make specific our commitment to the conception that good soldiers are good persons. What we should mean when we commit ourselves to integrity first is that we understand the importance of both personal integrity and professional integrity, as two compatible faces of our moral character.

# part five

# CHARACTER
## *in*
# SOCIETY

ARIANNA HUFFINGTON is a nationally syndicated columnist and the author of many books, including *Greetings from the Lincoln Bedroom; The Fourth Instinct; The Female Woman; After Reason; Maria Callas; The Gods of Greece;* and *Picasso: Creator and Destroyer.* A native of Greece who headed the famed Cambridge Union debating society while she studied in England, she is today a fixture in American political discourse and has made numerous appearances on television programs ranging from *Larry King* and *Oprah* to *48 Hours* and *Roseanne.* During the campaign year of 1996, she teamed with comedian Al Franken to provide coverage for Comedy Central, and she also worked with Franken on the "Strange Bedfellows" segment for the TV show *Politically Incorrect.* She is chair of the Center for Effective Compassion, which advocates greater community involvement to solve social problems.

*23*

# Does the Personal Character of Our Leaders Really Matter?

*Arianna Huffington*

CHARACTER — EVEN WHEN the word is not uttered — has dominated the political conversation in America in recent times. Yet at the end of the day, does the personal character of our political leaders really matter, or is it irrelevant provided there is peace and prosperity in the land? Is character important only when things are going badly?

Too often we confuse character with flawlessness. "Is it to be the cherub or the tiger?" Winston Churchill asked Graham Sutherland when he was about to sit for the portrait Lady Churchill later destroyed. In that short question he summed up a great truth: no human being is hewn out of a single block. And no great man or woman, whether a politician, a philosopher, or an artist has been of a piece.

In fact it is an inescapable truth of history that the greatest men have been enigmatic composites of virtue and vice. So, in our zealous post-Freudian age, "show me a great man and I will dismantle him for you" has become one of our best loved national pastimes.

Demystifying the giants of the past was, until recently, our favorite game. Systematically, and with a bizarre kind of vindictiveness, our attention was diverted from the greatness of Tolstoy, Dostoyevsky, Newton, and Molière and focused on the "discovery" that Tolstoy was schizoid, Dostoyevsky epileptic, Newton paranoid, and Molière consumptive. And this list doesn't include the scandalous sex habits and shockingly bad parenting.

Although we enjoy wallowing in revelations about the greats of the past, we launch our heartiest assaults against our current leaders. We relish every opportunity to reduce our highly visible politicians to terminally flawed creatures. In fact, if you would like to have your character praised and your flaws neglected, your best bet is to die. For a short while, especially after a sudden death, there is a reprieve. A statesman is a dead politician, the saying goes. And we see this tendency to vilify in life and glorify in death fully demonstrated in the cases of entertainer and congressman Sonny Bono, Kennedy family scion Michael Kennedy, and commerce secretary and political operative Ron Brown.

No doubt the time will come when their characters will be exhumed and dissected. But during the media honeymoon that follows tragic death, Michael Kennedy was a fearless athlete, Sonny Bono was the embodiment of wit and wisdom, and Ron Brown (whose friends just days before his death were proclaiming on national television that he was "unable to distinguish between public service and private gain") was extolled as "a magnificent life force," "an inspirational leader," a "Renaissance man of politics." Even Richard Nixon got a eulogy from President Clinton.

The inescapable conclusion to be reached from the coverage of our public figures is that as a nation we need to grow up. Now growing up does not mean character shouldn't matter to us. Far from it. It does mean, however, that we shouldn't magnify each transgression until it eclipses everything else, until nothing else can be seen—and especially nothing good.

Maybe the solution is to have an obituary writer vet every scandal story. Is the scandal so enormous that it eliminates everything positive, or can there at least be a sidebar about the rest of the person's life?

When someone complained to President Lincoln about General Grant's drunkenness, Lincoln suggested that the person find out what brand Grant drank and send a case to every one of Lincoln's other generals. Today, by spotlighting political leaders' private weaknesses, we're in danger of being led by men and women who have no private weaknesses, or indeed, private thoughts, private ideas, or private values—in fact by smiling, handshaking robots programmed with all the requisite poll numbers and focus group results. But it is not all the public's fault. Part of the reason for our fascination with authority in dishabille, with the private lives and foibles of our political figures, is that their stature is so shrunken these days there is little to differentiate them except speaking style and sexual tastes.

The problem with the leaders of today is not that they are flawed but that they are bad leaders—because the essence of good leadership is the ability to see the iceberg before it hits the ship of state. Václav Havel, the president of the Czech Republic and one of the few great modern political leaders, called recently for "postmodern politicians," who will speak the truth and put principle above party. "Firsthand personal insight into things" and "the courage to be one's self and go the way one's conscience points" are two of the qualities he identified as essential for effective leaders. Such leaders have character and moral authority even when they fall into temptation. As Havel did. In the fall of 1996, the Czech tabloid *Blesk* reported for the first time that there was more than had been previously told to the relationship between Havel and a forty-three-year-old actress, Dagmar Veskronova. She had allegedly been his mistress for a few years before his wife's death. Now they are married.

So what is the difference between President Havel's infidelities and President Clinton's? The difference is to be found in looking at each man's entire character—which can only be seen in each man's entire life. Havel, the imprisoned hero of the Cold War, had the capacity for sacrifice and the courage to put principle above self—essential aspects of character. The opposite was ironically defined in a speech that Havel gave in Salzburg in July 1990. He painted this portrait of the political leader corrupted by power: "In short, he believes that he has something like an unconditional free pass to anywhere, even to heaven. Anyone who dares scrutinize his pass is an enemy who does him wrong." It is this hubris that has throughout history created around leaders a corrosive environment of lies and cover-ups and has led to a progressive breaking down of character.

After all, what we learn, both from our own lives and from the lives of public figures, is that character is not something static. James Q. Wilson summed it up in *The Moral Sense:* "To say that people have a moral sense is not the same thing as saying that they are innately good. A moral sense must compete with other senses that are natural to humans—the desire to survive, acquire possessions, indulge in sex, or accumulate power—in short, with self-interest narrowly defined. How that struggle is resolved will differ depending on our character, our circumstances and the cultural and political tendencies of the day. But saying that a moral sense exists is the same thing as saying that humans, by their nature, are potentially good."

We build up our moral muscle—our character—by exercising it. We become virtuous by the practice of virtue, responsible by the practice of responsibility, generous by the practice of generosity, and compassionate by the practice of compassion. And we break down our moral muscle with every flabby choice and decision we make.

Plato wrote that most people want power, not virtue, and must be trained to prefer virtue. Freud, in contrast, enthroned sexuality as the strongest universal force and said it too must be channeled into the proper avenues.

True character therefore involves discipline, restraint, and sacrifice. True character subordinates the lust for power and sex to a higher spiritual purpose—the giving of oneself to others. The act of transcending ourselves—not just our problems, cares, and fears but also our pleasures, hopes, and joys (and lusts)—is at the heart of character. In every major religion, giving and service mark the path back to God, back to a world in which we are no longer strangers and alone but members of a vast but tightly knit family.

In a study on altruism, Ervin Staub analyzed men and women who had risked their lives during World War II to protect Jews hiding from the Nazis. What turned an ordinary bystander into an intrepid defender? "Goodness, like evil, often evolves in small steps," Staub wrote. "Heroes evolve, they aren't born. Very often the rescuers made only a small commitment at the start—to hide someone for a day or two. But once they had taken that step, they began to see themselves differently, as someone who helps."

Indeed, heroes evolve, but they could not evolve if the seed for heroism, for goodness, for transcending self-interest, had not been planted a long time ago. It is this capacity, this potential to love others more than ourselves, that is our common heritage, waiting like a seed to be watered by the first tender drops of compassion. So it is the obligation of us all, as a society, as communities, and as parents, to plant this seed in our children and watch them grow into the leaders of tomorrow. The bounty flowing from our efforts may range from death-defying rescues to daily acts of kindness and wisdom. As for the season of spring of a man or a woman, the time when each will become a leader of true character, this is the mystery of grace. The seed may bear forth year after year, or it may lie fallow, wedged in a corner of an arid soul. Yet as in the seed that lay buried in a sealed urn in a pharaoh's tomb, the potentiality—the eternal impatience to be born—is there. When the conditions necessary for germination were met some five thousand years later, the seed burst forth into life, as if it were planted with last year's crop.

Such is the character and nature of our leaders, as it is in all humans: complicated, unpredictable, full of potential—and capable of breathtaking heroism and appalling villainy. When we recognize character as a dynamic unfolding process leading us closer or further away from our true selves, then we will recognize that our public figures, like the rest of us, are on a similar journey. To expect flawlessness and perfection is to be stuck at an infantile stage of all-good fairy godmothers and all-bad witches. At the same time, to argue that character doesn't matter is to embrace the twentieth century's moral relativism, according to which we are nothing more than a bundle of neurons and chemical responses.

As for the media coverage of our public figures, would it not transform our public discourse if, even as we raise legitimate questions about their conduct, we also acknowledge their qualities and contributions? Could we not praise what is praiseworthy at the same time that we investigate what needs to be investigated and condemn what should be condemned?

In other words, could we not grow up?

STEPHEN L. CARTER is the William Cromwell Professor of Law at Yale University, where he has taught since 1982. His work has been hailed by a broad cross section of Americans, from Marian Wright Edelman and William F. Buckley to John Cardinal O'Connor and Bill Clinton. His book *The Culture of Disbelief: How American Law and Politics Trivialize Religious Devotion* (1993) was the first book by a nontheologian to receive the Louisville-Grawemeyer Award in religion. His other works include *Civility* (1997), *Integrity* (1996), *Reflections of an Affirmative Action Baby* (1991), and *The Confirmation Mess: Cleaning Up the Federal Appointments Process* (1994). Carter also contributes regularly to the *New York Times* and the *New Yorker* and is a frequent guest on television talk and news shows. He is a fellow of the American Academy of Arts and Sciences.

*24*

# In Defense of Privacy

## Stephen L. Carter

NOBODY IS UTTERLY good or bad. This is a crucial fact to keep in mind when we try to depict a person's overall character. We are, each of us, a complex set of selves, integrated—more or less—into a whole. Yet the whole is all but impossible to evaluate. So we look at the Reverend Martin Luther King Jr. and we are likely to judge him highly, based on the power of his prophetic ministry, despite evidence of tawdry morality in his personal life. We look at—oh, say, Adolph Hitler—and judge him as evil because we know of his murderous hatefulness that led to the deaths of millions. We do not much care whether he carried candy in his pockets to give to children, as some of his biographers claim.

When we make moral evaluations of famous people, we often focus on a single dimension of their character. For our evaluations

*Note:* © 1998 Stephen L. Carter.

of the famous are often not meant to be thorough moral profiles but teaching tools. We tend to single out the traits we want to avoid or emulate. So we use George Washington as a man too complicated to be categorized.

## The Moral Character of Political Leaders

Discussion of the private morality of our political leaders reached new heights during the presidency of Bill Clinton. Highly publicized accusations that he had a long-term adulterous affair with Gennifer Flowers and that he sexually harassed Paula Jones in his years as governor of Arkansas were capped by an intensive investigation of charges that, as president, he had an improper sexual relationship with Monica Lewinsky, a White House intern. With all the righteous indignation generated, one would think he was the first president to be charged with improper sexual conduct. Yet even a cursory review of the private lives of past presidents reveals substantial evidence that Franklin Roosevelt, Dwight Eisenhower, Lyndon Johnson, and John Kennedy had extramarital affairs. Thomas Jefferson, many believe, fathered children by one of his slaves. And Grover Cleveland confessed to having an illegitimate child.

Much of the press and most of Clinton's most ardent detractors expressed amazement that through the worst of the Monica Lewinsky charges, he maintained extraordinarily high approval ratings for the job he was doing as president. Yet it may be quite sensible to look at President Clinton and his predecessors—or for that matter any people currently in public life—and distinguish between their public selves and their private selves, evaluating each independently. Our willingness to make this sort of private-public distinction affects more than presidents. It affects the very language we use to describe which public figures are morally good and which are not. It goes, really, to our deepest understanding of the existence and nature of the private sphere—the sphere into which, in the best American tradition, one simply does not pry.

The wall between public and private is an important one to maintain, even if it means we will sometimes ignore personal traits or conduct that could well diminish our opinion of the overall person. We should maintain this wall not to protect public figures from the judgments that might naturally flow from their conduct but because we should prize and protect the idea of privacy. Privacy, after all, is vital to our essence. With our humanity comes an entitlement to a region where we can freely think, speak, and behave, with confidence that we are, for that instant, on our own. This is not to deny the importance of norms of conduct in holding the community together. Norms are crucial. Community is crucial. The links we form to others are crucial. But so are spaces to be ourselves. Moreover, a life without privacy would be psychologically intolerable.

## The Importance of Privacy

A person of character is guided by conscience. A good definition of conscience is that which guides our actions when nobody except God is looking. The idea that there *is* such a space, inaccessible to all but God, is precisely the idea behind privacy. In the first important essay on privacy as a legal concept, Louis Brandeis and Earl Warren described it simply as the right to be left alone. That, surely, is true privacy: to own a space in which one will not be bothered. The shape and size of that space need not concern us now. What exceptions we might write in are, for the moment, beside the point. I propose only that the need to preserve that space is urgent.

There is of course a social cost to honoring a domain of privacy. We will lose information we might want to know, even relevant information one could argue we ought to know about our leaders. I believe, however, there will be a higher social cost if we eliminate the private space altogether.

Agreeing that we should draw a line between private and public life doesn't solve all our problems, however. Private behavior can often affect the public sphere. For example, Clinton cabinet member Henry Cisneros ran into legal (and political) trouble over an extramarital affair after allegations that during his security clearance interviews he misled the FBI about payments he was making to his former mistress. His adultery became a public matter because of the charge that he lied about it. One could argue that if an area of life is truly private, we should scarcely be surprised that people lie in order to protect it. Lies, of course, raise moral problems of their own. But people are human, and in a land as frequently puritanical as this one, the temptation to lie when caught is considerable. We shouldn't condone these lies, but I think we should react with something less than astounded fury when we discover that some poor soul, caught doing in private what he would rather keep from public knowledge, yields to the first and very human instinct to lie.

Of course, if we truly believe in privacy, we must also allow people to say, "This is nobody's business but mine, and I refuse to answer your question about it." Unfortunately this is not possible today under the rules of litigation. Much of the Monica Lewinsky brouhaha, for example, focused on the question of whether President Clinton lied when he testified in a deposition in an unrelated civil suit that he had not had a sexual relationship with her. But if sexual relationships—even adulterous ones—should remain in the private sphere, then shame on the lawyers who ask such questions and shame on all of us for creating a legal system in which it is possible to ask them. I am not claiming that the question of whether a politician—or anybody else—has violated a marriage vow is irrelevant to understanding his or her moral persona. I am simply insisting that a respect for privacy means denying ourselves the opportunity to use that information in our moral evaluation.

I am well aware of the argument that people who choose public lives necessarily surrender their right to privacy to the public's right to know. Journalists vigorously assert their duty to ferret out anything that bears on the character of public officials, and the courts make it very difficult for any public figure to win invasion of privacy and defamation cases. But whatever might be the correct rule of journalistic ethics or constitutional law, the right rule of moral judgment is different. We should not measure the morality of the famous with one set of tools and the morality of our friends, our neighbors, and ourselves with a different set. Put most simply, if it is relevant to evaluating the morality of a president to know whether he had an affair, then similar information is relevant when we evaluate the morality of a news anchor or college professor.

Unfortunately we are whiplashed by double standards. Back in 1993, the press was busy assaulting the moral fitness of Zoe Baird, President Clinton's nominee for attorney general, because she failed to pay Social Security taxes for her nanny. When I spoke with a member of the editorial board of a publication that had called on Baird to withdraw her name (which she ultimately did), this editor confided that she herself had a nanny for whom she was not paying Social Security taxes, but added that her situation was different because she was not trying to become the nation's chief law enforcement officer. How persuasive is this distinction when she was presuming to sit in moral judgment on an individual whose moral offense was exactly the same as her own?

I think we commit a great offense against common sense by our strident insistence on banning from government service anybody who has ever sinned. Since we ourselves are all fallible, we should be more forgiving of the fallibility of others, including those in public life. By accepting occasional moments of moral weakness as the human condition rather than a mark of turpitude, we might teach our children important lessons about the complexity of moral life.

The principal reason for caring about the moral conduct of public figures is that their behavior helps set a tone for the rest of the society. The level of morality we tolerate from those in government service is a cue to the level of morality we expect in our culture. Such cues as this one, in turn, help us in the vital project of the moral training of children. When children see a world in which there are clear moral expectations, they come to understand morality; the coherence of the moral world around them helps create a coherence in their inner moral world. However, as Robert Coles has explained with some elegance in his book *The Moral Intelligence of Children*, when children see a world without clear moral expectations, they often grow up without clear moral compasses of their own. To allow our children to grow up without clear moral guidance is wicked—and that is the reason that we must demand high moral standards of people in public life. But we ought to demand the same high moral standards from all adults. The project of raising good children is one in which the entire society necessarily participates. It is culture, not government, that determines what moral rules children learn. Culture is the sum total of what we truly value, and we see its bite when we see what lines we draw in life. It does no good at all to assure young people that we will not tolerate lying by the president if we freely tolerate it among our relatives, friends, and colleagues. Indeed, to insist on a high moral standard for government officials and tolerate a low moral standard for everybody else is a bit like vaccinating only government officials against the flu while ignoring the people to whom children are most frequently exposed: we should profess neither surprise nor outrage when our children become ill.

It is a tricky matter to insist that the employees of the state meet moral standards that the rest of us are free to flout. Public officials are drawn from the same cultural cauldron that produces the rest of us. If we tell them that they and not we must be sinless, we will most likely discourage from service only those who really are morally better than the rest of us—people of true integrity who have, like all of us, done some wrong in life but who are not willing to have the scandal-hunting press destroy their reputations and perhaps their families. Instead, we will find ourselves stuck with people of less integrity, who are quite willing to lie if the private wrongs they have done become publicly known.

## A Line Between Public and Private

Moral judgments about the character of our leaders are important. But if privacy is to have any meaning, we must be willing to reach those judgments with incomplete information. To protect the private sphere is not to dismiss its relevance but to acknowledge its importance. So if we choose to ignore extramarital affairs by government officials, the reason is not that adultery doesn't matter, but rather that privacy does. If on the other hand we think adultery matters enough that it justifies the invasion of privacy, we should take that view about everybody, not just those who are in the public eye.

What matters is that we draw a line—that we decide what part of life can be kept private and what part should be open to public scrutiny and judgment. We should not draw the line in haste or for the sake of ratings or political advantage. We should not continue to construct a world in which public officials come in only two varieties: those who have been disgraced and those who have not yet been caught. Nor should we continue the mischievous double standard of morality: one standard for those who are covered by the press, and who must be perfect, and another for the rest of us.

SENATOR PETE V. DOMENICI is serving his third decade in the U.S. Senate and his second decade as chairman (and ranking Republican) of the Senate Budget Committee. The son of thrifty Italian immigrant grocers, he worked hard and long to eliminate the country's budget deficit. Equally disturbed by evidence of out-of-control personal behavior, he now works to close the nation's "character deficit." His bill establishing federal grants for character education programs became law in 1994. His concerns also extend to improving care for the mentally ill and federal protection for abused spouses and children. He is the recipient of numerous awards and honors, including the Russell Chilton Hill Memorial Award from the Character Education Institute and the Lifetime Achievement Award from the U.S. Psychiatric and Mental Health Congress.

# 25

# Addressing the Character Crisis

*Senator Pete V. Domenici*

M Y GRANDCHILDREN are terrific. A blessing. I want the best the world has to offer for them. But as they get older I have a growing concern about the world they will inherit. Our nation has grown so fast and so great in the twentieth century. The technological advances of our age virtually ensure that they and their generation will live longer and better lives than any of the people who ever populated the earth. But at the same time, I see the perils presented by the contemporary and complex world.

As a United States senator, I have challenged myself to help pave the way and open the door for all those who dream of a better life, not only for themselves but for their children and grandchildren. One aspect of this is helping steer the fiscal and social policies of our government in ways to make this better life possible. But I found myself

---

*Note:* © 1998 Pete V. Domenici.

asking about the ultimate good of such lofty governmental policies when there is a crisis of character in our society.

## The Failure to Teach Character

The foundation of good character, traditionally built at home by parents and fortified by the schools and community, seems now to be crumbling. My parents, who were both born in Italy, imbued the lives of my four sisters and me with character education. We were taught and expected to be respectful, honest, responsible, and caring.

We were taught, for instance, to have respect for our parents and family. My mother and father taught us to be responsible for ourselves from the earliest days. We were responsible for school, our behavior, and studies. We were given chores to do at home and at my father's grocery business and were expected to get them done. We were taught the difference between right and wrong and tried hard to live by those guidelines. Honesty was expected of us in all aspects of our daily lives. It goes without saying that caring was everywhere. The message was cemented at school and by our relationship with the community around us.

As I started my own career and family, I believed the character traits I was taught were what all people wanted for themselves and their children. But I soon learned that was not the case.

There has been an undeniable trend in this country, a growing erosion of self-discipline, self-restraint, and responsibility, particularly among our young people. We read with horror of senseless crimes committed by juveniles; we see the behavior on our raging roadways. We pay for these social changes through the excesses of substance abuse. On the whole, we have relaxed our cultural emphasis on community and self-control in favor of an emphasis on self-expression and selfishness. According to the Josephson Institute of Ethics 1996 Report Card on American Integrity, "there is a hole in the moral ozone and it is getting bigger." The Josephson study shows that the present fifteen- to thirty-year-old generation is more likely to engage in violent, dishonest, and irresponsible conduct than previous generations.

Knowing this, I worry for my grandchildren's generation and shudder at the long-term consequences for our nation.

Today, we Americans enjoy more freedom and privilege than we have ever known. But increased liberty brings with it additional personal responsibility. We have a civic responsibility to each other. Ancient civilizations knew this. As one Greek philosopher said, "A man's character is his fate." Similarly, a nation's character is its fate. That national character is equivalent to the citizenry's everyday exercise of virtue. How we maintain and improve the values that animate that virtue—the sum of our nation's character—is one of the great dilemmas we face.

## A Workable Solution

Many of my colleagues in Congress share my deep concern about the moral compass of our nation's youth, but there has been a reluctance to speak out publicly. There has been a fear that talking directly about the morality of the nation would be perceived as treading on personal beliefs or interfering with the proper role of families or religious organizations as the primary teachers of values and ethics. Those who speak about values risk being labeled as puritanical, extremist, dogmatic, and censorious. As a consequence, discussions of ethics, values, or character have been generally approached with extreme caution. Indeed, the desire not to offend our fellow citizens often seems to have left us collectively speechless about concerns that the fundamental character of our society is deteriorating. This may have left the impression that the nation no longer respects basic values passed from one generation to the next.

It was in this light that in 1993, I learned of the Character Counts Coalition, the alliance of education and youth-serving organizations dedicated to bolstering the character of this and future generations. I first read about the coalition in a column by William Raspberry, and

I was intrigued to find that former Congresswoman Barbara Jordan and actor Tom Selleck had come together as joint spokespersons for the group, formed by Michael Josephson of the Josephson Institute.

The coalition promoted a format that transcended political and ideological beliefs, emphasizing the use of the six pillars of character to educate children and communities about the basic traits of good character: trustworthiness, respect, responsibility, fairness, caring, and citizenship. The program attempts to fill a void in our society by fortifying the teaching of the basics of good character and reinvigorating classic truths for a new age.

My first personal encounter with the program in action was at Albuquerque's Bel Air Elementary School, the nation's first school to adopt the program. As I visited teachers and students to see how the program worked, I discovered teachers loved it because they could use its simple tenets in their lesson plans, regardless of the course of study, to discuss the values or ethics issues without fear of offending someone. The children loved it because the values were understandable and applicable to their home and school lives. Disciplinary problems were diminished, and there was a greater sense of optimism and community at the school.

I came back to Washington convinced of the merit of the six pillars of character. They integrate easily into existing programs and activities and, more important, transcend cultural, religious, and socioeconomic differences. Finally we had an effective way on both the local and national levels to discuss and address the nation's crisis of character.

I drafted a National Character Counts Week resolution and asked my colleague Sam Nunn to join with me in forming a bipartisan character counts working group in the U.S. Senate to assist in this important effort. The original group consisted of myself and Senators Nunn (D-GA), Robert Bennet (R-UT), Thad Cochran (R-MS), John Danforth (R-MO), Christopher Dodd (D-CT), Joseph Lieberman (D-CT), and Barbara Mikulski (D-MD). I then contacted Representatives Tony Hall (D-OH) and Tom Wolf (R-VA) to lead a bipartisan group in the

House of Representatives and to pass this resolution there. By fall 1994, the Congress had passed the resolution to designate the third week in October as the first National Character Counts Week.

The passage of that first resolution was a turning point for character education. Members of Congress now had a legislative and philosophical vehicle to speak more forcefully in support of good character—nationally and in their home states and districts. The Senate has passed similar resolutions every year with wide bipartisan support.

But more than supportive resolutions were needed, so Senator Chris Dodd and I successfully amended the Elementary and Secondary Education Act of 1994 by creating the federal Partnerships in Character Education Pilot Program. This grant program provides states with funding to develop character education programs. We anticipate the program will be expanded in future years so that it can reach more schools.

The annual National Character Counts Week resolutions and the grant programs allow national figures to responsibly support grassroots character education. We know that our voices are best heard when joined with those in America's towns and cities. Good character can be endorsed and supported by government, but in the end it is the families, schools, and communities that will make the difference. Good character does not begin and end with the ringing of the school bell. It must encompass all facets of society so the messages of trustworthiness, respect, responsibility, fairness, caring, and citizenship become imbedded in each person's psyche.

## An Inspiring Example

As a consequence of the national support, then-mayor Martin Chavez of Albuquerque and I helped set up a task force of leaders from Albuquerque businesses, churches, labor unions, public and private schools, law enforcement agencies, community organizations, and the media to keep good character at the forefront of the public's consciousness.

Soon thereafter, the entire city of Albuquerque, led by a character counts leadership council, officially voted itself a character counts city.

Similar partnerships have now been started throughout the nation, although I am very proud that Michael Josephson refers to New Mexico, with its phenomenal statewide endeavor, as the "crown jewel" of the program. Dozens of communities and schools have adopted character education as a central theme in children's education. Their actions prove without a doubt that people are willing to promote character education to improve the quality of communal and individual life. In 1998, almost 200,000 public and private school children in my state will have daily exposure to the character counts message—in homes and schools, on billboards and in creative community events, and in social clubs and organizations.

If you haven't seen it, it is hard to believe the positive and pervasive impact of this initiative that teaches and promotes the six pillars of character community-wide. In Albuquerque, for example, the water utility bills stress a value each month. Radio and television public service announcements promote the message, and children are constantly engaged in written, artistic, and musical activities that reinforce the core values. When the Character Counts Coalition introduced a new children's video called *Kids for Character*, Sandia National Laboratories sponsored more than one hundred free screenings for children and parents.

Now an ambitious effort is being made in New Mexico to establish a program called Character Counts in Business. It started with a pilot project featuring businesses committed to integrating the six pillars of character into every phase of their operations, from human resources to marketing to customer relations. This new effort is based on the premise that it takes an entire community working in concert to emphasize responsibility, trustworthiness, and other traits of good character.

The pillars of character are no longer just six simple words in New Mexico. Children and adults alike are rewarded when they practice these character traits. Good character is promoted not as a slogan but as a way of life. I truly believe that New Mexicans in general have bought into the premise that the strength of a society is the sum of the strength of its individual members.

I am very proud of the effort made by many communities in New Mexico to make the six pillars of character part and parcel of their children's education. Without hesitation I can say my involvement in this program has been one of the most important and rewarding ventures of my career as a public servant.

I remain concerned about the crisis of character in this nation, but I am encouraged by the success of the program in New Mexico and around the nation. With its success, more people are reemphasizing the importance of self-discipline, hard work, and civic responsibility in their day-to-day lives. Our social institutions—families, churches, schools, neighborhoods, and civic organizations—have traditionally provided our children with love, order, and discipline. They have taught self-control, compassion, tolerance, civility, honesty, and respect. We must encourage our children to embrace these fundamental pillars of our society and, in doing so, reenergize these essential institutions so their critical and time-honored tasks can be carried out. I truly believe the fate of our democratic nation depends on it.

The people I've met—young and old, rich and poor, workers and retirees—believe a common language of values helps make their homes and towns a better place to live. They are giving their time, talent, and energy to a cause that will offer decades of tangible rewards—a society with good character. Their efforts give us hope that the current generation will mature in a nation that is better than the one they inherited.

COLIN GREER is president of the New World Foundation in
New York. A former college professor and administrator, he is
the coauthor (with Herbert Kohl) of *The Plain Truth of Things*
and *A Call to Character* and the author of *The Great School
Legend*, and *Choosing Equality: The Case for Democratic
Schooling*, which won the American Library Association's
1988 Eli M. Oboler Intellectual Freedom Award. A founding
editor of both *Change* and *Social Policy* magazines, he is a contributing editor to *Parade* and a columnist for *Child* magazine.
He has consulted to publishers, foundations, and educational
groups and has developed briefing papers on the relationship
of philanthropy and government for First Lady Hillary Clinton
and on education and public policy for U.S. Senator Paul Well-
stone. He is working on a new book about human rights and
the moral imagination for Harvard University Press.

*26*

# Awakening Our Moral Imagination

*Colin Greer*

MORAL LIVING REQUIRES successfully resolving conflicts between selfish and selfless behavior, conflicts such as spending more time with one's family versus spending more time pursuing a career, helping the homeless versus ignoring their plight, and publicly opposing bigoted remarks versus keeping safely silent. The qualities possessed by *moral* people, as evidenced by their choices and behavior, might be called character. Good people, people of character, engage the world, try to act compassionately and responsibly, and are ready to make personal sacrifices when necessary.

Whether or not we act morally is very often derived from the poverty or richness of our imaginations, how we see not just what *is*, but what *can be*. Our imaginations often determine our actions, and therefore have a moral component. But without the mediation of values, our imaginations wander in a myriad of directions not necessarily connected to any ideals of *right living*. Indeed, our imaginations can take us to hellish places—driven by fear, longing, or despair. When fear smothers other emotions, or the wounds of humiliation and rejection overwhelm our longing for connection with others, our imagination mutates into hatred. We can end up hurting those close to us and disparaging those who are needy—perhaps because they remind us of our own pain and threaten the brittle security we have won for ourselves.

The good news is you can imagine anything: you can start over, and you can learn from your mistakes. But to be a person of character, you must take action, even if only corrective action. There's an old Jewish imperative that sums this up, "compassion, truth, and then action, not guilt."

Imagination doesn't function when you're sleeping. In his book *My Experiments with Truth,* Gandhi says moral living is not about being right but about being awake—awake to suffering in the world and aiming to reduce it and not to add to it. Hence he preferred forgiveness to revenge, preferred the impulse to make amends over willful pride. Gandhi strove to pursue the truth of this belief in his life. He didn't claim to have had more than a glimpse of what he called this "truth force," but he was sure that he was right in devoting his life to pursuing it. Gandhi was certain that a person of high moral purpose, a person of character, must be committed to helping make this truth manifest in the world.

If making this truth manifest requires such effort, that means, of course, that it's quite possible (in fact, very tempting!) to fall short and be selfish. But in moments of weakness it's worth remembering (or *imagining*) that our character is ultimately expressed by what we tolerate—including the misery and abuse of others.

When I think of character, I find myself thinking of the inner life of a person. As David Mamet recently wrote of character, "It is not a construct you are free to amend. You can develop it, you can learn from mistakes, but finally, it has no other meaning than: the readiness to act, to resist, to assent, to assert, to proclaim, to support, to deny, to bear.

These are the components of character. Your character is developed and presented by the decisions you make and the actions you take. It's about who you are in the world and who you are deep within your self."

## Imagination

How we deal with ourselves, with intimates, and with strangers returns us to the subject of the human imagination. So much of what we love and fear we anticipate first in our fantasy of how other people are motivated, what we can expect of them, and how defensive or compassionate we feel we must or can be. Over the years, scholars of human behavior have given us numerous ways to think about our talent for both competition and altruism. Due to our power to symbolize, to delay gratification, and to empathize, we are able to stop our selfish impulses. Such discipline of the imagination is absolutely crucial if we are to live in a truly humane society. The psychologist Ernest Becker and the philosopher Philip Rieff have both argued well that there must be limits—and the values that set those limits are the force that makes human society possible. Those values express themselves in our imagination and, put into action, are the stuff of character.

But values can also be engaged to protect us against people we see as the other; they can be the basis for demonic fantasies that have at times caused great havoc. Our imaginations are full of positive and negative narratives. The negative can dominate when our undisciplined imagination runs wild with fear and blame; our altruism can be mobilized when our imagination is tempered by values and the heartfelt generosity we are all capable of.

All too often, competitive, uncharitable, or habitual instincts dominate our imagination. This can occur even when we regard those closest to us: think how a parent's expectation about a child's second year (the "terrible twos") can be a self-fulfilling prophecy, built on a negative narrative of imagined though not-yet-experienced behavior. We often deal with people of a different race, religion, ethnicity, gender, or age according to powerful narratives we have stored in the library of our imagination. Yet such stereotypes can dramatically change, and have: think here of the once-common notion that slaves were not fully human or that women were naturally subservient. In each case, appropriate value-based behavior evolved after the moral scope of people's imaginations had been forced to change. People were forced to change what they imagined others could be. In the process, they imagined themselves as more tolerant and fair-minded.

## Acting on Values Versus Splitting

We often direct our fears at a target group ("the other side") and blame the members of this group for the various problems du jour (emancipation, immigration, welfare, illegitimacy, and so on).

This comprehensive blaming involves what psychoanalysts refer to as *splitting*. It is also sometimes known as *scapegoating*. Splitting siphons off all the bad from the self (an individual or group) and allocates it to an agreed-upon blame object. At the same time, all that is good is retained for oneself or one's own group. Herman Hesse put it this way: "Whenever we hate someone, we are hating some part of ourselves that we see in that person. We don't get worked up about anything that is not in ourselves."

Silence in the face of splitting can be enormously destructive, to the individual's and the society's moral character. The imagination is fueled by possibilities. So it is important to counter sometimes obsessive media attention to hateful behavior with stories of what is being done to make the world more loving. Communities across the country are showing imaginative responses to counter racism, anti-Semitism, and homophobia. Just as the abolition and civil rights movements grew gradually, willfully, and strategically over time, so have new movements against hatred and intolerance. At the personal and social level, people are emphasizing their altruistic potential over and against the propensity to split the community and scapegoat a few. In South Carolina, David Kennedy, an African American minister, took into his home a local Klan figure who had fallen on hard times and homelessness. Reverend Kennedy's altruism was a shock to the town and to the man in question, because they had not *imagined* such a thing was possible.

In Great Falls, Montana, values of compassion and tolerance led to a surprising and altruistic community response when a predominantly black church was daubed with racist graffiti. After the incident the church's congregation doubled as people from neighboring churches came in support. A rally followed (which was also meant to counter antigay activity in the area). Local newspapers publicized the community response, schoolchildren discussed the issues in class, money was raised for repairs, and community members wrote letters of support. "Dear friends," said one person, "I support you and send you prayers of love and courage. This country's full of good white people who would stand by you, any place, any time, as you would for us." A fifth grader wrote, "Whoever did this must not think very good of themselves if they have to tear down others to make them feel good about themselves."

These people, and countless others who fight for tolerance, recognize the humanity we all share. They imagine us as one community. They imagine another's pain as their own. They have tears in their eyes when they see mindless victimization. And they've learned to act on those tears—just as they would act to apply medicine to a bleeding wound. They understand the wisdom of most of our religious and secular humanist traditions that says we are more alike than we are different and that the things we fear in others are typically present or potentially present in ourselves.

"If you don't fight hate, hate wins," as Nobel Prize–winning peace advocate and novelist Elie Wiesel once told me. "It occupies the imagination, conquers it, and limits who we can be and what we can achieve together. The only way to fight it is to speak up and denounce its ugliness. Hate is everywhere because it is a part of human nature . . . the worst part. But it is also part of human nature to oppose it vigorously—with every fiber of our being. When people do that, they express what is best in us."

## Success

Material success raises issues about character in the way it promotes or detracts from our focus on the least privileged in society. We might enjoy imagining ourselves as winners: rich, beautiful, talented, and powerful. But how often do we imagine ourselves, compassionately, as none of those things? Yet our character may depend on our having done so. In addition, a culture that lionizes the materially successful can prompt the downtrodden to feel they are not bound by the moral standards of this society that rejects them. When splitting and denial suppress compassion and understanding, then suffering is accentuated, and those with means help to demean their own humanity.

Sometimes it is difficult to accurately imagine the lives of society's less fortunate. As essayist Simone Weil writes: "Nothing is so rare as to see misfortune fairly portrayed; the tendency is either to treat the unfortunate person as though catastrophe were his natural vocation, or to ignore the effects of misfortune on the soul, to assume, that is, that the soul can suffer and remain unmarked by it, can fail, in fact, to be recast in misfortune's image."

Billionaire currency speculator and philanthropist George Soros puts it this way, "Money-making success is what people very often want most. Right now our culture prizes winners above all; they get the greatest respect; it often doesn't matter what they've done to succeed. So whatever you get away with is OK as long as you win. I'm admired for my success at money-making, but that kind of adoration is ultimately dangerous."

Mindlessly celebrating supposed winners and victors is dangerous, and people of character know this. Archbishop Desmond Tutu of South Africa, recipient of the Nobel Peace Prize, has long rejected vengeance and the right to punish as the inevitable tribute owed the victors in the struggle to defeat apartheid. Or witness Yitzhak Rabin's rejection of an Israeli victory march through Arab territory after the 1967 war. "We do not celebrate the death of our enemies," he said. In Rabin's restraint we see a person of character fully manifest—a person whose action is entirely synonymous with the values of justice and compassion he espouses.

## Facing the Millenium: A Challenge

As an educator and parent I've seen over and over how values such as compassion, idealism, and justice can become rhetorical and divert us from actually *doing* the right thing. George Soros says he learned from his mentor, the philosopher Karl Popper, that one of the great dangers confronting a free people comes when they believe in the absolute nature of the values they espouse. When values are used to confirm one's own righteousness and to blame and judge others, the whole point of the moral imperative has been lost. Our collective imagination dies with this prejudicial, rigid certainty. "The fallibility of the human condition" is the common ground we all share, Soros says. And this realization, says this great philanthropist, is the beginning of altruism. "We have to be concerned for each other," he says, "and it is to our values that we have long looked for guidance in that."

It is through caring contacts with adults that young people can learn about strength of character without also learning the rigidity that follows the punishment and forced feeding that once typified moral education. Youngsters need opportunities to think important things through in discussion with adults they respect in safe and non-didactic settings.

Values can so easily become self-righteous fortresses against others—splitting them off from us, assigning them dark places in our imaginations. We have to be on the alert for the occupation of our imagination by wrong and misguided narratives about ourselves and others. A punishing attitude can freeze the options open to us. Once we identify certain kinds of people as bad, especially when we are young, we can be locked into attitudes and behaviors toward them that are justified only by our stereotypes. Hence a forgiving attitude must constrain and direct imagination's wild play. This means that the value-based actions we take are best informed by an approach that recognizes the human tendency, and therefore our own tendency, toward the splitting response. We must instead imagine ourselves as one community—and act on that belief.

As we close out a century of unparalleled barbarism, we could well use a new renaissance of character. To encourage this millennial imperative, we must use what we know about disciplining our imaginations with values. We must emphasize *empathy* and *idealism* to heal and repair the world; *courage* and *discipline* to take action and adhere to the principle of doing no harm; *honesty* and *loyalty* to bring a forgiving attitude to our affairs with others and make human lives more valuable than things. Finally, we must bring *compassion* to our action in the world. Action based on the commitment not to pass on suffering is basic to a person of character.

LLOYD V. HACKLEY is chairman of the CHARACTER COUNTS! Coalition and former president of the North Carolina Community College System, chancellor of Fayetteville State University, and vice president of the University of North Carolina system. A twenty-year veteran of the U.S. Air Force, he chairs President Clinton's Advisory Board on Historically Black Colleges and Universities and serves also on the National Commission on Civic Renewal and the Advisory Board of the National Center for the Kenan Ethics Program. He also sits on such corporate boards as BB&T Bank, Blue Cross/Blue Shield of North Carolina, and Tyson Foods and on the boards of the North Carolina Methodist Home for Children and the Josephson Institute of Ethics. He has frequently appeared before legislative and community bodies to address issues relating to minorities, disadvantaged students, and character education.

# 27

# Community Action for Children's Character

*Lloyd V. Hackley*

M OST OF US have had an experience with a person, organization, or event that changed us fundamentally, sometimes forever. Such a defining moment occurred for me about five years ago when I was invited to visit a meeting of the advisory board of the National CHARACTER COUNTS! Coalition. I was encouraged to attend because of my experience in involving the community in the education process. While I was chancellor of Fayetteville State University in North Carolina, we initiated more than twenty mentoring, tutoring, and scholarship programs to link the campus with the surrounding community and help children build skills, self-confidence, and aspirations for the future.

I was somewhat skeptical about what national organizations, even well-intentioned ones, could effectively do for local communities with real problems. But I came away from that first meeting with the advisory board impressed with its diversity and with the high-minded, nonpartisan focus of the coalition on improving the ethical life of young people. But what really impressed me was the coalition's focus on grassroots action based on programs using specific language.

I noticed parallels between the mission of the coalition and the spirit of my Roanoke, Virginia, hometown, which represented all the glory and tragedy of America, where there were still people alive in my African American community who had firsthand knowledge of slavery. It was a traditional community, where academic achievement, athletic excellence, and, yes, character were all valued and inextricably bound.

The Aspen Declaration (the founding document of the coalition) and the "rules" in my community both emphasized the welfare of children, the fact that the well-being of America required citizens with good moral character, the need for specific and concrete guidance for children's moral development, the necessity for the entire community to work in concert to assist families and children, and the importance of good role models.

America defines its ideal self in its sacred documents. Yet the ideals outlined in the Declaration of Independence, the Constitution, the Gettysburg Address, and so on have no life unless they are passed on to each succeeding generation. These ideals must be lived, modeled, and taught if we are to create American citizens worthy of the legacy. America will survive as a free democratic society only if its fundamental values are fully understood and practiced by each succeeding generation.

Through the ages, adults—parents, community residents, school personnel, church members and ministers, and law-enforcement officers—have wrestled with the problem of rearing successful and decent children. Laments about children's behavior from two thousand years ago sound much like what we hear from today's adults. There are some strong indications, however, that today's young people may have exceeded their predecessors in antisocial and criminal behavior, both in degree and kind.

The test of a nation's religious, political, and educational systems is the character of the human beings they produce. I agree with the belief that if a nation injures its children's intellect, it is bad; if it injures their character, it is vicious; and if it injures the development of their conscience, it is criminal. And who could argue with Gandhi, who pointed out that education without character and leadership without principle will corrupt a society?

## Leading by Example

Leadership by example is the only true leadership. As Justice Louis Brandeis once said of the extraordinary responsibility of public servants: "Our government is the potent, the omnipresent teacher. For good or for ill, it teaches the whole people by example. If the government becomes the lawbreaker, it breeds contempt for the law, it invites every man to become a law unto himself."

Families and schools introduce children to America's ideals and heroes, past and present. In communicating to young people the purpose of the presidency or of other offices, parents and teachers naturally find it useful to tell stories about some of the outstanding officeholders of the past—highly sanitized stories. But when children observe contemporary presidents, governors, senators, and representatives, they do not separate the office from the officeholder. When leaders misbehave, a trust is broken, and the institution itself becomes suspect. For the democratic process to work and be embraced by future generations, leaders must be committed to living the principles and civic virtues that define America in its ideal. They must be people of character. Others will follow their example; that's why we call them leaders.

National and state leaders always have had a powerful influence on America's moral culture. *Newsweek* columnist Meg Greenfield stated recently that what individual families have been trying to get their children to learn is simple and easy to understand—a sense of proportion, decency, and restraint, along with the discipline to live these virtues. She concluded by telling her readers, however, "Our leaders are not giving you much help."

Numerous surveys have revealed that the majority of American adults have grown increasingly distrustful, angry, disaffected, pessimistic, and cynical toward our leaders as a group—whether cultural, political, corporate, educational, media, special interest, or lobbyist. Once adults sense a crisis of moral authority in leadership, real or imagined, they are less likely to pass on lessons of civic virtue to succeeding generations. Instead, these adults will pass on messages of cynicism and doing whatever it takes to win or to avoid responsibility—because these attitudes apparently work for the "leaders."

There are at least three ways adult behavior can affect the inculcation in children of America's ideals. First, children hear what their parents say about people who have been elected, appointed, or hired to carry out public business. Second, children become aware through the media of leaders' behavior. And third, children notice the behavior of adults, especially parents, relatives, neighbors, teachers, the clergy, and coaches.

Just like adults, even our best and brightest high school students have low levels of confidence in public leaders and institutions. These young people consider the greatest crisis facing America and their own generation to be the decline in moral and social values.

Not surprisingly, the hypocrisy practiced by adults so successfully shows up among young people too. Despite their stated dissatisfaction with adult behavior, ethics, and morality, huge percentages of young people admit that they lie to their parents, cheat on tests, and steal from stores. Alarmingly, the young people who state a commitment to religious principles and an understanding of right and wrong do not behave significantly better than their nonreligious peers do.

## Teaching Values at the Local Level

Is there any hope? Absolutely! There is no doubt in my mind that parents, schools, and communities can succeed in rearing decent children, even in today's increasingly complex world. But, to paraphrase Albert

Einstein, the people and the processes that made the problem cannot be expected to correct the situation. If we keep on doing what we have always done, we will keep on getting what we have always gotten.

The power and influence of state and national elites notwithstanding, the solutions to the matter of rearing successful—and decent—children will have to be found at local levels. The community is the place where fundamental human relationships take place. Our own neighbors have the greatest stake in helping us build just and caring communities that nurture people, bridge differences, foster civility, and promote the common core values of trustworthiness, respect, responsibility, caring, fairness, and citizenship. And as was clear in the community where I grew up and as emphasized today by the Character Counts! Coalition, these values cannot be taught passively or remotely. The lessons must be purposeful, pervasive, repetitive, consistent, concrete, and creative. Children have to see other children performing decent acts and being recognized for them. As Aristotle said, people become virtuous, kind, and brave by behaving in those ways.

There is good reason to be optimistic about the local approach to improving children's character. Americans still believe in the ideal of a democratic system of decision making based on the exercise of trained virtue and natural self-interest. This bedrock belief gets stronger the more one ignores remote centers of administrative and legislative power and focuses instead on where people live. Studies have determined that children have a greater amount of confidence in their parents than in any other group of people, including sports, music, and movie stars. Celebrity worship and trust are not synonymous. Many surveys also have indicated that parents want to be good parents but they are confused and often frightened by the complicated political, social, and economic problems of contemporary America.

Many parents behave in ways that hurt their children's development of good character. Nevertheless, it is much more sensible and pragmatic to assist parents and communities in doing better than to try to "fix" the nation's children by attempting to improve the behavior of state and national leaders and other remote role models.

One major lesson parents still need to learn is that "Do as I say and not as I do" has never been an effective, or ethical, child-rearing strategy. When children become aware of the gap between what is said and what is done, trust is broken. More than two thousand years ago, Plato said that the best way to rear decent children is to make certain that they never see adults behaving in an indecent manner. To teach children how to do right, adults must first heed their own rhetoric.

If we expect to save our children from the stranglehold of ignorance, violence, materialism, and dog-eat-dog greed, we have to be honest with them. We must admit when and where we have fallen short. But at the same time we must be setting clear and specific expectations. If we want children to show greater respect for other people's dignity, rights, freedom, and property, then we must be very clear in our lessons—for instance, that violence (including the psychological violence of racism and sexism) is wrong because it is the epitome of disrespect.

Children are not born knowing how to respond appropriately to questions that will test their intellect or their morality, but they are born with the capacity to learn all they are likely to need to know about decency and decimals. Unquestionably, the most reliable predictor that a child in even the worst circumstances will learn how to be decent and successful is the active, long-term presence of two caring parents. The second most reliable predictor is the presence of at least one caring adult. (And it is important to note that this adult does not have to be the child's parent, or even of the same race, gender, or economic class). The third most reliable predictor that a child will do well is the presence of a caring community. In fact, a caring community will strongly influence the effectiveness of the first and second predictors.

In our focus on caring adults, we must distinguish between role models and mentors. No one can volunteer to be a role model. Children admire and emulate whom they will, across the spectrum from decent to indecent. Role models reflect what children can become;

they are a destination. Mentors guide the process of choosing role models; they are a road. Mentors help the less experienced learn how to achieve their desired—and desirable—ends.

Given the pervasiveness of self-destructive addictions, greed, bad sportsmanship, violence, and cheating, individual families find it extremely difficult to fight alone to save their children and create safe neighborhoods. They must have the support of their neighbors to build a caring, child-centered community. In order for each child to be safe, all the children must be safe. Then adults can teach children values, good manners, a work ethic, good health habits—and that character is no less important than calculus.

Education systems do not create communities; communities create education systems. The most important educational organization is not at the national, state, or even the district level. It is the local PTA, or other parent-teacher-student association, formed around a small grouping (an attendance zone) of elementary, middle, and high schools. Only at this level can people together create a crusade for academic, athletic, and moral excellence that touches and supports all the children and also their teachers, mentors, and coaches.

A positive response to changing unethical behavior and the cynicism it engenders will not develop by chance. It requires deliberate, unending, cooperative action. The community is the only place where this action can take form and a better society can be brought about. Only by focusing on our own behavior and on community cooperation can we help our children bond with each other, bond with adult leaders, and bond with the best America says it is and ought to be, in the pursuit of a more decent society.

GOVERNOR JANE DEE HULL is the governor of Arizona and was the first Republican in sixty-five years to be Arizona secretary of state and the state's first female Speaker of the House. Known for her candor and tough pioneer spirit, Hull has long focused on ethics, first as a state representative in the state legislature and then as Speaker, taking decisive action after some legislators were caught up in the "AZSCAM" FBI sting in the late 1980s. She is well respected for her dedication to children's issues, focusing on the quality of their health and education. She serves on the boards of numerous community and service organizations, including Arizona Save a Life Alliance (which promotes organ donation), Children's Action Alliance, and Kids' Voting of Arizona. She and her husband have four children and eight grandchildren.

# 28

# The Challenge of Public Service

*Governor Jane Dee Hull*

I'VE BEEN A POLITICIAN for more than twenty years. I say that not as a confession but as a statement of pride. Despite the well-worn clichés and easy cynicism about the ethics and character of politicians, I am an unrepentant public servant.

My love for politics took hold when I was campaigning for Barry Goldwater in the 1964 presidential election. Since then I've been hooked on the prospect of having a say in the policies that affect the everyday lives of my family, friends, and the citizens of Arizona. After years as a precinct committeewoman getting out the vote, I won a seat to the Arizona House of Representatives in 1978. Eight years later I was elected Republican whip, the first woman ever to become part of the majority leadership in Arizona. In 1989 my colleagues elected me Speaker of the House. After three years as Speaker, I served as chairwoman of the Ethics Committee until I resigned from the house to run for secretary of state. I was elected. In an unexpected turn of events I became governor when the previous governor resigned due to several federal convictions.

I've seen a great deal during my political career, from petty and major corruption to extraordinary demonstrations of integrity and courage. Yes, some of the people I've met fit the stereotype of the self-serving local politician, but I've also met men and women of exemplary character. Of course a political career marked by success and integrity takes a special type of person. First, political office is certainly no place for you if you are extremely materialistic. Though the media sometimes like to characterize political office as a lucrative job, there are very few successful politicians who could not make many times their public salary on the "outside."

Second, you have to have a high tolerance for criticism and controversy. It's unavoidable. I find some solace in the observation of a highly ethical politician who was chided by a colleague for going to such great lengths to avoid not only improprieties but even the appearance of improper conduct. "Do you really expect that you will avoid criticism by all this extra care?" the colleague asked. "No," was the reply, "I simply expect to know that I will be unworthy of the criticism."

Third, you must have a high degree of tolerance for scrutiny into your private affairs and submit all details of your financial life for public consumption. I often hear people lamenting that politicians inevitably embark on a moral downslide after they enter office. However, I think many politicians bring their long-standing personal problems with them into office, problems that are then exposed in the bright light of public life. A politician today has to be ready to answer for anything he or she has ever done that might be considered improper. Nothing will be sacred. You will even be held accountable for the behavior of your extended family! Every comment, picture, letter, and bit of gossip is fodder for the rumor mill and a candidate for the front page. I doubt there is a person on this earth whose reputation could survive unscathed that type of scrutiny. Moreover, in this era of "gotcha" journalism you cannot expect either the benefit of the doubt or the presumption of innocence. In politics, character attacks and accusations of any sort are so heavily publicized that in many cases the ultimate outcome hardly matters.

Fourth, the moral universe that elected officials must live in is fraught with temptations and pressures that test character on a daily basis. Here are some of them:

- *Compromise.* Compromise is an essential aspect of politics. As in the boardroom, deals are cut to get things done. There is nothing inherently unethical about compromise. In fact, in a democratic system that must accommodate differing views and opposing interests, it is unethical to ignore other voices. The challenge is to assess objectively and with a cool head exactly what is being compromised. Half a loaf is usually better than none, but compromises of principle exact too high a price. There are many considerations when making compromises: the viability of the bill; promises you have made to constituents, public interest groups, and colleagues; the spirit of the law; unintended consequences; and fairness to minority positions. Did the deal go too far? Was the goal lost in the pursuit of a "win"?

- *Corruption and rationalization.* Politics offers an endless variety of temptations to subordinate the public interest to personal gain. Accepting these temptations is corruption. In its simplest form, corruption is bribery and extortion, but in politics, abuse of power is usually much more subtle, especially when people want influence. Rarely do they offer a quid pro quo—I'll give you this if you do that. However, an improperly motivated citizen can disguise a payoff as a personal favor, a paid trip, a gift, a discount, a business opportunity, a campaign donation—you name it. The problem gets even tougher when a lobbyist is also a good friend or when a powerful constituent or generous benefactor requests a special favor. It is so easy to rationalize in these situations. To maintain your character, it is necessary to be ever vigilant and to consider not only your own motives but the motives of the person you are dealing with. And it's not enough to know you have done nothing wrong. You have to think about how the transaction will be interpreted by journalists.

- *Dirty politics.* It has been said that "just because you *can* doesn't necessarily mean you *should*." Politics can be as rough as any contact sport, and many politicians fight dirty. Mudslinging takes many forms—name calling, mischaracterizing facts, distorting or lying about an opponent's positions or actions, making untrue accusations or unfair innuendoes. It takes great strength of character to endure such tactics. It takes even more strength to resist the temptation to fight fire with fire or to act as though the end justifies the means.

- *Special rules.* A public servant may have more opportunity to behave unethically simply because elected officials are governed by so many rules. For example, Congress requires its members to report any visit to a friend's home that exceeds forty-eight hours. I would bet that there is not a member of Congress who has not broken this rule. Because such visits are illegal, they must be classified as unethical, even if the rule does not seem to be a fair or rational standard. Even allowing a friend to pick up a lunch tab can be a violation.

## Responding to Unethical Behavior

Arizona is a wonderful state to live in, yet those familiar with recent Arizona political history, or for that matter politics in general, know that not every public official consistently lives up to the highest standards of public service ethics. Often you can take the temperature of a culture from the opening acts on late-night television. I knew politics in Arizona was suffering from a high fever when Jay Leno began to mention us by name. It all started some years ago with a scandal that became known as AZSCAM, where several state legislators were convicted of accepting bribes. Then came the impeachment and federal indictment of the governor, who used public funds to pay off personal debts, and the conviction of yet another governor, my immediate predecessor. This sort of criminal behavior, coupled with various ill-advised off-the-cuff remarks from officials, left all public servants exposed to sarcastic one-liners, judgments, and ridicule.

I was speaker of the Arizona House of Representatives when some of my colleagues, some I called close friends, were caught in AZSCAM. I immediately ordered those indicted to no longer vote on issues until they were cleared of all charges. Later I became the house ethics chairman, a post that would give me the opportunity to help clean up the legislature's soiled image. I called together community leaders, political leaders, legislators, and others to define a code of ethical behavior appropriate for elected officials and their staffs. Our guiding principle was that there was hope, that the majority of people want to do right. To help them do right, all guidelines had to be crystal clear. Our group created a user-friendly ethics manual to help lawmakers in their daily decision making.

## Confronting Public Cynicism

Despite such efforts—and similar efforts taken by public servants elsewhere—public and media skepticism abounds. There seems to be prejudice against everyone who seeks public office, and the position of elected official seems to rank somewhere below tax collector and tabloid TV reporter in the public's esteem.

The public's disdain for politicians has become mundane, commonly thought to be hardly worthy of comment or reflection. Nothing could be further from the truth. This reflexive, unthinking mistrust and disgust reduces civic activism, voting, and law abidance. As a result we are producing a generation of timid and fearful political candidates who are unwilling to make the tough choices that duty requires of them. And many principled people are unwilling to make the financial and privacy sacrifices needed to enter the political arena because it seems like such a thankless task. This is not healthy for the country.

I am not saying we ought to go easier on people who abuse the public trust or that the press and public should lower their expectations. I simply suggest that we need a fairer, more balanced, and more generous approach to the way we treat our public servants. Life offers many chances at bat, and no one bats .1000. We all make bad decisions. Yet our culture tends to turn elected officials' careers, personal lives, mistakes and misunderstandings, and everything else into media entertainment.

Quixotically, people demand the highest of ethical behavior from politicians yet do not believe politicians are capable of it. We as citizens must learn to judge fairly and reasonably—and we must be accountable to the highest standards ourselves before we hold others accountable. In the end it will take character to judge character. What is important is to keep scandals in perspective and not lose sight of the vast majority of honest, hardworking men and women who sit in state legislatures and Congress.

## Doing One's Best

The only way a public figure can deal with the challenges of public office is to make a personal decision to do his or her absolute best to maintain integrity. Ultimately we can control only our own actions.

In my own case, I think of character in terms of guiding principles that help me assess a situation and govern my behavior. These principles operate in the background. I do not run hundreds of "character checks" a day. Rather I rely on my instincts about right and wrong, instilled in my brain and heart by experience, intellect, and religious teachings. I do, however, occasionally pause to assess the ethics of my conduct a bit more explicitly to see where I might have done better. My approach to thinking about and dealing with ethical principles and the consequences of choices has also benefited from a Josephson Institute seminar some years ago, which helped me isolate the core values that are the basis of my own character: honesty, integrity, fairness, kindness, empathy, accountability, respect, and reliability—the list goes on and on. As a woman, wife, mother, eight-time grandmother, and former teacher, I have worked all my life to make these principles the guiding force in my life and in the lives of my children, grandchildren, and students. I have also placed these virtues at the center of my political career, as have many of my colleagues throughout the nation. Sometimes, that is quite a challenge.

In public service, perhaps more than in any other setting, individuals have the opportunity to put some of the harder virtues into practice—listening with an open mind to opposing viewpoints, dealing respectfully with anger and disappointment, verbalizing beliefs and principles, and striving to deal fairly and honestly with everyone. A responsible public official must handle all financial matters with precision and openness. Accountability requires one to be willing to admit to mistakes publicly. The key is never to lose sight of the reason why one is in politics: to serve the community by ensuring that laws and bureaucracies improve the present and future of one's neighbors and neighborhoods.

I resolved once I became governor that the cloud that hung over Arizona's capital was going to be dispersed by a new standard of conduct. I hired staff as committed as I believe I am to the core values of responsibility, integrity, commitment, and efficiency. I challenged all state agencies to conduct business according to these values. I tore down all of the artificial barriers that prohibited people from talking to one another, and I encouraged open meetings and public discussion. I believe that most people strive to behave in an ethical manner. It is that assumption that I mean to exploit. I expect the highest of ethical standards. I set an example in both my personal and professional life.

And I still unhesitatingly encourage people who want to make a difference to enter the arena of public service. Despite the many trials and tribulations involved in seeking, retaining, and wielding public power, being an elected official is, in the end, a wonderfully rewarding life. If I were to mentor a young woman considering a public service career path, I would begin by showing her all the opportunities to affect policy and law in a manner that reflects her highest beliefs and principles. I know of no other career that provides as great an opportunity to affect directly the lives of so many people. And I would tell her how interesting and stimulating it is to meet and work with people from all segments of our society.

For most of the dedicated people I know, commitment to public service in the face of the heavy personal costs is itself a demonstration of character. There are great psychological rewards from knowing that you are on the front lines, fighting to improve the quality of life in cities, counties, states, and the entire country. Quite simply, it's meaningful work.

SANFORD N. MCDONNELL is the former chairman and chief executive officer of the McDonnell Douglas Corporation, a leading aerospace company that is now part of the Boeing Company. During his forty years at the company, McDonnell helped focus national attention on the importance of ethics and served as the first president of the Malcolm Baldrige National Quality Award. Since retiring in 1988, he has focused his attention on restoring overt character education to the nation's schools. In 1988, he organized the PREP (Personal Responsibility Education Process) program in the St. Louis public schools, which now involves 426 schools and almost 250,000 students. In 1993, he became the founding chairman of the Character Education Partnership. He is a past national president of Boy Scouts of America and the recipient of numerous professional and civic awards.

*29*

# Character and Freedom

❦

*Sanford N. McDonnell*

I N 1983, AFTER YEARS of telling young boys to practice the values of the Scout Oath and the Scout Law (to be trustworthy, loyal, helpful, friendly, courteous, kind, obedient, cheerful, thrifty, brave, clean, and reverent), I asked myself how well my behavior reflected that code of ethics. I found there was a lot of room for improvement. Then I asked myself, "Surely our employees at McDonnell Douglas know that we want them to behave ethically, but by what values?"

We had a code of conduct as all organizations have, a "thou shalt not" code; but we didn't have a positive "thou shalt" code of ethics. So I gave a task force the Scout Law and told them that I didn't want the McDonnell Douglas code to read like the Scout Law, but did want it to cover the twelve points of that law. After a number of iterations the task force came up with the following code of ethics, which covered all the points except "a scout is reverent." (As a Christian I would like to think that all of our employees believe in God, but I had to agree with the task force that we should not use our executive position in the corporation to pressure our employees to be reverent.)

### McDonnell Douglas Code of Ethics

Integrity and ethics exist in the individual or they do not exist at all. They must be upheld by individuals or they are not upheld at all. In order for integrity and ethics to be characteristics of McDonnell Douglas, we who make up the Corporation must strive to be:

- Honest and trustworthy in all our relationships;
- Reliable in carrying out assignments and responsibilities;
- Truthful and accurate in what we say and write;
- Cooperative and constructive in all work undertaken;
- Fair and considerate in our treatment of fellow employees, customers, and all other persons;
- Law abiding in all our activities;
- Committed to accomplishing all tasks in a superior way;
- Economical in utilizing company resources; and
- Dedicated in service to our company and to improvement of the quality of life in the world in which we live.

Integrity and high standards of ethics require hard work, courage, and difficult choices. Consultation among employees, top management, and the Board of Directors will sometimes be necessary to determine a proper course of action. Integrity and ethics may sometimes require us to forgo business opportunities. In the long run, however, we will be better served by doing what is right rather than what is expedient.

We adopted that code of ethics at our April 1983 board of directors meeting. And we didn't just hang it on the wall. We set up a mandatory eight-hour training program—beginning with me and those reporting directly to me—to teach us all how to apply the code in our daily business lives. By the time I retired in 1988, we had trained well over 50,000 employees. This training program was just one part of the corporation's comprehensive, proactive ethics program. Initially it was received with some skepticism, but soon our employees realized we were serious. And then they began to appreciate that along with all the pressure we put on them to meet the bottom line, we were also insisting that first and foremost they must always take the ethical high road. The program grew more and more effective each year and is stronger than ever today in our merger with the Boeing Company.

## The Historical Perspective

After starting this ethics program, I felt the need to check into the character of the young people coming out of the schools into the community and into McDonnell Douglas and other companies. In the process of that investigation I went back into history and found the following background of character education.

In 1748, Baron Charles de Montesquieu published his magnum opus, *The Spirit of Laws,* a work that had a profound effect upon our founding fathers. In it, Montesquieu developed the concept of the separation of powers, which formed the basis of our Constitution over two hundred years ago. In his work Montesquieu also explored the relationship that must exist between a people and their government, without which that form of government cannot survive. For example, a dictatorship depends upon fear, and when fear disappears, the dictatorship is overthrown. A monarchy depends upon the loyalty of the people and dies when loyalty dies. The most desirable form of government is a free republic, obviously; but it is also the most fragile form of government because it depends upon a virtuous people.

Virtuous people, people of character, live by high ethical values. But what do we mean by ethics? One of the best definitions I have come across was given by Albert Schweitzer: "In a general sense, ethics is the name that we give to our concern for good behavior. We feel an obligation to consider not only our own personal well-being but also that of others and of human society as a whole." Therefore, in a free republic the leaders and a majority of the people must be committed to doing what's best for the nation as a whole. When that commitment breaks down, when the people consider only their personal well-being, they can no longer be depended upon to behave in the best interests of their nation. The result is laws, regulations, red tape, and controls—things designed to force people to be trustworthy. But these are instruments of bondage, not freedom.

Benjamin Franklin underlined this concept of Montesquieu's when he said, "Only a virtuous people are capable of freedom." And throughout most of our history, certain basic, ethical values have been considered fundamental to the character of this nation and to the people who made it up. These values were passed on from generation to generation in the home, the school, and the religious institution—each one undergirding and reinforcing the others. We had a consensus not only on values but on the importance of those values; and from that consensus, we knew who we were as a people and where we were going as a nation.

In 1831, Alexis de Tocqueville came to this country to find out what it was that made this upstart new nation so progressive and prosperous. He traveled all over the country and talked to people of all walks of life. He hated slavery and considered the true America to be the Northern, free states. In his classic *Democracy in America,* published in 1835, he wrote of that true America, "America is great because she is good, but if America ever ceases to be good America will cease to be great."

## The Need for Character Education

Today in America we have far too many twelve-year-olds pushing drugs, fourteen-year-olds having babies, sixteen-year-olds killing each other, and kids of all ages admitting to lying, cheating, and stealing in epidemic numbers. We have crime and violence everywhere and unethical behavior in business, the professions, and in government. In other words we have a crisis of character all across America that is threatening to destroy the goodness that, as de Tocqueville recognized, is the very foundation of our greatness. That is the bad news, but the good news is that we know what to do about it. And that is getting back to the core values of our American heritage in our homes, our schools, our businesses, and our government and indeed in each of our daily lives.

It is the schools that have the greatest potential for overcoming the crisis of character that is raging all around us. When our country was founded, Harvard, Yale, and Princeton were already in existence as theological seminaries whose whole thrust was to teach the values of the Judeo-Christian faith. And from kindergarten through the university, character education was considered just as important as intellectual knowledge. For many reasons, formal character education has been largely absent from our public schools over the last thirty to forty years. We can't teach religion in the public schools anymore, but we can teach the universal values common to all the great religions. With that conviction, seven public school districts in the St. Louis area formed a business-education-community partnership in 1988 and initiated a character education program called PREP (Personal Responsibility Education Process). The program has now grown to thirty-two public school districts representing 426 schools with over 247,000 students. Where PREP has been implemented properly, it has produced very encouraging and sometimes dramatic results. Drug problems, teenage pregnancies, and absenteeism have gone down, while discipline and academic performance have gone up. It is obvious that if you don't have law and order in the classrooms then teachers won't be able to teach anything. However, if you create a moral and caring community environment in the school, kids feel better about themselves, and they work harder. The teachers are happier, the students are happier, the parents are happier, and the community is happier. It is a win-win program. The unmistakable conclusion? Character education should be an integral part of the county's entire formal education system, from kindergarten through graduate school.

## Seven Effective Practices

To take my local experience with character education to another level, I became the founding chairman of the Character Education Partnership, a nonprofit organization dedicated to promoting character education and to helping communities and cities throughout the country set up character education programs in grades K–12 in their schools.

The Character Education Partnership defines good character as "understanding, caring about and acting on core ethical values such as honesty, responsibility, respect, kindness and caring for others." Kevin Ryan, a professor and a member of the board of directors of the Character Education Partnership, has an even simpler definition of character: "knowing the good, loving the good and doing the good." Both definitions make it plain that building good character must involve the cognitive, the emotional, and the behavioral: the head, the heart, the hand. Developing character in this comprehensive sense requires a comprehensive educational approach—one that uses all aspects of schooling (the academic subject matter, the instructional process, and the management of the school environment) as opportunities for character development.

What are some of the essential practices of a successful character education program?

• First and foremost the teachers must be role models: they must be caregivers, and they must be moral people.
• Second, the teachers and the parents in each school or district must come to consensus on what values they want the students in the school to learn and what those values mean. Once people work through this process, the school community will have ownership of the values chosen, and no one can criticize them, because everyone in the community will have had the opportunity to participate.
• Third, the teachers must teach the school values through the curriculum and in every other possible way, and the students must

be encouraged to engage in moral reflection through reading, writing, and discussion.

• Fourth, students should be involved in deciding the rules and the rule enforcement that they feel will make their classroom a good place in which to be and in which to learn. In other words, a micro, civil, and democratic society is created in the classroom. When students help establish the rules they have ownership of them, and they use peer pressure to help the teacher keep order and discipline.

• Fifth, teachers should practice moral discipline, using the processes of creating and enforcing the rules as opportunities to foster moral reasoning and respect for others.

• Sixth, cooperative learning should be used to teach kids how to help each other learn and how to work together. And, certainly students should be taught how to resolve conflict in fair and nonviolent ways. Beyond the classroom the principal and her staff should use the total school environment to support and reinforce the values taught in the classroom. For example, service projects in the school and the community help students learn to care by giving care.

• Last but not least, the parents, the religious institutions, the businesses, and indeed the entire adult community should be recruited as partners in character education.

Above all, I believe the school itself must embody character. It must be a moral community that helps students form caring attachments to adults and to each other, because these are the relationships that nurture both the desire to be a good person and the desire to learn.

Character without knowledge is weak and feeble, but knowledge without character is dangerous and a potential menace to society. Today's America won't achieve the goodness celebrated by de Tocqueville if we graduate from our schools young people who are brilliant but dishonest, who have great intellectual knowledge but don't really care about others, who are great thinkers but are irresponsible.

America can be both great and good if we teach our young to do what is right, to tell the truth, to serve others, to work hard, to have courage when hardship comes, to try again when they fail, and to never ever give up. That is character education.

Character education is one of the most important, if not the most important, answer to our national crisis of character, and it is absolutely essential to any truly effective education reform movement. As citizens we all know what to do. We are doing it in many parts of the nation, but we need to get on with character education as fast as possible in every school in America.

George Washington once said, "To personally understand and maintain the American way of life, to honor it by his own exemplary conduct, and to pass it intact to future generations is the responsibility of every true American." Let each one of us decide how to discharge that responsibility to these great United States of America.

# part six

# VALUES
## *and the*
# MEANING
## *of*
# CHARACTER

GREG EVANS has made a name for himself with his obsession with fear and excitement, uncertainty and intrigue, awkwardness and discovery—in other words, with adolescence, the focus of his nationally syndicated cartoon strip *Luann*. All about reality (only funnier), *Luann* helps readers, especially teenage ones, find the humor in doubt, fear, romance, school, friends, and family. Evans has also employed his multiracial characters, from geek to jock to brainiac, to illustrate brochures that help adolescents deal with such complex health issues as AIDS, drugs, and teen pregnancy. "I feel I have a responsibility, considering who my readers are," the cartoonist father of two young adults has said. "I always try to enlighten and inform without being preachy."

# 30

# *Luann* and the Meaning of Character

## *Greg Evans*

I N MY COMIC strip, *Luann*, there are fifteen characters, counting Luann's dog, Puddles.

That's a lot of characters. Does that mean my strip has character? Do my characters have character? Do *dogs* have character? As the creator of *Luann*, do I have character?

Many questions. But before any of them can be answered, we need to define character.

To me, character means living a life that makes the world a better place.

This doesn't mean you have to discover a cure for AIDS or find a way to end world hunger or invent a VCR that people can actually understand. It doesn't mean you have to be rich or powerful or good-looking or even smart. It doesn't require any special traits or talents. All it requires of us is a desire to *not* mess up the world—and a sincere effort to be people who give more than they take.

In my strip, the main character, Luann, is a teen girl who laments that all the really popular people have lots of everything: personality, spunk, spirit, friends, clothes, hair. And she wonders what *she* has lots of. To which her friend Bernice replies: "You have lots of ordinary."

Fortunately, ordinary is good enough. You don't need to be an extraordinary person to have character. There are some extraordinary athletes, actors, politicians, and tycoons who are sorely lacking in character. Yet there are millions of average people, young and old, rich and poor, able-bodied and disabled, who have character. No one is perfect; perfection isn't required. Just a desire to do good. But, you may say, nearly all of us *want* to do good, yet we don't, for one reason or another. That's because, along with desire, we must have the will and the courage to act on that desire. It's so easy to talk or plan or dream about what we *could* do. But talk is just good intentions and warm air unless it's backed with meaningful action. To have character, we must commit ourselves to a course of action and stick with it.

Let's look at Luann, since I happen to personally know her. Luann is definitely not perfect. She argues with her parents, she fights with her brother, she forgets to do her homework, and she struggles to connect with her dream guy, Aaron Hill. It's a daily battle to just stay afloat, and often Luann feels as though she's doing more sinking than swimming.

At times she probably thinks it would be easier to just surrender—there are certainly plenty of temptations to surrender to. But Luann's a fighter and a survivor. She doesn't give up, drop out, and give her life away to things that will harm herself, her family, or her community.

It's as though she's in a 10K charity run. Sooner or later, as she jogs along, she's faced with pain, fatigue, doubt, and all sorts of physical, mental, and emotional challenges—just as in real life.

It would be *so* easy to quit.

But she doesn't. Deep inside her, she knows that she must stay in the race. She knows it's good for her, good for the charity, good for the world.

That's character.

Another example of character is Luann's good friend Delta. Delta is an African American girl who, unlike Luann, has her act together. She seems to have life's problems all figured out. She's poised, confident, and has a good self-image. In one strip, Luann says, "I wonder if we will EVER become confident, self-assured women?" Delta replies, "What do you mean, 'we'?"

But self-confidence isn't what shows Delta's character. It's her genuine concern for others that sets Delta apart. She cares about her school, her town, the world—and she *does* something about it. She runs for student office. She volunteers at a girl's club. She has her sights set on a life of public service. She genuinely wants to work to make the world a better place. And she will.

There are many degrees of character: from those rare individuals who have tons, like Delta, to those who have an average amount, like Luann, to those who apparently have none. Like Tiffany.

Tiffany is Luann's worst nightmare. For one thing she competes for Aaron Hill. As if that's not bad enough, she's gorgeous: perfect figure, perfect hair, perfect nails, perfect wardrobe. But it's not her looks or money that betray her lack of character; it's that she's perfectly obnoxious.

In one strip, Tiffany says to Luann, "I know you like Aaron, but he likes ME." Luann asks, "And you feel the same?" To which Tiffany replies, "Yes. I like me, too."

She's totally self-centered. If it doesn't involve Tiffany, it's not important. This sort of self-absorbed attitude doesn't allow room for character. As a result, Tiffany is a deceitful, scheming, competitive busybody whose only goal in life is to make the world a better place— for Tiffany.

Somewhere just slightly above the scale from Tiffany is Luann's older brother, Brad. Brad is basically a good guy, but he's a little too lazy and unmotivated to have real character. Plus, he has a habit of inflating his own ego by deflating others'. When he tells Luann that he can't tell if she's coming or going, and she replies that she's not *that* busy, he says, "I'm talking about your figure." Not the kind of caring attitude that breeds character.

Several years ago I did a story about Luann's best friend, Bernice. An extremely cute older guy named Derek started coming on to Bernice, and she felt she had found true love. But she soon discovered that Derek was wooing her just so he could stash drugs in her locker. She protested, and Derek tried to win her over, first with charm, then with a kiss, finally by attempting to get her hooked on the same drugs he was hooked on. But Bernice resisted, and although she dearly loved Derek, she turned him in. Then, rather than wallow in self-pity or anger, Bernice helped Derek into a drug rehab program.

Bernice showed real character in this story and, in the end, so did Derek. They both made the world a little better. Not by solving global warming or ridding the world of junk mail but simply by doing what's right. You don't have to do big things to have character. You can do something small and simple. Like a comic strip.

When I started Luann in 1985, I knew that chronicling the life of a teen would be a roller-coaster ride, a ride I'd experienced only secondhand, as the parent of two teens. When I was a teen, back when TVs were small and radios were huge, life was like *Leave It to Beaver.* We didn't yet know about the dangers of sunburn, cholesterol, fatty foods, smoking, alcohol, drugs, guns, gangs, and driving without a seat belt. Today, being a teen is life threatening. I remember being worried about The Bomb when I was young. This great nuclear threat could wipe out whole cities and even overpower the school's cafeteria food. We went through drills of hiding under our desks—as if a desk would shield us from the blast—but it all seemed somehow unreal and distant. Ominous, yes, but also abstract and not really possible.

Today's teens face genuine danger everywhere they go: in schools, playgrounds, malls, streets, and even their homes. This hazardous environment could be seen as hostile to the development of character. Or it could be seen as a ripe opportunity. That's how I see it.

And that's why I feel a certain responsibility in my strip to enlighten as well as entertain. Scientists have shown that, although difficult, it is possible to survive adolescence. But when you're a teenager, you feel as though the woes of the world are on your shoulders and no

one else understands all your problems. The truth is, there are millions of teens carrying the same woes and problems. My goal in Luann has always been to hold up a mirror so that readers can see themselves and realize that they're not alone. And maybe that can help people a bit.

If I can provide a little smile, a little peace, a little sigh of relief in the face of life's challenges, then I feel that I've made the world a little better place to be in.

So I'm pleased to say that, yes, I guess I do have character. Not as much as Delta, maybe, but it's not a competition. Any amount is good. Building character is a lifelong journey of small steps.

As for Puddles the dog, well, that's another essay.

ALAN M. DERSHOWITZ is Felix Frankfurter Professor at the Harvard Law School. Profiled by many major magazines, he has been described by *Newsweek* as "the nation's most peripatetic civil-liberties lawyer" and by *Time* as "the top lawyer of last resort in the country—a sort of judicial St. Jude." His clients have included Anatoly Shcharansky, O. J. Simpson, Claus von Bulow, Michael Milken, Leona Helmsley, Jim Bakker, Christian Brando, Mike Tyson, and Patricia Hearst. His best-selling books include *The Best Defense; Chutzpah; The Advocate's Devil; The Vanishing American Jew; Reasonable Doubts; Taking Liberties;* and *Reversal of Fortune,* and he has written hundreds of articles for publications ranging from the *New York Times* to *Penthouse* to *TV Guide* to the Harvard, Yale, and Stanford *Law Reviews.* A consultant to several presidential commissions, he has lectured around the world, from Carnegie Hall to the Kremlin.

# 31

# Good Character Without Threat or Promise

*Alan M. Dershowitz*

FOR MOST PEOPLE, the question why be good? is a simple one. Because God commands it, because the Bible requires it, because good people go to heaven and bad people go to hell. The vast majority of people derive their morality from religion. This is not to say that all religious people are moral or of good character—far from it. But it is easy to understand why a person who believes in a God who rewards and punishes would want to try to conform his or her conduct to God's commandments. A cost-benefit analysis should persuade any believer that the eternal costs of hell outweigh any earthly benefits to be derived by incurring the wrath of an omniscient and omnipotent God. Even the skeptic might be

---

*Note:* © 1998 Alan M. Dershowitz.

inclined to resolve doubts in favor of obeying religious commands. As Pascal put it more than three hundred years ago: "You must wager. It is not optional. You are embarked. . . . Let us weigh the gain and the loss in wagering that God is. Let us estimate these two chances. If you gain, you gain all; if you lose, you lose nothing. Wager, then, without hesitation that He is."

I have always considered "Pascal's Wager" as a questionable bet to place, since any God worth believing in would prefer an honest agnostic to a calculating hypocrite. To profess belief on a cost-benefit analysis is to trivialize religion. Consider, for example, the decision of Thomas More to face earthly execution rather than eternal damnation. When the king commands one action and God commands another, a believer has no choice. This is the way More reportedly put it: "The Act of Parliament is like a sword with two edges, for if a man answer one way, it will confound his soul, and if he answer the other way, it will confound his body."

More followed God's order and gave up his life on earth for the promise of eternal salvation. For his martyrdom—for his goodness— More has been accorded the honor of sainthood.

I have never quite understood why people who firmly believe they are doing God's will are regarded as "good," even "heroic." For them the choice is a tactical one that serves their own best interests, a simple consequence of a cost-benefit analysis. Thomas More seemed to understand this far better than those who have lionized him over the centuries.

To a person who believes that the soul lives forever and the body is merely temporary, it is a simple matter to choose the edge of the sword that will cut off earthly life but preserve the soul. Heaven and hell are forever, while life on earth, especially for a man of More's age, lasts only a few years. Therefore, if More truly believed in reward and punishment after life, he was no hero. By choosing death over damnation, he demonstrated nothing more than his abiding belief; giving up a few years on earth for an eternity in heaven was a wise trade-off that should earn him a place of honor in the pantheon of true believers, but not in the pantheon of heroes.

The basic question remains. Why is it more noble for a firm believer to do something because God has commanded it than because the king has, if to that person God is more powerful than any king? In general, submission to the will of a powerful person has not been regarded as especially praiseworthy, except, of course, by the powerful person. Would Thomas More have joined the genocidal crusades in the eleventh century just because God and the pope commanded it? If he had, would he justly be regarded as a good person? Nor is this question applicable only to Christian believers. I have wondered why Jews praise Abraham for his willingness to murder his son when God commanded it. A true hero who believed in a God who rewards and punishes would have resisted that unjust command and risked God's wrath, just as a true hero would have refused God's order to murder "heathen" women and children during the barbaric crusades.

The true hero—the truly good person—is the believer who risks an eternity in hell by refusing an unjust demand by God. The great eighteenth-century rabbi, Levi Isaac of Berdichev, was such a hero. He brought a religious lawsuit against God, and told God that he would refuse to obey any divine commands that endangered the welfare of the Jewish people. By doing so, Levi Isaac may have risked divine punishment, but he acted heroically. He stood up to a God who he believed had the power to punish him but who he also believed was acting unjustly. In challenging God, he was following the tradition of the heroic Abraham, who argued with God over His willingness to sacrifice the innocent along with the guilty of Sodom, rather than the example of the compliant Abraham, who willingly obeyed God's unjust command to sacrifice the innocent Isaac.

This then is the conundrum of judging goodness in a religious person who believes in divine reward and punishment. Those religious leaders who select martyrs and saints cannot have it both ways. They cannot declare someone to be both a hero and a believer, because the two honors are logically inconsistent. The undoubting believer is less of a hero for choosing death over eternal damnation. The real hero is necessarily less of an undoubting believer. Real heroes are those who face death for a principle—say, to save the lives of others—without any promise of reward.

Only if More were in fact a hypocrite, feigning belief in the hereafter but really a secret disbeliever, would he deserve the status of hero, but then of course he would be denied the accolade given for true belief—and for honesty.

There is, to be sure, an intermediate position. More could have been someone who tried hard to believe but could not suppress doubts. If that were the case, his decision to choose death entailed some degree of risk. Maybe he was giving up a bird in his earthly hand, namely what was left of his life, for two in the heavenly bush, namely a chance at a possible heaven. But this, too, would be a calculation, albeit a more complex and probabilistic one. (I am not suggesting that religious martyrs always think this way consciously, but surely they experience this mix of belief, calculation, and action at some level.)

This is not to argue that believing persons cannot be truly moral. They certainly can. Perhaps they would have acted morally without the promise of reward or the threat of punishment. This is to suggest, however, that to the extent conduct is determined by such promises and rewards, it is difficult to measure its inherent moral quality, as distinguished from its tactical component.

But what about atheists, agnostics, or other individuals who make moral decisions without regard to any God or any promise or threat of the hereafter? Why should such people be moral? Why should they develop a good character? Why should they not simply do what is best for them?

Even the Bible provides a model for such people. The author of Ecclesiastes explicitly tells us that he (or she, since the original

Hebrew word for Ecclesiastes is *Koheleth,* which means "female gatherer") does not believe in any hereafter.

> I have seen everything during my vain existence, a righteous man being destroyed for all his righteousness and a sinner living long for all his wickedness.
>
> . . . [T]he fate of men and the fate of beasts is the same. As the one dies, so does the other, for there is one spirit in both and man's distinction over the beast is nothing, for everything is vanity. All go to one place, all come from the dust and all return to the dust. Who knows whether the spirit of men rises upward and the spirit of the beast goes down to the earth?

Not surprisingly, Ecclesiastes concludes that "there is nothing better for man than to rejoice in his works, for that is his lot, and no one can permit him to see what shall be afterwards." And Ecclesiastes goes on to recommend hedonistic selfishness as a response to the absence of a hereafter: "I know that there is no other good in life but to be happy while one lives. Indeed, every man who eats, drinks and enjoys happiness in his work—that is the gift of God."

Ecclesiastes is wrong. Even if there are no heaven and hell, there are good reasons for human beings to do better than merely be happy. The truly moral person is the one who does the right thing without any promise of reward or threat of punishment—without engaging in a cost-benefit analysis. Doing something because God has said to do it does not make a person moral; it merely tells us that person is a prudential believer, akin to the person who obeys the command of an all-powerful secular king. Abraham's willingness to sacrifice his son Isaac because God told him to does not make Abraham moral; it merely shows that he was obedient. Far too many people abdicate moral responsibility to God, as Abraham did. Accordingly, for purposes of discussing character and morality, I will assume that there is no God who commands, rewards, punishes, or intervenes. Whether or not this is true—whatever true means in the context of faith—it is a useful heuristic device by which to assess character and morality. Just as Pascal argued that the most prudent wager is to put your eternal money on God, so too, it is a useful construct to assume God's nonexistence when judging whether a human action should be deemed good. There is a wonderful Hasidic story about a rabbi who was asked whether it is ever proper to act as if God did not exist. He responded, "Yes, when you are asked to give charity, you should give as if there were no God to help the object of the charity." I think the same is true of morality and character: in deciding what course of action is moral, you should act as if there were no God. You should also act as if there were no threat of earthly punishment or reward. You should be a person of good character because it is right to be such a person.

I am reminded of the cartoon depicting an older married man marooned on a deserted island with a younger woman. He asks her to have sex, arguing "no one would ever know." The woman responds, "I would know." The "I would know" test of good character is a useful one.

What then is the content of good character in a world without the threat of divine or earthly punishment and without the promise of divine or earthly reward? In such a world every good act would be done simply because it was deemed by the actor to be good. Good character in such a world would involve striking an appropriate balance among often competing interests, such as the interests of oneself and of others, of the present and of the future, of one's family (tribe, race, gender, religion, nation, and so forth) and of strangers. Since the beginning of time, civilized humans have struggled to achieve that golden mean. The great Rabbi Hillel put it well when he said: "If I am not for myself, who will be for me, but if I am for myself alone, what am I?"

Good character consists of recognizing the selfishness that inheres in each of us and trying to balance it against the altruism to which we should all aspire. It is a difficult balance to strike, but no definition of goodness can be complete without it.

**DENNIS PRAGER** has been broadcasting his unique brand of "thought radio" in Los Angeles for fifteen years. He now also has a national radio show and is the author of several highly praised works, including *Think a Second Time; The Nine Questions People Ask About Judaism; Happiness Is a Serious Problem;* and, with Joseph Telushkin, *Why the Jews? The Reason for Anti-Semitism.* Called "one of the three most interesting minds in American Jewish life" and "one of the five best speakers in America," he teaches Torah at the University of Judaism and has lectured in Russia and Israel. He was appointed by former president Ronald Reagan to the U.S. Delegation to the Vienna Review Conference on the Helsinki Accords. He has made videos on such subjects as race and character. His favored lecture topics include marriage, happiness, human suffering, intolerance, and capital punishment.

# 32

# The Moral Character of Religious and Secular People

*Dennis Prager*

A WIDELY HELD BELIEF among secular intellectuals is that good religious people are at a lower level of character development than good secular people—because the religious believe that God rewards good and punishes evil while the secular do not believe in a God who rewards good and punishes evil. For example, the belief in reward and punishment marks the lowest stage of one's moral development, according to Lawrence Kohlberg, the late famed Harvard scholar. Others argue one's essential goodness— what we might call one's moral character—is best measured by one's motives. That is, the good person who believes in divine reward and punishment is simply not as good a person as the good secular person, who performs his good acts selflessly, without fear (of hell, bad karma, an unfortunate reincarnation, and the like) or ulterior motive (of salvation, eternal life, a corner office, and the like).

At first glance this argument seems to make sense. But under scrutiny it reveals itself as only a secularist's desire to prove the supremacy of his character. You may think this is so much intellectual or theological quibbling. But no. This debate has ramifications not only for our own behavior but for how we try to build a better society by encouraging good behavior in others.

## The Impact of Belief

The first defect in the secularist's argument is a simple empirical one. The belief in divine reward and punishment has only a minimal impact on the moral behavior of nearly all religious adults. This startling fact is easily demonstrated: if the belief in divine reward and punishment were instrumental in motivating moral conduct, nearly all religious people would be exceptionally ethical. Unfortunately, however, that is not the case. Indeed, secular thinkers concede as much, as they often contend that religion has a minimal impact on most people's ethics. (If these secularists did not believe in the impotence, or inefficiency, of religious values, they would be frauds for advocating secular values.)

The secularists cannot have it both ways. They cannot argue that good religious people who believe in divine reward and punishment have an inferior character to good secular people and at the same time argue that religion doesn't make people better. Either one must argue that the belief in divine reward and punishment causes people to behave better but that these people do not deserve particular credit for their ethical behavior. Or one must argue that such religious beliefs do not tend to make people behave better; in which case the religious people who act ethically do so primarily for other reasons, and one must then ascribe as much moral character to good religious people as to good secular people.

The latter argument is demonstrably the case. The belief in divine reward and punishment has little impact in the day-to-day ethical behavior of most religious people (though, to repeat, we can all wish that it did, because all of us presumably want people to act morally for whatever reason).

## Why There Is So Little Impact

The first and most important reason why belief in divine reward and punishment has so little behavioral impact is that the personal reward or punishment is promised for the afterlife. While some religious people irrationally believe that if they act religiously, God will reward them in this life (by, for example, rendering them immune to a fatal disease or to being hit by a drunk driver), all rational religious people know that religious people are as likely as anyone else to be hit by a drunk driver or get cancer. The belief in divine reward and punishment applies only to some unknowable afterlife and is therefore only a belief, not a certainty.

The second reason is that religious people hold other, at least as powerful, beliefs that minimize the behavioral impact of the belief in divine reward and punishment. For example most religious people believe that if they repent, God will forgive them. Consequently very few religious people walk through life fearing punishment in the afterlife. Indeed, some Protestant Christians believe they are saved irrespective of how they behave. They believe they are rewarded—saved—according to their faith alone. According to the secularists' thesis, then, these Protestants who act ethically would have a much greater moral character than decent religious Jews, because religious Jews believe that God does reward and punish behavior (one of the Thirteen Principles of the Jewish faith is that God rewards the good and punishes the bad). Obviously such ranking of religions is ridiculous and irresponsible—yet this is what the logic of the secularists' argument demands. And consider this: nearly all religious people believe that one should do good and desist from doing bad more out of love for God than out of fear of punishment or desire for reward.

A third reason for the minimal behavioral impact of the belief in divine reward and punishment is that nearly all religious people who begin doing good out of a belief in an afterlife reward sooner or later do good because they have acclimated themselves to doing so. It is preposterous to argue that if a religious person who has spent a lifetime doing good and resisting the bad were to be convinced suddenly that there is no eternal reward and punishment, this person would then begin lying, stealing, and murdering.

## Reasons to Believe in Reward and Punishment

Of course all this leads to another question: If the belief in ultimate reward and punishment plays such a small role in most religious people's behavior, why do religious people hold this belief, and why do their religious leaders and traditions teach that God rewards the good and punishes the bad?

They do so to give order to the moral chaos of our world and thereby prevent people's despair. I, for one, would sink into despair if I believed that Hitler had the same fate—death and then oblivion— as the millions of innocent men, women, and children that he had murdered. The thought that the murderers and torturers of the world get away with all their evil and that the good who suffer are in no way rewarded for their good works or compensated for their unjust suffering would drive me to despair. In fact, I have always wondered how secular people do not despair, given their belief that the evil are not punished and the good are not rewarded. How sensitive to human suffering can these people be that they are able to lead relatively happy lives while believing that the universe is deaf to suffering and utterly oblivious to good and evil?

The primary purpose of the religious belief that God rewards good and punishes bad, then, is not to shape every action of the religious adult but to assure humanity that God did not create a universe oblivious to injustice and evil.

None of this implies that a belief in reward and punishment in an afterlife has no effect on any religious people. It probably does affect some, and for goodness' sake, I certainly hope it does—we need all the good we can get in this world. But for most religious people who choose good, in the final analysis, love of God and the habit of doing good and resisting evil play a much stronger role than does fear of God's punishment or the certainty of His reward.

## The Flaw in Assessing Motives

The argument that the moral character of the religious person who believes in divine reward and punishment is inferior to the moral character of the secular person who has no such motivation is wrong for another reason—it presumes that motivations for behavior are entirely knowable.

This presumption has no basis. Few of us know all of our own motives, let alone those of other people. It takes years of intensive psychoanalysis (not merely psychotherapy) to begin to understand what really motivates our behavior, and it is virtually impossible to know the motivations of others even when they are intimates, let alone strangers.

Why should we therefore assume that the nonbeliever's motives for doing good are purely altruistic? Perhaps the secular person who acts ethically does so because he fears being caught, or he lacks courage to violate the law, or he wants to impress his mother, or he wants to be known as an ethical person, or simply because he was raised in an environment so ethically preoccupied that behaving unethically is actually more difficult for him than acting ethically. Or perhaps he acts ethically simply because it makes him feel better about himself (which it always does). Why do any of these motives imply a higher moral character than that of the believer in divine reward and punishment?

In fact, they do not.

Why, then, given our general inability to know people's motives and the real possibility of nonaltruistic motives among secular people who act ethically, do so many secular intellectuals assess motives of ethical behavior and find religious motives less noble? One reason may be a desire to disparage religious arguments (just as many religious people desire to disparage secular arguments). But the major reason is the century-long tendency among secular intellectuals to assess motives rather than behavior.

That is why secular intellectuals composed the one group in the Western world that significantly supported Communism—and simultaneously loathed capitalism. Many secular intellectuals assessed Communism and capitalism not by their moral results but by their presumed motives. Communism, these people believed and argued, emanated from noble motives—equality, justice, concern for the downtrodden; while capitalism, they believed and argued, emanated from selfish motives—greater and greater profits.

Yet capitalism has been the socioeconomic engine of every democracy, and it has produced unprecedented wealth for virtually all its citizens, whereas Communism led to the slaughter of more people than any ideology in history, including Nazism (if only because the Nazis had less time). Nevertheless, legions of Western professors, writers, and artists have at various times passionately embraced murderous Communist regimes, such as those of Joseph Stalin and Mao Tse-tung, and despotic regimes, such as those of Ho Chi Minh and Fidel Castro.

Again, the intellectuals did so in large part because of their tendency to place greater importance on motives than on behavior. This same tendency accounts for the belief that the moral character of those who believe in divine reward and punishment is an inferior one.

Character consists of doing the right thing when not doing the right thing is more tempting and immediately rewarding. Having character consists of valuing the good more than one's own desire, of being honest when dishonesty is personally beneficial, of exercising self-control when the impulse toward self-gratification is more powerful. Precisely identifying the motives of a person who engages in these character-filled choices is rarely possible. Even if such identification were possible, the only importance in doing so would be to encourage the building of such motivation in others—not in order for us to pass judgment on it.

When I interviewed the greatest people of character I have ever met—non-Jews who risked their lives to rescue Jews during the Holocaust—I asked those who were not religious why they did it. In every case the response was, "Because it was the right thing to do. I couldn't do otherwise." They felt that they had no choice, that they could not have lived themselves if they hadn't acted as they did.

If we are to assess character by motives, then, why are we to assume that these secular moral heroes had greater moral character than the religious moral heroes who also risked their lives to save Jews? Because the latter may have believed in a just God who governs the universe and therefore rewards the good and punishes the evil? We could just as easily disparage the secular heroes' moral character for acting as they did because they "couldn't do otherwise."

## Religious Character Is More Reliable

While assessing motives is of interest primarily to secular moral thinkers, the true test of character is its moral reliability. And here, the religious person is often decisively superior.

As the ancient Talmudic dictum holds, "The person who is commanded and acts [right] is greater than the person who is not commanded and acts [right]." Why? Because the person who does good because he feels commanded is obeying a code that is greater than himself. Even if he does not feel like engaging in the act of goodness, he will do so. Conversely, the individual who does not feel obligated to heed any outside command does the good that he does because he feels it is right and feels like doing it.

In the final analysis, which individual is more morally reliable—the one who always does what he feels is right or the one who acts in accordance to a moral code to which he feels obligated?

Although we should give credit and gratitude to anyone who does good in this world, if our greatest concern is that goodness increase and prevail, we cannot rely on those who answer only to themselves and to their consciences. When you have to answer only to yourself, it is all too easy to err and it is all too easy to rationalize away anything.

Any woman walking alone in a dark alley and seeing ten men walking toward her would be far more relieved to know that these men felt commanded to obey a higher law of ethical behavior than to know that each of these men did whatever he personally felt was right.

None of this is written with the slightest desire to impugn the character of good secular people. Good secular people are beacons in a dark world—not to mention infinitely superior to mediocre and bad religious people.

Rather, it is written for two other reasons. One is to respond to the widespread belief among secular intellectuals (who carry such sway in our culture) that religious moral character is morally inferior to secular moral character when both lead to identical acts of goodness. The other is to make the case for the greater reliability of religion-based morality. For the vast majority of people, consistently choosing the good and the noble in life over powerful temptation is the result of belief in a moral order, faith in a transcendent moral source, and acceptance of guidelines from a moral code that emanates from that transcendent source. Yes, a handful of individuals will consistently know and act upon the moral good even though they believe that the universe is morally blind, even though they believe that there is no higher source of morality than their own conscience. But such individuals are too rare to be depended on for creating a better world.

For a better world, we are far better off relying on those individuals whose moral character has been molded by discipline before a greater moral code and been shaped by a belief in a just universe. If we are forced to judge between moral characters, this is the deeper and more reliable one.

RABBI WAYNE DOSICK is the spiritual guide of the Elijah
Minyan and an adjunct professor at the University of San
Diego. He is the award-winning author of six books, including *The Business Bible: Ten New Commandments for Creating an Ethical Workplace; Golden Rules: The Ten Ethical
Values Parents Need to Teach Their Children;* and *When Life
Hurts: A Book of Hope.* He lectures and conducts workshops
on spirituality, ethics, life transitions and transformations, and
evolving human consciousness, bringing the message that contemporary society can be transformed when we bring the transcendent world of the spirit and enduring ethical values into
our businesses, public institutions, faith communities, families,
and children, and into our own hearts and souls.

*33*

# Love Your Neighbor

## *Rabbi Wayne Dosick*

A FISH STORY.

My wife, Ellen, and I went into a fine restaurant for dinner. We said to the waitress, "We have tickets for the theater, so we have a amount of limited time to eat. Could you please recommend something on the menu that will not take very long to prepare?"

She pointed out a number of menu items, including one that I had never seen before, fish kabob. The menu described it as "small pieces of grilled halibut on a skewer with pieces of tomato, onions, green peppers and mushrooms." It sounded appetizing and unique, so I ordered it.

First, the waitress brought us small dinner salads and a basket of delicious rolls. Soon the fish kabob arrived. It was as the menu

*Note:* © 1998 Wayne Dosick.

promised except that interspersed between the fish and the vegetables were pieces of bacon.

Now, I observe the Jewish laws of keeping kosher, so I am prohibited from eating any pork products. So I said to the waitress, "Because of my religious beliefs and practice, I cannot eat this bacon. And because we have to get to the theater, we don't have time to order anything else. So please just bring me the check."

If you were that waitress—or that waitress's manager—what would you have done?

Most probably, you would have come to me and said, "Sir, I am so sorry that this unfortunate error occurred. And I am so sorry that you did not have time for dinner. Please accept my apologies. There is, of course, no charge, and here is a coupon for free appetizers next time you come to our restaurant."

But rather than a sincere apology and an invitation to return, I got a check. And the check was not just for the few pennies worth of the small dinner salads and pieces of bread that we had eaten. I got a check for $15. In a stunning display of twisted wisdom, the waitress and her manager decided that we had eaten two salads à la carte—$7.50 each!

You can imagine that it will be a long time before I—or any of my friends and associates I tell about this incident—will return to that restaurant.

Another fish story.

Ellen and I went into another restaurant at another place and another time. From the extensive menu, I ordered sea bass. Within a very short time, the waitress returned to our table. "Sir," she said, "I am so sorry. In the minute it took me to place your order in the kitchen, we ran out of sea bass."

I expected her to hand me the menu and ask if I would like to make another selection. But instead she said, "But don't worry. My manager told me to tell you that we are upgrading you to salmon."

Now, I've been upgraded to an airplane seat before but never to a piece of fish. Yet that restaurant cared enough about pleasing its customer that it offered a more expensive menu item in place of what it could not provide. And you can imagine that I—and any of my friends and associates I tell about *this* incident—will be patronizing this restaurant on a regular basis.

One of the best-known injunctions from the Hebrew Bible is "Love your neighbor as yourself" (Lev. 19:18). It is such a wise adage that most religions and cultures have a version of it as part of their faith teachings. Christianity instructs, "Do unto others as you would have them do unto you." Islam teaches, "No one of you is a believer unless he loves for his brother what he loves for himself." Buddhism admonishes, "Hurt not others with that which pains thyself." Hinduism teaches, "Do nothing to thy neighbor which thou wouldst not have him do to thee thereafter. And Confucius said, "What you do not want done to yourself, do not do unto others."

Even though this admonition seems to make perfect sense, we cannot always know what is in another's mind or heart; we cannot always know how another would like to be treated, for—in the well-known adage of Native Americans—we can never really know another's needs or wants until we walk in his or her moccasins. Yet, if we change the grammatical formulation of the Hebrew verse a bit, we come up with an unequivocal, irrefutable adage: "Love your fellow human being. He or she is just like you."

Every human being wants to be respected and treated with decency and dignity. Every human being wants to be told the truth and be dealt with in fairness and in integrity. Every human being wants to be honored as a child of the universe, as a child of God.

The folks at the second restaurant knew this. They regarded Ellen and me as they would regard themselves. They knew we would be disappointed that our menu selection was not available, and they peremptorily defused what might have been an unpleasant situation by offering us a very palatable alternative.

The folks at the first restaurant did not care about their customers' feelings or needs. They cared only about their own convenience and their own self-interest. They regarded Ellen and me not as people but as product. They were seemingly unwilling to accept any responsibility—or the consequences—for their actions.

How hard would it have been for the folks at the first restaurant to act as did the folks at the second restaurant, recognizing that they manifest love for their fellow beings by responding to their needs and caring about their feelings?

Religious and spiritual traditions focus on the whole human being and on the entirety of the human experience. The Bible is filled with teachings and laws not just about faith and belief, not just about rituals and ceremonies, but about the everyday conduct of our everyday lives—at home and in community, in business and in commerce.

These religious precepts—the core teachings of moral conduct—seem to be widely accepted and warmly embraced by the vast majority of Americans. While only 30 percent of Americans attend organized religious services at a church, synagogue, or mosque on a regular basis, more than 90 percent of us report that we believe in God and in God's mandate of clear, unequivocal standards of ethical behavior. Even if we do not place our religious and spiritual sentiments into the confines of "organized religion," we are keenly aware of the presence of the divine in our midst, and we know that the spirit of God is within us.

Thus we clearly understand when we are enjoined, "you are not to lie" (Lev. 19:11), and, "you are not to take up an empty rumor" (Exod. 23:1). Is there anyone among us who thinks that lying or spreading gossip is a higher good than being honest and telling the truth?

We are enjoined, "you are not to steal" (Lev. 19:11), and, "you are not to commit robbery" (Lev. 19:13a). Is there anyone among us who thinks that taking something that does not belong to us is a higher good than respecting and safeguarding another's property?

We are enjoined, "you are not to commit corruption in justice, in measure, weight or capacity; you shall have scales of equity" (Lev. 19:35), and, "you shall have a stone-weight that is perfect and equal" (Deut. 25:15). Is there anyone among us who thinks that cheating in business is a higher good than acting with complete honesty and integrity?

We are enjoined, "you are not to keep overnight the working-wages of a hired hand [a day-laborer] until morning" (Lev. 19:13b), and, "if you take your neighbor's coat as a pledge [collateral for a loan] return it to him before the sun goes down, because it is his only garment; in what else shall he sleep?" (Ex. 22:25–26). Is there anyone among us who thinks that exploiting the most vulnerable in our society is a higher good than treating each and every person with respect, dignity, and honor?

We know what is right.

We know what is wrong.

Yet how meticulous are we about bringing God's word, God's standard of ethical behavior, God's definition of right and wrong out of the sanctuary into the streets, into the marketplace, into our everyday dealings? How often do we bring our sense of God's presence and our understanding of God's will through the office door or the factory gate, onto the assembly line, or into the executive suite?

A soap maker once came to a rabbi and said, "Rabbi, Rabbi, what good is religion? Religion teaches honesty. But just look at how many dishonest people there are. And religion promises peace in the world. But just look at how many wars there have been. What good is religion?"

The rabbi answered, "My dear soap maker, there are so many wonderful soaps in the world. And just look at how many dirty people there are."

Religion and its teachings—just like soap—work only when we use them.

Ethical values sourced in religious teachings are not just for a sacred time or a holy place. They are to be the foundation, the touchstone, the guides, and the goals of our everyday lives.

Disregarding religion's ethical precepts—doing what is wrong even when we know what is right—has repercussions that go far beyond the marketplace, far beyond our daily business dealings. It has consequences that reach to those most precious to us and that ripple and reverberate far and long.

When Bobby was five, he and his father went for a drive in the country. At a crossroads, Bobby's father drove right through the red light without bothering to stop.

Bobby said, "Daddy, in school my teacher taught us that we are supposed to stop at every red light."

Bobby's father replied, "Oh, don't worry, son. There's no traffic on this road, and besides, there are no police cars around. No one will ever see us going through the red light."

When Bobby was twelve, his mother took him to the movies. As they were going into the theater, she said, "Bobby, if the usher asks you how old you are, tell him that you are eleven. I bought you a child's ticket."

When Bobby was sixteen, he overheard his father on the phone with the family accountant. "That's right, Charlie," said Bobby's father, "forget that I told you about the extra income from the stock option deal. There's no record of it anywhere, so there's no reason to pay the extra tax."

When Bobby was eighteen, he went off to the state university. Three months later his parents received this letter from the dean of the college:

Dear Mr. and Mrs. Smith:

I regret to inform you that your son Robert has been expelled from our university. He violated our school's honor code when he was caught cheating on his midterm exam.

Bobby's mother cried out, "Bobby? Cheating on an exam? How could it be? We brought him up in such a good home. Where did he ever learn to cheat?"

And Bobby's father sighed and shook his head and sadly asked, "How could Bobby do this to us?"

Our children are very, very smart. They watch us and they learn from us. We cannot fool them by being one person at work and trying to be another person at home. Our ethical values and our moral conduct permeate our every place and our every moment.

As we are, so our children will be. At stake in our every word and our every deed is the moral climate in which our children will grow, the ethical mandate they will receive, the moral foundation on which they will build the next generation.

Are a few dollars more profit, a few hours more power, a few minutes more prestige, worth our children's moral inheritance?

Are they even worth our children's respect?

If we ever have any doubts about our ethical choices and our moral conduct, we can ask ourselves the question given to us by modern technology: What if my every word and deed of today were being recorded by a hidden video camera? And what if the tape from that camera were to be played on tomorrow night's television news? And what if I had to call my parents or my children and say, "I am going to be on national television"? Would I be happy and proud? Or would I be embarrassed and humiliated?

The answers to those questions tell us if we are doing right.

But as helpful as that image may be, we really do not need the threat of technological wizardry to guide us. For in our heart of hearts, in the deepest places in our souls, we know what is right; we know what is wrong.

There is only one question that we have to constantly ask ourselves: If I know what is right—and I do—why would I ever do what is wrong?

To remember our ethical mandate, to remember our moral destiny, there is one word to remember always: ETHICS.

E    EVERYWHERE

T    all the TIME

H    be HONEST

I    act with INTEGRITY

C    have COMPASSION

S    for what is at STAKE is Your Reputation, Your Self-Esteem, Your Inner Peace.

CHARLES COLSON is founder and chairman of Prison Fellowship Ministries, one of the world's largest volunteer organizations, serving the spiritual and practical needs of prisoners in
seventy-five countries. He was special counsel to President
Nixon for four years, and spent seven months in prison on a
Watergate-related charge of obstruction of justice. He is also
the founder of Justice Fellowship, which works with legislators and policymakers to reform the penal and justice systems,
and Neighbors Who Care, a support system for victims of
crime. His numerous awards include the Templeton Prize for
Progress in Religion and the Others Award from the Salvation
Army. He has written thirteen books, including the best-seller
*Born Again* (1976), which was made into a movie. He donates
the royalties from his books, which have sold over five million
copies, to Prison Fellowship.

# 34

# Knowing What Is Right Is Not Enough

❦

*Charles Colson*

AS A FORMER MARINE I was honored to address two thousand officers of the Second Marine Division at Camp LeJeune, North Carolina. I'd been a young lieutenant in that very place many years before. Now I had been asked to address the topic of ethics, and I urged a commitment to absolute ethical standards. Otherwise, I argued, America will suffer an accelerated decline into crime, drug abuse, and family breakup that could destroy liberty or public order or both.

At the end of my talk, a tall, erect master sergeant walked into the aisle, took the microphone, and asked, "Mr. Colson, which is more important, loyalty or integrity?" For a Marine, holding fast to the creed *Semper Fidelis*—always faithful—this is not an abstract question. In the Marines I learned an intense loyalty that has never

---

*Note:* © 1994 Charles Colson.

left me—loyalty to country, to comrades, to the cause. Marines are known for their unquestioning obedience to orders. So this question got to the heart of things: should any moral commitment take precedence over the commitment of a Marine?

I wish that someone had posed that blunt question to me when I was in the Nixon White House. At age thirty-nine, I was asked by President Nixon to be his special counsel. Within a short time I occupied the office next to the president's. At the time I considered myself a man with an almost puritanical moral code. My father had drilled into my conscience the necessity of telling the truth. (After testifying forty-four times under oath, I was the only major figure involved in the great Watergate scandal who was never accused of perjury.) I had been scrupulously taught high ethical standards, and so in the White House I refused to take gifts, placing everything I owned in a blind trust (losing a lot of money in the process). Above all, I was absolutely certain that no one could corrupt me, a former Marine who knew the meaning of loyalty and duty.

My self-righteousness was accompanied by a conviction that the reelection of the president was vital to America's interests: it was the only way to end the Vietnam War honorably and get back our prisoners.

I was honest and I was zealous. However, these virtues weren't tempered by the humility to question the means by which I was pursuing my objectives. I was blinded by a conviction of my own integrity, and before I knew it, despite the best of intentions and strong values, I ended up in the midst of the biggest political scandal in American history—one that forced a president out of office and sent me to a prison cell.

Thus, from personal experience, I could answer the master sergeant's question. I told him that loyalty, if not attached to a cause that is moral and just, can be the most dangerous of all virtues. Nothing is more seductive or destructive than a virtue misapplied. When we human beings believe that our cause is just—in my case the cause of a president I respected—we are capable of infinite self-justification. Our conscience becomes not a guide but an accomplice. Intending to do good, we end up neck-deep in compromise.

Clearly, it is possible to be self-righteous without being righteous. Clearly, being a man or woman of character requires something more than an intellectual commitment to noble goals and high ethical standards. It requires something more, as I discovered, than the echoes of a father's advice or even a Marine code.

What is this something more? It is the disposition to do what is right. It is not enough to *know* what is good; we must also *love* the good and have the will to act in accord with it. This could hardly be more urgent, given the collapse of character in American life. We see an epidemic of broken marital promises, leaving women in poverty and children in emotional chaos. We see a growing number of brutal juvenile offenders, with vacant eyes and hollow souls, who have lost all contact with mercy and morality. We see scandals in government, business, and academia, which have become so commonplace they have lost their power to shock. In every class and community the breakdown of character is the storm in which we're attempting to navigate.

## Character in an Age of Relativism

The problem is that contemporary culture, with its emphasis on personal autonomy and relativism, is loath to make any judgment, much less judgments that assess a person's adherence to standards such as justice, courage, or prudence. Thus we have created the great impasse of modern life. Character is proving indispensable, yet our society finds it nearly impossible to define character. Seventy percent of Americans, according to the Gallup Organization, say there are no moral absolutes that apply in all situations. Seventy-two percent say there is no such thing as "truth."

The institutions that have traditionally reinforced character have surrendered to the same spirit of relativism. Only 11 percent of elementary and secondary schoolteachers surveyed by the National Education Association say they try to teach right and wrong. The institutions of American public education offer almost no moral training during the morally formative years—a silence filled by the trendy moral anarchy of television, music, and movies.

I've seen the most dramatic evidence of the reign of relativism on college campuses, where relativism is not a controversial contention but an unquestioned assumption. A few years ago I was asked to give a lecture on ethics at Harvard Business School, where a debate was raging on how to teach business ethics. The day I arrived, Harvard's Aldrich Hall was packed. Hundreds of students and faculty were sitting at desks and standing in the aisles or against the walls. I told them, in no uncertain terms, that their ethics courses were a waste of time and money because they taught that right and wrong are up for grabs, to be determined subjectively. Such subjective values, I argued, will never withstand the pressures of life. When I finished speaking, I braced myself for some tough questions. But to my shock, not a single person pressed me with a tough argument. As one student later told me, "They didn't know what to ask." The students either had not thought about the issues or lacked the basic intellectual framework to challenge me. As law professor Stephen Carter once explained to me before a similar presentation I made at Yale, "Students today are taught that law is amoral—that moral issues like the ones you'll raise are irrelevant." Even the dyed-in-the-wool secularists won't bother to debate, Carter warned me. "They'll listen to your point of view, acknowledge that you're entitled to it, but conclude that it's really of no consequence. They won't bother to argue because they don't think it matters. All points of view are equal."

This easygoing, apathetic relativism is the culmination of a process of moral deregulation that began in the 1960s. The purpose of life and law was recast to maximize individual expression and choice above "oppressive" social norms. Liberty was defined as the death of standards. Tolerance was defined as moral neutrality. Divorce became a personal freedom and right; illegitimacy became "nonmarital child bearing"; unwed mothers became "single-parent families." Moral convictions were reduced to personal tastes. Preferring any lifestyle above another became the ultimate form of bigotry.

In this postmodern worldview, the supreme virtue is choice, which should always be maximized. But we should remember that choice is morally neutral; it is *what* we choose that makes all the difference to individual dignity and social order. Relativistic freedom can quickly become slavery to compulsion, appetite, and self-interest. Choice unguided by moral absolutes can swiftly become a cluster of debasing addictions—to materialism, drugs, and sex. Children whose souls are stunted in the shadow of relativism are left without noble ideals and moral goals to raise their sights above immediate self-gratification. Promising young lives are wasted on whims and wants, leading to the dark valley of an empty life. Taken together, these disorders coalesce into the disorder found in society. When young boys, for example, are "free" to invent their own values, we end up with scenes from William Golding's *Lord of the Flies* transported to the streets of our cities. "A society in which men and women are morally adrift, ignorant of norms, and intent chiefly upon gratification of appetites, will be a bad society," warned historian Russell Kirk, "no matter how many people vote and no matter how liberal its formal constitution may be."

That is precisely what has happened to Americans: we no longer celebrate virtue, and we mock honor and truth. The very basis of character—individual and corporate—has been eroded.

## Four Prerequisites to Character

So how can character be recovered and renewed? There are at least four prerequisites, none of which is easy to satisfy.

First, we must rediscover a belief in binding, unchanging moral truths. Our crisis of character is understandable, even predictable, in the absence of absolutes. Obeying moral laws is often hard, involving self-denial, even sacrifice. If that sacrifice is not seen as inherently good and just and true, it makes little sense. In a relativistic environment, ethics deteriorates into utilitarian or pragmatic concerns, which are no match for self-interest. The belief that character is a matter of choice and taste cannot help but alter our moral sensibilities, eroding our sense or responsibility.

Our word ethics derives from the ancient Greek word *ethos,* which means "stall"—a hiding place, the one place a person could go to find rest and security. Our word morals comes from the word *mores,* which means "customs." Ethics, or ethos, is what is normative, what ought to be. Morals is what actually is. Unfortunately, in American life today we are totally guided by polls charting the shifting practices that actually exist.

And this leads to a practical problem. If we lose our belief in what ought to be, we can never challenge or change what is. If we want to condemn adultery or date rape, cheating or racism, we must be able to appeal to an objective rule, some transcendent basis of authority—not a subjective feeling or a majority decision that might change tomorrow. *Re*form has no meaning when form is lacking. If we lose our ability to know what is absolutely right, we lose our ability to know what is absolutely wrong. Philosopher Peter Kreeft writes that of all the symptoms of decay in our civilization, subjectivism is the most dangerous of all. "A mistake—be it a moral mistake or an intellectual mistake—can be discovered and corrected only if truth exists and can be known."

Second, we must restore a sense of shame and stigma in our society. In a free nation, not everything that is wrong can or should be illegal. But this does not mean that the broader society should be indifferent. In the past, for example, social shaming rather than the law was the means of limiting ills such as drunkenness or sex outside marriage. The same could be said of drug abuse or divorce or child abandonment. When social disapproval is strong, it is more effective than laws, policies, and the courts. It enforces an informal social order by defining some behavior as worthy of contempt. "So long as there is shame," it has been said, "there is hope for virtue."

Third, we need to respect and strengthen the character-forming institutions of society, particularly the family, supported by the church and local community. Intellectual virtue—knowing what is good—

is not enough. As Aristotle said, "We become just by doing just acts, temperate by doing temperate acts, brave by doing brave acts." It is in families that we learn not just moral beliefs but moral habits, reinforced through years of loving discipline. In an ideal world those habits of heart and mind will be supported by other adults: teachers, neighbors, mentors, youth group leaders, and coaches. Edmund Burke said, "A man's habits become his character." We need to show special concern for the institutions that instill moral habits and to express outrage when government or the entertainment industry undermines the work of those institutions.

Finally, I want to return to the problem I posed at the start. I had the advantage of these institutions and ideals—a belief in moral standards, a sense of shame at bad behavior, and a family that took moral instruction seriously. But it wasn't sufficient, because my heart and will had not embraced what my intellect had learned. That's why I believe our ethical system cannot be separated from our relationship with God. Our relationship with God helps us breach the chasm between *knowing*, what we might call our ethical system, and *doing* (or character), how what we believe is manifested in our lives. My relationship with God motivates and empowers me to live in accordance with what I believe, or more accurately, what God teaches.

In an essay published in 1947, C. S. Lewis likened the composition of the properly ordered human soul to that of the human body: the head (reason) must control the belly (appetites) through the chest (the will and heart—or the "spirited element"). Under relativism, Lewis says, the head is no match for the appetites of the stomach; there is no force or power strong enough to dispose the will to do what we know in our heads to be good.

Relativism creates "men without chests." The theme is powerfully portrayed in the movie adaptation of Tolstoy's *War and Peace* when Pierre, the hapless central character (played by Henry Fonda), wanders aimlessly in the midst of war. Everything has gone wrong in his life, there's chaos all around him, and he muses aloud, "Why is it that I know what is right and do what is wrong?" The heart and the will (the "chest") must somehow be transformed so that we can love and do what is right.

## Character and God's Grace

The same lesson is reinforced every day in my work with prisoners at Prison Fellowship Ministries. I started Prison Fellowship after being released from prison in 1976. I had become convinced that only a personal relationship with God can break the cycle of hopelessness, despair, and self-centeredness that casts men into prison. Through the work of PF volunteers, thousands of men and women have been transformed. As St. Paul put it, they have become new creatures in Christ. They've left their old predatory life behind for a life devoted to serving others.

Without such an inner transformation, there is little hope for any meaningful change. That is why all our government efforts at rehabilitation fail: men and women who are impulsive, unsocialized, violent, and morally rootless require more than new skills or psychological therapy. They need a new system of values, created not by their choices but by God's grace. The result is a drop in recidivism from 41 percent to 14 percent among those who participate regularly in our Bible study programs (verified in an independent study by the National Institute of Mental Health).

The application of this principle goes far beyond prison walls. David Klinghoffer, literary editor for the *National Review,* has written in the *Wall Street Journal,* "A person does not accept a new, rigorous system of moral action because it might in the long run prop up civilized society." No, a person submits to a moral system "because he believes the system is, in a fundamental sense, true—very likely because he believes it is the will of God."

This isn't to say that it's impossible for a person to be good without God. People can be guided by natural law, a universalized application of Judeo-Christian tradition and the accumulated wisdom of human experience. They can know what is right (in every human being there is a sense of right and wrong). Atheists jump on grenades to save their buddies in a foxhole. I do not believe, however, that an individual can consistently and dependably live a virtuous life without God. That may sound dogmatic to some and perhaps even arrogant, though I hope not. The reason I make such an assertion is the very point Tolstoy made. Most people have at least a fair idea of what they ought to do in a given situation; we do have knowledge of right and wrong, and conscience does convict us. But things such as self-centeredness, desire for pleasure, and desire for power stand between each of us and doing what we ought to do. They are formidable barriers, and something even more powerful must intervene. For the Christian, that something is a someone. That someone is Jesus Christ. Through the act of love in which He died, He reconciles us to God.

And in that reconciliation two very important things happen: first, our consciences are quickened. We *want* to do the right thing, as an act of gratitude to the One "who loved me and gave His life for me." Even more important, He dwells within us if we are sincere about our faith. And He empowers us to overcome that which stands between us and *doing* the right thing.

There is nothing triumphalistic in this. Christians are sinners; in fact their recognition of this may well be more acute than non-Christians'. I have indeed faced temptations often as a Christian and struggle still with pride and self-righteousness. It is a struggle, not surprisingly, because forming human behavior and living ethically are not easy tasks. There is nothing more deceitful than the human heart, nor more rebellious than the human will.

But if my experience is any guide, our real hope for restoring character lies in once again recognizing the eternal truths of Judeo-Christian revelation as the binding authority for informing conscience, and trusting the supernatural power of Christ to cause us to *want* to do what we know is right.

THOMAS LICKONA, a developmental psychologist and professor of education at the State University of New York at Cortland, has done award-winning work in teacher education and currently directs the Center for the Fourth and Fifth R's (Respect and Responsibility). He has also been a professor at Boston and Harvard Universities and a past president of the Association for Moral Education. A frequent guest on radio and TV talk shows, he sits on the CHARACTER COUNTS! Coalition Advisory Council and the boards of the Character Education Partnership and the Medical Institute for Sexual Health. His publications include *Moral Development and Behavior* (1976), *Raising Good Children* (1983), and the best-selling and definitive *Educating for Character: How Our Schools Can Teach Respect and Responsibility* (1991). His work has been featured in a *New York Times Magazine* cover story and several educational videos.

# 35

# Sexual Responsibility and Character

*Thomas Lickona*

WHAT DOES SEX have to do with character? Popular belief holds that sexual conduct is simply a matter of personal freedom, lifestyle choice, and private values that have nothing to do with ethics. But like it or not, choices people make about sex are laden with moral considerations. In his essay, "Character First," Kevin Ryan says, "How we live our sexual lives is intrinsically a moral matter. Sex both involves and affects others."

The personal and social consequences of sexual activity involve physical, emotional, and spiritual issues that cannot be ignored by a person of character. Every decision to have sexual contact with another person raises issues of responsibility, personal integrity, and respect. In sexual relationships, as in all relationships, ethical principles of caring, fairness, honesty, promise keeping, and loyalty always come into play. As Ryan observes, "An important part of being a sexually mature person is to be a person with character, including self-control, responsibility and even courage."

Down through the ages, self-control—including sexual self-control—has been considered a mark of good character. The sexual revolution that began in the 1960s, however, sought to replace the traditional emphasis on sexual self-restraint with an emphasis on sexual freedom. People would be free to make love with whomever they wished without the strictures of marriage (a monogamous, public, legally binding commitment). The sexual revolution promised greater happiness, but three decades years later it is painfully clear that our society suffers from a plague of problems stemming from the abandonment of traditional norms of sexual morality. The problems include:

- *Rape.* It is increasing four times as fast as any other violent crime (according to a 1993 *CBS Evening News* report). In a 1988 survey by the Rhode Island Rape Crisis Center, two-thirds of boys grades 6 through 9 and 49 percent of the girls said it was "acceptable for a man to force sex on a woman if they have been dating for six months or more."

- *Teen pregnancy.* Each year, more than a million teenage girls, most of them unmarried, become pregnant.

- *Nonmarital births.* They are up from 5 percent of all births in 1960 to more than 30 percent today (according to the report "Marriage in America," published by the Institute for American Values, 1995).

- *Abortions.* There are a million and a half each year, a third of them performed on teenagers. The United States has the highest teen abortion rate in the developed world (according to a 1989 United Nations study).

- *Sexually transmitted diseases.* There are 12 million new cases each year, most of them in persons under twenty-five (according to the Centers for Disease Control).

- *Emotional and behavioral problems.* Teen sex is increasingly part of a syndrome of troubled behaviors that include drug and alcohol abuse, riding with a drug-using driver, getting suspended from school, running away from home, and committing suicide (according to the February 1991 issue of *Pediatrics*).

- *Sexual harassment.* Four out of five high school students said they have experienced "unwelcome sexual behavior" in school (according to a 1993 study by the American Association of University Women.)

- *Sexual abuse of children.* An estimated one in four girls and one in six boys is sexually abused at least once before age eighteen by a trusted adult.

- *Marital infidelity.* Persons who are sexually active before marriage are more likely to give in to the temptation of sexual affairs after marriage (according to studies reported over the past decade in the *Journal of Marriage and the Family*).

Surveying this moral landscape, the essayist William Schickel, writing in the *Ithaca Journal,* observes: "Chastity, like honesty, is a civic as well as a personal virtue. When a society loses chastity, it begins to destroy itself." Chastity is a necessary human virtue, Schickel argues, necessary for all human beings everywhere.

As a psychologist and character educator, I spend a lot of my time talking to teachers and parents about what they can do to help young people develop good character. I also frequently speak to teenagers about character issues. On these occasions, I am most often asked to talk about sex and its connection with character. My goal is to give teens a way of thinking about sexual morality that I believe will help them make good sexual decisions, ones that will help build character and lead a good and happy life. I address five questions that young people often ask about sex.

*Isn't everybody doing it?* Though teen sex is not uncommon, everybody is *not* doing it, and the numbers who aren't are going up. A 1995 federal study (*The National Survey of Family Growth*) found that 50 percent of fifteen- to nineteen-year-old girls said they had *not* had sex (up from 45 percent in 1990). Among boys in the same age group, 45 percent said they had not had sex (up from 40 percent in 1988). Moreover, according to a number of different studies, students who get good grades, students who have goals for the future, students who abstain from drugs and alcohol, and students who often attend religious services are all significantly less likely to have had sex than students who do not have these qualities. So kids who are virgins have plenty of company—good company.

*If you really care about the other person, isn't sex a natural way to express your love?* Love means wanting what is best for the other person, seeking the greatest good for that person. How do you know when somebody really loves you? When they want what is truly best for your welfare, your happiness. Measured against this standard, is having sex without being married truly an act of love? One way to answer that question is to think about the harmful consequences that can come from sex between unmarried persons. Consider these lines from a pamphlet titled *Love Waits*:

> Love is patient, love is kind. Love wants what is best for another person. Love never demands something that will harm you or the person you love.
>
> Love will never cross the line between what's right and wrong. It's wrong to put one another in danger of having to deal with hard choices . . . choices that could change your lives, your goals and your plans forever.
>
> Having sex before marriage may feel right for the moment. But the possible costs of an unexpected pregnancy, abortion and sexually transmitted disease—as well as the deep hurts that can come from a broken relationship—outweigh the feelings of the moment. The feelings are temporary; their consequences are long-lasting.

All good things are worth waiting for. Waiting until marriage to have sex is a mature decision to control your desires. If you are getting to know someone—or are in a relationship—remember: If it's love, love waits.

*But if you use protection, doesn't that make sex responsible?* No matter what type of contraception is used, pregnancies can occur. But that isn't all. Even with so-called protection, one can still transmit or catch one of more than twenty sexually transmitted diseases (STDs). People of character do not jeopardize the health and well-being of others, especially those they love.

Condoms fail to prevent pregnancy 15 percent of the time, according to the journal *Family Planning Perspectives.* According to Kristine Napier in *The Power of Abstinence* (1996), the failure rate for teens is higher still.

What about sexually transmitted disease? A survey of more than one thousand teens found that two-thirds thought that condoms provided 100 percent protection against STDs. Nothing could be further from the truth:

- Researchers at the University of Texas Medical Branch at Galveston, in an analysis of eleven different studies, found that condoms on the average failed 31 percent of the time to prevent transmission of the AIDS virus. Reporting this finding in *Social Science and Medicine* (June 1993), Susan Weller stated, "It is a disservice to encourage the belief that condoms will prevent sexual transmission of HIV."

- In the November 1997 edition of the Italian journal *Medicine and Morals,* the French priest-physician Jacques Suaudeau reports that "the risk of contracting an HIV infection while using a condom is at least 10 to 15 percent," based on his review of eighty-eight studies, most of them from American sources.

- Medical studies show that condoms provide little or no protection against what are now two of the most common STDs: human papilloma virus (HPV, the cause of virtually all cervical cancer) and chlamydia (which, undetected, can lead to pelvic inflammatory disease, scarring of the fallopian tubes, and consequent inability to conceive a child).

The physical and financial consequences of unwanted pregnancy and sexually transmitted disease, however, are only part of the picture when we are considering ethical principles of respect and responsibility. A person of character must also consider the mental, emotional, and spiritual consequences of temporary sexual relationships. There is obviously no condom for the heart, mind, or soul. The psychological and spiritual repercussions of uncommitted sex vary among individuals but are never to be taken lightly. They include:

- The worry about pregnancy and sexually transmitted diseases.

- The emotional upheaval associated with an unexpected pregnancy.

- The stress of premature parenthood or the self-sacrifice of adoption if the baby is carried to term.

- The impact on education and career if one undertakes the financial and other moral responsibilities of parenthood.

- The trauma and aftermath of abortion if the pregnancy is aborted.

- The feelings of regret and self-recrimination that often follow a broken sexual relationship.

- The feelings of being used; the corruption of character that comes from being a user; the lies told to get sex or the deception of others about one's sexual activity.

- The loss of self-control and the consequent loss of self-respect; the lowered self-esteem that accompanies finding out you have a sexually transmitted disease (which may be incurable).

- The shaken trust and fear of commitment because of having been burned; the rage over betrayal, sometimes leading to violence; the depression, sometimes leading to suicide; the ruined relationships (because sex often comes to dominate and eventually end a relationship); the stunted personal growth (because premature sex can hinder identity development); the infertility resulting from sexually transmitted disease.

- The debasement of sex, which, when divorced from commitment, loses its sense of specialness.

- For the religious, the guilt over having violated one's moral standards; the sense of having sinned against God's law and jeopardized one's soul (Catholic and Protestant Christianity, Judaism, and Islam all teach that God reserves sex for marriage only).

You don't see these consequences of sex outside marriage depicted on TV or in the movies. You don't read about them in *Redbook* or *Sassy*. But they are very real.

In short, condoms don't make sex physically safe (you can still get pregnant or sick), emotionally safe (you can still get hurt), or ethically loving (you can't claim to love someone if you're gambling with that person's health, life, and future happiness).

*If you're planning to get married, isn't sex OK then?* This is a tough question for a lot of people. One way to answer it is to ask, What is the intrinsic meaning of sexual intercourse?

When you have sexual intercourse with someone, you are being as physically intimate as it is possible to be with another human being. Within what kind of relationship does this ultimate intimacy make sense? In a loving marriage, sexual union expresses a total commitment. You join your bodies because you've joined your lives. In body language, sex says to the other person, "I give myself to you completely." Within the marriage commitment, that's really true.

By contrast, sex before marriage is like saying, "I give myself to you completely, but not really." It's a form of lying with your body—and lying is hardly a mark of good character. You aren't completely committed yet; even if you're engaged, you can always get disengaged. About half the people who get married have been engaged at least once before.

In thinking about sex before marriage, it also helps to understand natural moral law. There is a moral law built into human nature, just as there is a law governing physical nature. When we follow this natural moral law, we live in harmony with ourselves and each other. When we act in ways that go against the natural law—when we lie, cheat, and steal, for example—we create problems for ourselves and others.

In the natural moral order, what are the natural consequences of having sex? Bonding and babies. If you have sex with someone you aren't married to, you may very well create or deepen a bond that ends up being broken. And even if you are trying to avoid it, you may create a life you aren't ready to assume responsibility for.

In her 1996 book, *The Power of Abstinence,* medical writer Kristine Napier sums up the benefits of saving sex for marriage:

- Waiting will make your dating relationships better. You'll spend more time getting to know each other.
- Waiting will help you find the right mate (someone who values you for the person you are).
- Waiting will increase your self-respect.
- Waiting will gain the respect of others.
- Waiting teaches you to respect others (you'll never pressure anyone).

- Waiting takes the pressure off you.

- Waiting means a clear conscience (no guilt) and peace of mind (no conflicts, no regrets).

- Waiting means a better sexual relationship in marriage (free of comparisons with other premarital partners, free of sexual flashbacks, and based on trust). By waiting, you're being faithful to your spouse even before you meet him or her.

- By practicing the virtues involved in waiting—such as faithfulness, self-control, modesty, good judgment, courage, and genuine respect for self and others—you're developing the kind of character that will make you a good marriage partner and attract the kind of person you'd like to marry.

To be sure, in today's pleasure-now culture, it's not easy for adults or youngsters to say no to sexual pressures and temptations. As philosophy professor Janet Smith of the University of Dallas points out, the willingness of couples to wait, to live chastely out of love and respect for each other, is a great testimony to their strength of character. Even youngsters who have already experienced sex can choose to be chaste; chastity is a moral choice and a spiritual state, not a physical condition. Growing numbers of young people are making this choice and experiencing its rewards. They are returning our society to a basic moral truth: in the most intimate areas of human behavior, right and wrong do exist; in sex, as in every other domain of conduct, character counts. In governing our own lives and also in teaching our children what is good, we shouldn't allow wishful thinking, misinformation, or political ideology to excuse our moral responsibility to take into account the physical, emotional, and social consequences of sexual behavior.

# part seven

# EDUCATING
## *for*
# CHARACTER

DANIEL GOLEMAN is a psychologist and journalist whose book
*Emotional Intelligence* topped the best-seller lists by arguing that
self-awareness, self-discipline, persistence, and empathy are more
important than IQ in determining success and happiness. The
book sold millions of copies worldwide and inspired more than
a thousand school districts to investigate teaching emotional
literacy. Goleman's other books include *Mind Body Medicine;*
*The Creative Spirit; The Meditative Mind;* and *Vital Lies, Simple
Truths: The Psychology of Self-Deception.* A fellow of the American Academy for the Advancement of Science, he has received
awards from the American Psychological Association, American
Psychiatric Association, National Association for Mental Health,
and National Alliance for the Mentally Ill. He has also reported
for the *New York Times,* taught at Harvard, and consults and
lectures internationally.

# 36

# What We Can Do About Emotional Illiteracy

*Daniel Goleman*

E ACH DAY'S NEWS comes to us rife with reports of the disintegration of civility and safety, an onslaught of mean-spirited impulse running amok. But the news simply reflects back to us on a larger scale our creeping sense of emotions out of control in our own lives and those of the people around us. No one is insulated from this erratic tide of outburst and regret; it reaches into all our lives in one way or another.

The last decade has seen a steady drumroll of reports portraying an uptick in emotional ineptitude, desperation, and recklessness in our families, our communities, and in our collective lives. A spreading emotional malaise can be read in the numbers showing a jump

*Note:* This chapter is adapted from Daniel Goleman, *Emotional Intelligence* (Bantam Books, 1995). © 1998 Daniel Goleman.

in depression around the world, and in the reminders of a surging tide of aggression—teens with guns in schools, freeway mishaps ending in shootings, disgruntled ex-employees massacring former fellow workers.

There is growing evidence that fundamental ethical stances in life stem from underlying *emotional* capacities. First, impulse is the medium of emotion; the seed of all impulse is a feeling bursting to express itself in action. Those who are at the mercy of impulse—who lack self-control—suffer a moral deficiency: the ability to control impulse is the base of will and character. Second, the root of altruism lies in empathy, the ability to read emotions in others; where there is no sense of another's need or despair, there is no caring. And if there are any two moral stances that our times call for, they are precisely these: self-restraint and compassion.

## Academic and Emotional Intelligence

I remember the fellow in my class at Amherst College who attained five perfect scores on the SAT and other achievement tests he took before entering. Despite his formidable intellectual abilities, he spent most of his time hanging out, staying up late, and missing classes by sleeping until noon. It took him almost ten years to get his degree. Academic intelligence has little to do with emotional life. The brightest among us can flounder on the shoals of unbridled passions and unruly impulses; people with high IQs can be stunningly poor pilots of their private lives.

One of psychology's open secrets is the relative inability of grades, IQ scores, or SAT scores, despite their popular mystique, to predict unerringly who will succeed in life. To be sure, there is a relationship between IQ and life circumstances for large groups as a whole: many people with very low IQs end up in menial jobs, and those with high IQs tend to become well paid—but by no means always. At best, IQ makes up about 20 percent of the factors that determine life success, which leaves 80 percent to other forces.

Even Richard Hernstein and Charles Murray, whose book *The Bell Curve* imputes a primary importance to IQ, acknowledge this when they point out that "the link between test scores and [career] achievements is dwarfed by the totality of other characteristics that [each person] brings to life."

My concern is with a key set of these other characteristics: *emotional intelligence*. Emotional intelligence encompasses such characteristics as being able to motivate oneself and persist in the face of frustrations; to control impulse and delay gratification; to regulate one's moods and keep distress from swamping the ability to think, to empathize, and to hope.

There is an old-fashioned word for this body of skills: character. Character, writes Amitai Etzioni, the George Washington University social theorist, is "the psychological muscle that moral conduct requires."

If character development is part of the foundation of democratic societies, consider some of the ways emotional intelligence buttresses this foundation. The bedrock of character is self-discipline; the virtuous life, as philosophers since Aristotle have observed, is based on self-control. A related keystone of character is the ability to motivate and guide oneself, whether in doing homework, finishing a job, or getting up in the morning. And the ability to defer gratification and to control and channel one's urges to act is a basic emotional skill, one that in a former day was called will. "We need to be in control of ourselves—our appetites, our passions—to do right by others," notes Thomas Lickona in writing about character education. "It takes will to keep emotion under the control of reason."

Being able to put aside one's self-centered focus and impulses has social benefits: it opens the way to empathy, to real listening, to taking another person's perspective. Empathy leads to caring, altruism, and compassion. These capacities are ever more called on in our increasingly pluralistic society, allowing people to live together in mutual respect and creating the possibility of productive public discourse.

## The Cost of Emotional Illiteracy

It had begun as a small dispute but escalated. Ian Moore, a senior at Thomas Jefferson high School in Brooklyn, and Tyrone Sinkler, a junior, had had a falling out with their buddy, fifteen-year-old Khalil Sumpter. Then they had started picking on him and making threats. Now it exploded. Khalil brought a .38 caliber pistol to school one morning, and, fifteen feet from a school guard, shot both boys to death at point-blank range in the school's hallway.

This chilling incident can be read as yet another sign of a desperate need for lessons in handling emotions, settling disagreements peaceably, and just plain getting along. Educators, long disturbed by schoolchildren's lagging scores in math and reading are now recognizing a different and more alarming deficiency: emotional illiteracy. And while laudable efforts are being made to raise academic standards, this new and troubling deficiency is not being addressed in the standard school curriculum. As one Brooklyn teacher put it, the present emphasis in schools suggests that "we care more about how well schoolchildren can read and write than whether they'll be alive next week."

Perhaps the most telling data of all are from a national sample of American children, ages seven to sixteen, comparing their emotional condition in the mid-1970s and at the end of the 1980s. Children, on average, were doing more poorly in these ways:

- *They had withdrawal or social problems:* preferring to be alone, being secretive, sulking a lot, lacking energy, feeling unhappy, being overly dependent.

- *They were anxious and depressed:* feeling lonely, having many fears and worries, needing to be perfect, feeling unloved, feeling nervous or sad and depressed.

- *They had attention or thinking problems:* being unable to pay attention or sit still, daydreaming, acting without thinking, feeling too nervous to concentrate, doing poorly on schoolwork, being unable to get their minds off particular thoughts.

- *They were delinquent or aggressive:* hanging around kids who get into trouble, lying and cheating, arguing a lot, being mean to other people, demanding attention, destroying other people's things, disobeying at home and at school, being stubborn and moody, talking too much, teasing a lot, having a hot temper.

What can we change that will help our children fare better in life? The abilities that make up emotional intelligence—including self-control, zeal and persistence, and the ability to motivate oneself—are skills that can be taught to children, giving them a better chance to pursue whatever intellectual potential the genetic lottery may have given them.

## Teaching Emotional Literacy in Schools

Academic intelligence offers virtually no preparation for the turmoil—or opportunity—life's vicissitudes bring. Yet even though a high IQ is no guarantee of prosperity, prestige, or happiness in life, our schools and our culture fixate on academic abilities, ignoring the emotional intelligence that also matters immensely for our personal destiny. Emotional life is a domain that, as surely as math or reading, can be handled with greater or lesser skill and that requires its unique set of competencies. And how adept a person is at those competencies is crucial to understanding why one person thrives in life while another of equal intellect dead-ends: emotional aptitude is a *meta-ability,* determining how well we can use whatever other skills we have, including raw intellect.

Schools, notes Etzioni, have a central role in cultivating character by inculcating self-discipline and empathy, which in turn enable true commitment to civic and moral values. In fulfilling this role, it is not enough to lecture children about values. Children need to practice values, and they get this practice as they build essential emotional and social skills. In this activity, emotional literacy goes hand in hand with education for character, for moral development, and for citizenship.

Understanding the need for emotional literacy expands our vision of the task of schools, making them more explicitly society's agent for seeing that children learn these essential lessons for life—a return to the classical role of education. This larger educational design requires, apart from adding specific material to the curriculum, using opportunities in and out of class to help students turn moments of personal crisis into lessons in emotional competence. The teaching of emotional literacy also works best when the lessons at school are coordinated with what goes on in the children's homes. Many emotional literacy programs include special classes for parents to teach them about what their children are learning, not just to complement what is imparted at school but to help parents who feel the need to deal more effectively with their children's emotional life.

Another way in which a focus on emotional literacy reshapes schools is in building a campus culture of a caring community, a place where students feel respected, cared about, and bonded to classmates, teachers, and the school itself.

In short, the optimally designed emotional literacy program begins early, is age appropriate, runs throughout the school years, and intertwines efforts at school, at home, and in the community.

Perhaps the most telling signs of the impact of emotional literacy classes are the data shared with me by the principal of a school with an unbendable rule that children caught fighting are suspended. As emotional literacy classes have been phased in over the years, the school has seen a steady drop in the number of suspensions.

The data suggest that although such courses do not change anyone overnight, as children advance through the curriculum from grade to grade, there are discernible differences in the tone of the school and in the outlook—and level of emotional competence—of the girls and boys who take them.

There have been a handful of objective evaluations, the best of which compare students in these courses with equivalent students not taking them. Another evaluation method is to track changes in the same students before and after a course, using objective measures of their behavior. Pooling such assessments reveals a widespread benefit for children's emotional and social competence and for their behavior in and out of the classroom. They learn

*To Have Emotional Self-Awareness*

- Improved recognition and naming of own emotions
- Better understanding of the causes of feelings
- Recognition of the difference between feelings and actions

*To Manage Emotions*

- Better frustration tolerance and anger management
- Fewer verbal putdowns, fights, and classroom disruptions
- More appropriate expression of anger, without fighting
- Fewer suspensions and expulsions
- Less aggressive or self-destructive behavior
- More positive feelings about self, school, and family
- Better stress management
- Less loneliness and social anxiety

*To Harness Emotions Productively*

- Improved ability to take responsibility
- Better focus on the task at hand and paying attention
- Less impulsive behavior; more self-control
- Improved scores on achievement tests

*To Have Empathy, to Read Emotions*

- Better ability to take another person's perspective
- Improved empathy and sensitivity to others' feelings
- Better skills for listening to others

*To Handle Relationships*

- Increased ability to analyze and understand relationships
- Better ability to resolve conflicts and negotiate disagreements
- Better ability to solve problems in relationships

- More assertiveness and skills for communicating
- More popularity: outgoing, friendly, and involved with peers
- More behavior that makes them sought out by peers
- More concern and consideration
- More pro-social behavior; harmonious behavior in groups
- More sharing, cooperation, and helpfulness
- More skill at being democratic in dealing with others

One further item demands special attention: emotional literacy programs improve children's *academic* achievement scores and school performance. This is not an isolated finding; it recurs again and again in such studies. In a time when too many children lack the capacity to handle their upsets, to listen or focus, to rein in impulse, to feel responsible for their work or care about learning, anything that will buttress these skills will help in their education. In this way, emotional literacy enhances school's ability to teach. Even in a time of back-to-basics and budget cuts, there is an argument to be made that these programs help reverse a tide of educational decline and strengthen schools in accomplishing their main mission and so are well worth the investment.

Beyond these educational advantages, emotional literacy courses seem to help children better fulfill their roles in life—as friends, students, sons, and daughters—and help prepare them to be better husbands and wives, workers and bosses, parents, and citizens.

## Preparing Children for Better Lives

My focus on the place of emotional and social deficits is not to deny the role of other risk factors, such as growing up in a fragmented, abusive, or chaotic family or in an impoverished, crime- and drug-ridden neighborhood. But there is a role that emotional competence plays over and above family and economic forces—it may be decisive in determining the extent to which any given child or teenager is undone by hardships or finds a core of resilience to survive them.

Long-term studies of hundreds of children brought up in poverty, in abusive families, or by a parent with severe mental illness show that those who are resilient even in the face of the most grinding hardships tend to share key emotional skills: a winning sociability that draws people to them, self-confidence, an optimistic persistence in the face of failure and frustration, the ability to recover quickly from upsets, and an easygoing nature.

Over the last decade or so "wars" have been proclaimed, in turn, on teen pregnancy, dropping out, drugs, and most recently, violence. The trouble with such campaigns is that they come too late, after the targeted problem has reached epidemic proportions and taken firm root in the lives of the young. They are crisis intervention, the equivalent of solving a problem by sending an ambulance to the rescue rather than giving the inoculation that would ward off the disease in the first place. Instead of mounting more such wars, what we need is to follow the logic of prevention, offering our children the skills for facing life that will increase their chances of avoiding these fates.

So far, we have not bothered to make sure every child is taught the essentials of handling anger or resolving conflicts positively—nor have we bothered to teach empathy, impulse control, or any of the other fundamentals of emotional competence. By leaving the emotional lessons children learn to chance, we risk largely wasting the window of opportunity presented by the slow maturation of the brain to help children cultivate a healthy emotional repertoire.

Despite high interest in emotional literacy among some educators, courses are as yet rare; most teachers, principals, and parents simply do not know of the possibility for them. The best models are largely outside the education mainstream, in a handful of private schools and a few hundred public schools. Of course no program is an answer to every problem. But given the crises we find ourselves and our children facing and given the quantum of hope held out by courses in emotional literacy, we must ask ourselves: Shouldn't we be teaching these most essential skills for life to every child—now more than ever?

And if not now, when?

ELIZABETH KISS is the founding director of the Kenan Ethics Program at Duke University, where she is an associate professor specializing in moral and political philosophy, human rights, feminist theory, and Central European politics. A Rhodes Scholar and the daughter of former Hungarian prisoners of conscience, she has been active in several human rights organizations. She previously taught at Princeton University and at Randolph-Macon and Deep Springs colleges and held fellowships at the Harvard Program in Ethics and the Professions and at the National Humanities Center. She serves on selection committees for the Rhodes, Truman, and Stuart scholarships and on the boards of Davidson College and the Duke University Center for Documentary Studies.

# 37

# In Praise of Eccentricity

*Elizabeth Kiss*

S HE'S *QUITE* A CHARACTER." We've all heard these words applied to the more eccentric and colorful among us. People who *are* characters can be amusing or inspiring, challenging or irritating. They are, in any case, memorable.

This sense of the word character may seem very distant from the concerns that motivate today's character education movement. This movement seeks to unite parents and teachers in our diverse communities around a common vision of the character traits we should all strive to nurture in young people. Here in the Durham, North Carolina, public schools, for instance, posters proclaim that "Character Matters," and list nine traits selected and defined by a community task force: citizenship, courage, fairness, honesty, kindness, perseverance, respect, responsibility, and self-discipline. The idea is that these are behavioral traits all of Durham's schoolchildren should learn in order to become productive citizens. Young and old, we should all strive to become persons of character by developing these traits, for they represent a widely shared idea of human goodness.

I want to suggest that both meanings of character—the common and the uncommon, the normative and the eccentric—have an important place within moral education. Only by linking them can we draw on the full richness and depth of a character-based approach to ethics and the moral life. And only if we acknowledge the value of both decency and eccentricity will we live up to the promise and challenge of character education in, and for, a democratic society.

Our security and well-being depend on people's willingness, by and large, to abide by a set of basic norms, to be trustworthy, caring, responsible, and respectful of others. We want children to absorb the idea that it is wrong to be dishonest, irresponsible, or indifferent to the fate or feelings of others, just as we want them to recognize that certain actions and attitudes, like cheating, stealing, murder, rape, torture, and racism, are morally intolerable. Character originally meant an engraver's mark or stamp, and we can view the basic virtues of good character as traits we want engraved on every child's heart and mind. To be sure, children are not just blank slates in this process, for they exhibit capacities for empathy and justice from a very young age. But character education reinforces and shapes these existing moral capacities.

While the first sense of character refers to a *uniform* standard of goodness and decency—we should all strive to be honest, kind, fair, and responsible—the second depicts character as a *distinctive* bundle of traits, the qualities and attributes that distinguish an individual. Each of us has a unique character, continually formed out of what happens to us and what we do with it. While every life builds on and intertwines with the lives of others, it has its own idiosyncratic contours. Each person's character is thus the sum of the qualities that distinguish him or her as an individual. Moreover, we might even say that some are more unique than others. That is, some people are so striking and memorable that we call them characters. The dictionary nicely sums up this meaning of character as "moral qualities strongly developed or strikingly displayed," and as "character worth speaking of."

## The Role of Uniformity

One of the great achievements of the character education movement has been its ability to identify a uniform standard of good behavior in an age of moral uncertainty. At a time when many of us are tongue-tied on ethical matters, it is empowering to recognize that we can unite with our fellow citizens, affirm basic norms of good character, and make a commitment to nurture them in our children and ourselves.

An explicit standard of good character can teach young people a great deal about ethics and the moral life. For one thing, children crave consistency, and character education can help provide them with a coherent set of behavioral expectations, ideally reinforced both at school and at home. A lot depends, of course, on *how* we try to teach good character. For instance, didactic techniques appropriate for working with small children may insult the intelligence of older students. And formal teaching, however skillful, will never be as powerful as efforts by adults to model good character and to create environments—at home, in school, and in the community—where good behavior is informally reinforced.

A focus on good character can do much more, however, than establish basic behavioral expectations. It can also provide a strong and nuanced approach to teaching young people about the moral life. As Joel Kupperman argues in his fine book, *Character,* the advantage of teaching the ethics of character over many other approaches to ethics is that it recognizes that morality is a lifelong project that involves our innermost lives. Being ethical is not just a matter of following rules, identifying principles, or producing the "right" answer to ethical dilemmas. It has to do with the kind of person I want to become, what most matters to me and why, and how I think and feel about myself and others. One way we convey these insights about character and ethics is by telling stories. Stories show us how and why people succeed, or fail, in being good and decent. They give us something to live up to, offering us portraits of people who exemplify one or another of the character traits to a remarkable degree—who are extraordinarily kind or who treat even their enemies with respect. But stories also teach the complexities of good character, revealing, for instance, that public virtue can be deceptive. Stories can move our vision of good character beyond a mere bundle of traits—the virtue-of-the-week approach favored by many schools when they initiate a policy of character education—toward a richer understanding of how character, developed over time and tested in ways both large and small, gives shape to a life.

The greatest moral educators, in my experience, are those whose words, deeds, and attitudes reinforce one another. What they say resonates because their characters shine through in the telling. These teachers haunt us, their words and gestures surface in our consciousness to guide, prod, or inspire—or at times to call us to account. I think, for instance, of an afternoon I spent as a child in the company of a carpenter who was putting his life together after years of homelessness and alcoholism. We sat in the late afternoon sun on the banks of a small pond, and he described desperate times. More haltingly, he also shared with me the pride he took in his work, his efforts to serve his new community, and his hopes for the future. He gave me a lifelong lesson about honesty, dignity, and moral possibility. In the classroom, too, I have had the good fortune to study with a handful of teachers whose efforts to make their students think harder, be more imaginative, and lead more deliberate lives were made irresistible by their own commitment to these ideals. I will never forget the moral dilemmas of loyalty, virtue, and corruption explored in Shakespeare's *Julius Caesar* (or, for that matter, what a direct object is) thanks to Ebba Jo Spettel's unflagging commitment to broaden her eighth graders' horizons. And I am grateful to philosophy professors who modeled the examined life and made me realize it really matters what I think and say.

Some have criticized the character education movement for overemphasizing didactic instruction to the detriment of critical reflection and for elevating obedience to authority above all other ethical considerations. These may be fair—and important—criticisms of specific efforts. But neither the vocabulary nor the underlying vision of character education entails these shortcomings. Taking good character seriously means inviting young people to engage in critical reflection on themselves and their society. Twelve-year-olds accustomed to thinking about fairness, kindness, and respect will have a good starting point for exploring the rights and wrongs of the world around them, whether their topic is classroom cheating, race relations in the classroom, or homelessness.

## The Value of Eccentricity

A uniform standard of good character has great value in promoting young people's moral development. As a framework for character education, however, it remains incomplete. What's missing is a recognition of how the uncommon, the extraordinary, and the eccentric play a critical role in creating a better and more decent world. Our efforts in character education will be deprived of the full richness and depth of character ethics if they ignore character in the second sense, as a matter of distinct individuality, of moral qualities strikingly displayed, and even of qualities that cause us to label people "odd," "extraordinary," or "eccentric."

To be eccentric is, literally, to follow a different orbit. An encyclopedia of the moral life of humanity would have to reserve several volumes for eccentrics. Where would we be without prophets, visionaries, nonconformists, ironists, and dissenters? The great ethical traditions, both religious and secular, as well as literature and the arts, are filled with eccentrics—complex characters who challenge, inspire, and irritate those around them. They flaunt conventional wisdom, stubbornly champion new and unsettling ideals, love those whom others deem unlovable, or are themselves considered strange and unlovable. Think of the defiance of historical or literary characters like Antigone, Jeremiah, St. Francis, Galileo, Thoreau, and Rosa Parks; of Socrates' incessant questions, Siddhartha's uncompromising quest for enlightenment, and Jesus' friendship and solidarity with such social pariahs as prostitutes and Samaritans. Today we may view these people as uncontroversial examples of good character. But we must not forget that many of the decent people of their own day considered them outlandish, dangerous, even wicked. They challenged established codes of goodness and decency and in the process played an essential role in transforming human values and ethics.

Of course, not all eccentrics are morally admirable. Nor, even if it were possible, should we set out to train a generation of eccentrics. What we can and should do is teach young people that the moral life of humanity has drawn vigor and insight from nonconformists' "defiant moral imagination," to borrow the phrase of theologian Mikael Broadway. Enduring moral insights can come from those we consider strange or deviant. Students of moral character must therefore be attentive to, and respectful of, the singular qualities that make human beings unique.

## The Importance of Being Different, Standing Tall

As a democratic activist in 1940s Hungary, my father, Sándor Kiss, was imprisoned first by the fascists and later by the communists. A modest man of quiet grace, he almost never spoke of these experiences. But once he described to me how, in the chaotic final weeks before the Nazis lost control of Budapest, he was herded into a courtyard with prisoners from other detention centers. The prisoners, weak from hunger and torture, were commanded to line up in rows. Two drunk officers swaggered down the line. "What's your name?" they roared to each man, slapping and kicking those whose response or demeanor displeased them. My father, then twenty-seven, found himself toward the back, standing beside an older man he knew from the Resistance, László Kabók. Kabók's name was well known; he was a prominent Social Democrat and a suspected Jew. In a whisper my father urged him to lie about his name. "I can't do that, son," the man whispered back, calmly. "Please, *Laci bácsi*," my father entreated, using an affectionate term for one's elders, "don't be a fool!" But when the officers reached him, *Laci bácsi* stood erect, looked them in the eye and loudly stated his real name. "And they dragged him off," my father said, his voice choking with the bitter forty-year-old memory, "and beat him to death."

Did *Laci bácsi* do the right thing? Is his story an uplifting example of moral heroism? Or does it reveal the futility of uncompromising integrity in the face of wickedness and injustice? Should he have been willing to make one small compromise so that he might have lived to seek out surviving loved ones and perhaps even done important political work in post-Fascist Hungary? The answer, surely, is not simple. What is clear, however, is the singular power and beauty of *Laci bácsi*'s defiance. His stubborn gesture flares unforgettably across time and distance. He is a character worth speaking of. And his story reminds us also of the tragic dimension of moral life, of how goodness can come to grief in the face of injustice, prejudice, and brutality.

An appreciation for human singularity and eccentricity provides us with a fuller picture of moral character and of its role in efforts to make the world more humane. It also helps us resist the perennial temptation to turn standards of good behavior into tools of injustice. All too often, visions of virtue or decency have been invoked to brand as immoral and dangerous anyone who is different. Such aggressive moral dogmatism—which, it is worth stressing, can occur on both the political right and left—is one of the greatest enemies of human dignity. Combating it requires us to cultivate open minds and hearts and to affirm the value of difference and dissent.

# What Character Education Should Look Like

Ideal character education upholds common standards of good behavior while affirming the value of the uncommon and the defiantly different. We live in a world of multiple perspectives, of value pluralism and moral disagreement. These are the inevitable results of our democratic freedom. The twin dangers facing us in this situation are moral dogmatism and nihilism: either that we respond with fear and anger, condemning those who disagree with us as morally depraved, or that we lose all sense of a moral center and assert that anything goes. Character education that affirms the value of both decency and eccentricity can help us move beyond both of these dangers.

How does this affirmation work in practice? Promoting the virtue of courage within character education programs, for example, invites reflection on how morality may require unpopular stands. One creative effort to nurture courage is the Seattle-based Giraffe Project, which has developed a character education curriculum that invites kids to become "giraffes" who "stick their necks out for the common good." Given children's tendencies to stigmatize peers who are different, it is also important for teachers to challenge patterns of exclusion in the classroom and beyond. In *You Can't Say You Can't Play*, Vivian Paley describes how, after a remarkable schoolwide debate, she introduced the "you can't say you can't play" rule in her kindergarten class. More generally, nuanced and diverse readings of history and literature can help children recognize how dissenters, prophets, visionaries, and other "characters" contribute to good and decent societies. And for older students, character education should, as Joel Kupperman argues, include exposure to multiple perspectives. This not only helps young people think critically about a variety of views; it also demonstrates to them that reasonable and conscientious people will sometimes continue to disagree, so that a key moral question becomes how people of good character negotiate such disagreements.

Character education is no panacea. By itself, it will not repair disintegrating schools, neighborhoods, or families; dry up the drug trade; or create jobs. But it can be an important part of efforts to invest in our children's development and well-being.

Democratic education is committed to the principle that every child—rich or poor, female or male, of whatever race, creed, or culture—is a unique human being who has embarked on a singular life journey and deserves our support. Standards of good character such as respect, responsibility, honesty, and citizenship are critical resources for this journey. So is the openness of mind and heart that enables us to appreciate and to cooperate with those different from ourselves. Character education that integrates these goals can help us live up to the promise of democracy.

ANN MEDLOCK is president of the Giraffe Project, which she founded in 1982 to publicize stories of people who have "stuck their necks out" for the common good and to teach youngsters what heroes really are. She was previously an editor of social studies textbooks and of the news service *Children's Express;* a teacher in Japan and the Congo; a writer for such publications as the *New York Times, Editor & Publisher,* and *Working Woman;* a consultant to organizations such as AT&T and the Rockefeller Public Service Awards; and a speechwriter for public figures ranging from U.S. politicians to the Aga Khan. But she calls her true profession "boat rocking." In her frequent speaking engagements and guest spots on television and radio, she promotes the soul-satisfying and world-healing effects of taking a chance and working for the good of others.

# 38

# The Courage to Stick Your Neck Out

*Ann Medlock*

M Y SELF-ASSIGNED JOB on the character front is storytelling. It's always been a natural thing to me (despite getting in trouble at home when the kindergarten teacher told my mother I was a big storyteller and Mom thought that meant liar). Since 1982, the channel for that storytelling (all of it true stories, I swear) has been a nonprofit organization called the Giraffe Project, which set out to tell the stories of people who stuck their necks out for the common good. Their stories would provide balance to the media's out-of-kilter preoccupation with crime and mayhem.

News is too often defined as "what went wrong today." Stories about people making headway against the challenges of our times

---

are deemed "soft," not worth serious media attention. The net effect of this media attitude is enormous: people are so overwhelmed by the onslaught of information about the worst that humans can do that they pull the figurative covers over their collective heads, convinced that they can have no effect on such all-pervasive chaos and disintegration.

That's the description of a sick society, a wasteland. In stories back to the dawn of time, the healing of the wasteland has come only when *someone* refuses to be passive and summons up the courage to ignore all the naysayers, go forth, and slay whatever dragon has scared everybody else into terrified passivity. We need those brave blazers of trails, those people who are true heroes.

And such heroes are here, all around us. People who refuse to be daunted by the odds, who plunge into the devastation and start setting things right. For news to be truly balanced, we have to know about them. To heal society's wounds, more of us have to become like them.

The mission of the Giraffe Project has always been to inspire more people to stick their necks out for the common good. We find people who are taking risks to solve tough problems in their communities or further afield, and then we tell their stories through the mainstream media—which, despite its often-negative content, is still the best way ever created to reach hearts and minds. The heroes we find, our "Giraffes," are the substance of our storytelling.

People have known for millennia that stories stick in the mind. Listeners might brush off any principles embedded in stories if those principles were to come at them as rules and admonitions, but stories reach the mind by way of the heart. We all remember feelings long after we've forgotten facts; because stories move us emotionally, we don't forget them.

The love of stories may be programmed into our genes, going back to the first campfires, where people gathered to tell each other about their days. And it's a pretty sure bet that a lot of those stories were about feats of courage ("and brave Mog jumped on the mastodon's back and slew it with a sharp stick to the eye, saving us all from starvation . . ."). The Giraffe Project's modern-day tales are portraits of character in action. Giraffes are brave, compassionate, responsible, independent, active, and outspoken. They look at the world around them with keen, caring eyes, observing for themselves what needs to be done and stepping forward to get it done, no matter what they have to give up or go through. They don't whine, they're not passive, and they don't pass the buck. That's character.

While those of us in the Project didn't originally set out to *teach* character, we soon found that teachers were seizing on Giraffe Project publications. They saw the stories as a way to teach by examples, reaching the mind via the heart. And they were desperate to counter their students' fixation on celebrities as heroes. It's one thing to be interested in people who sing, shoot hoops, model, or make pots of money; it's a whole other thing to apply the word *hero* to them. In his book *The Image* (1963), historian Daniel Boorstin draws this necessary distinction between heroes and celebrities: "Celebrity-worship and hero-worship should not be confused. Yet we confuse them every day, and by doing so we come dangerously close to depriving ourselves of all real models. We lose sight of the men and women who do not simply seem great because they are famous but are famous because they are great. We come closer and closer to degrading all fame into notoriety."

Today's youngsters need true heroes who can be lodestars, guiding kids as they try to navigate a culture filled with violence, drug abuse, the worship of money, and the scarcity of good jobs. When they don't have such guiding stars, is it any wonder they feel there's no way out, much less up? The consequent frustration takes form in the rising tide of crime, addiction, and suicide among the young; in the alarming number of pregnant girls looking for meaning in early motherhood—and in the missing fathers of those new lives, who've cut and run from responsibility.

We knew we had lodestar stories to tell, stories that could help kids see what brave, meaningful lives were about, that could inspire them to live such lives themselves. It was clear that we had to go into the schools with a formal curriculum. Hence the K–12 Giraffe Program that starts by telling kids these compelling stories.

The hundreds of Giraffe stories in our files range in scope from the fourth-grade girls who labored in the playtime of others to raise money for Romanian orphans to the veteran seaman who first applied Gandhi's nonviolence teachings to stopping illegal whalers, putting himself and his *Zodiac* between whales and the powerful harpoons aimed at them. We tell kids about a waitress who has placed over four thousand unwanted newborns with Down's Syndrome in loving families and helped thousands more shocked new parents see that they can keep and love their Down's syndrome babies. We give them a young ex–drug dealer who turned his life around and started a legitimate business that employs other street kids, helping them make the same turnaround.

The logical next step is to move students from passive mode to active, from listening to stories to telling stories themselves. So the program sends them out to spot Giraffes in their own communities and then tell the stories they find to their classmates.

Knowing that example plus experience is the best learning of all, we make sure that they don't just get ears and eyes full of words but actually go into action. We ask them—once they're full of stories of people who've already taken action—to look around them and see what needs fixing. In this finale of the program, they decide for themselves what problem concerns them, and create a service project that addresses that problem.

Kids going through such a process are "enCouraged" to be brave, compassionate, responsible, independent, active, and outspoken. They discover that their concerns and their actions count; they experience making something good happen. Character becomes part of their own being, not something external imposed on them.

We're heartened when we hear from and work with the many teachers and youth leaders who share this approach to teaching. Their goal is not to silence and regiment children, physically or metaphorically. They know that manipulating children into "behaving" doesn't foster character. They know that simply imposing order on children does not prepare those children for the dignity and responsibility of citizenship in a democracy.

Michael Rothenberg, the pediatrician and child psychiatrist who coauthored *Baby and Child Care* with Benjamin Spock, told us: "Character-building has to be done from the inside. It's not in fact character-building when bigger and stronger people say to weaker people, 'Behave, because I say so and I'm bigger and stronger than you are.' When the child has it inside, it comes out as, 'I'm doing this because I want to do it, because I like to do it." His view nicely complements the insight from education scholar Thomas Lickona that the essence of good character is "knowing the good, loving the good and doing the good." A child can't be forced to love the good; that love has to be brought forth from within the child.

When you give kids stories of people they can love, get them to look in their own worlds for such people, and then help them become such people, you're looking at kids who know, love, and do good because they want to, because they like to.

A kid who wants to do good has to be brave. When we first went into the schools, we found that the children soaked up stories of courageous people even more eagerly than we had imagined they would. But we shouldn't have been surprised. We should have remembered that kids need moral courage to resist peer pressure. Do you remember being eight or twelve or sixteen and listening to the kids you most wanted to have like you, as they cooked up something really bad? Remember knowing it was wrong? Being terrified of saying so? Terrified of having them all hate you? Of having them spread the word through the whole school that you were a dork?

Whether you found the courage to say no, kept quiet and eased away, or actually went along with the antisocial enterprise, it's valuable to remember those feelings. Because we're all former children, we can, if we try, recollect how frightening it was to go against peer pressure. As educators, as parents, as citizens, it's right and fitting that we be mindful of how much courage it takes kids to be ethical, of how much it can cost them in the coin of their realm—peer approval. It's a betrayal of our own experience to act as if doing the right thing were as easy as "Just say no." Slogans are an insult to children's reality.

The national CHARACTER COUNTS! program, with its six pillars of character—trustworthiness, respect, responsibility, fairness, caring, and citizenship—rightly recognizes moral courage as essential to living a life of character. The program makes it clear that the ethical life is often easier talked about than lived; that people of all ages need courage to do the right thing. Hear, hear! I assume everyone but a few saints can agree with CHARACTER COUNTS! that it's not easy to lead an ethical life, to be people of character. It's a difficult thing for anyone—and a huge challenge for kids. But there is disagreement on *why* it's difficult. Some say it's because we humans are inherently bad and must have imposed controls; I think it's because our inherent goodness gets buried under overlays of cultural detritus.

We live in a culture in which the media fill us with stories of wrongdoing and in which business has convinced most of us that we're "consumers," the maddening label that's replaced "citizens" in our vocabulary. A multibillion-dollar part of that culture sees kids only as buyers of CDs, sneakers, and hamburgers. However, several years as editor-in-chief of *Children's Express,* "the news service by kids, for everybody," assured me that kids are capable of far more than the consumer culture asks of them. *Children's Express* editors recruited kids at random on playgrounds and then watched them scoop adult reporters on major national news stories. We saw those kids bloom in the light of our expectation that they could do more than respond to advertising pitches, that they could do a hard job well. They responded by revealing their magnificence.

Now I'm seeing again how much expectation affects what kids do. If adults look at a room full of young faces and see miscreants in need of reshaping into decent folk, guess what the kids give us. But when we assume that no matter what the presenting attitudes might be, beneath them there are good hearts, the kids can let that goodness come forth. Our own attitudes can determine what kids are willing to show us of themselves.

Starting with an expectation that at heart, kids are good—even the "bad" ones—we can proceed to find ways through the cultural junk, through the attitudes, to that good heart. Their minds and actions will follow.

A lot of the people who don't share that view will tell you they have good reason for thinking kids are rotten to the core. And it's painfully clear that many good people who work with kids are up against a wall. Time is short, demands are high, and many are confronted with hostile, even violent students. Nobody said teaching at the end of the twentieth century was easy—combat pay and medals are probably in order.

But there is an even greater danger in the classroom today: if the national call for character education becomes nothing more than a way to establish some order in an out-of-control realm, "success" will be a generation of obedient, malleable drones. In a democracy, that's a prescription for national disaster.

The antidote, I believe, requires a good measure of courage from all of us who work with kids: we have to trust them, even if we're afraid they aren't trustworthy. We've watched teachers tentatively step out on this tightrope, hoping it's true, afraid it's not. But they take the chance—and end up telling us they don't recognize their own students. Most heartening, the best stories come from teachers of the "worst" kids.

Typically, these teachers' classrooms are the dumping ground for every disorderly kid who's been flunked, suspended, and generally written off. The usual drill is to nail down everything that can be moved, try to maintain discipline, and hope maybe the kids will learn *some* academics while you keep them from hurting each other.

But teachers who've taken the risk of thinking such kids can be reached, not just controlled, have been amazed by what can happen. The kids love hearing stories, love finding stories, love doing service projects they've invented to fix problems they really do care about. Their dukes are down, their hearts are open, their minds engaged. And they learn something important about themselves and their value in the world.

In the Giraffe Project we've seen such kids get concerned that local voter registration was practically nil; their response was to create a relentless campaign that signed up hundreds of local adults. Another class full of "incorrigibles" decided that there was a safety hazard at a nearby street crossing; they clocked cars, researched the laws, did the math, wrote petitions, phoned officials, made a presentation to them, and dragooned them into coming to the crosswalk in question. They got a light installed, astonishing their former teachers, who hadn't been able to get the kids to talk, read, listen—or even answer roll call—much less so fully engage the world around them.

Seeing this kind of potential in kids may be a reach for some. Approaching kids' minds through their hearts is an uncomfortable road to travel if you've always approached them solely through reasoning. The whole idea of evoking the students' own courage and caring, of bringing out their own concerns and their own solutions, their own desire to do something meaningful, is not "normal" if you're accustomed to simply telling them what's what. It may be impossible if you believe that the kids don't have it in them.

But if you have the courage to trust in them and to open their hearts, they will amaze you. And they will become great citizens—brave, compassionate, responsible, independent, active, outspoken participants in this magnificent democracy.

CHRISTINA HOFF SOMMERS, a W. H. Brady Fellow at the American Enterprise Institute in Washington, D.C., and professor of philosophy at Clark College in Worchester, Massachusetts, is known for her provocative writings on moral education, feminism, and American culture. She has published many scholarly articles in such publications as the *Journal of Philosophy* and the *New England Journal of Medicine,* and she is the author of *Who Stole Feminism? How Women Have Betrayed Women* and the editor of *Vice and Virtue in Everyday Life,* a textbook in moral philosophy used in college ethics courses nationwide. A contributor to such major newspapers as the *Wall Street Journal, Washington Post,* and *USA Today,* she has also appeared on numerous television shows, from *Nightline* and *20/20* to *60 Minutes* and *Oprah.* Her newest book is *The War Against Boys.*

# 39

# What College Students Don't Know

*Christina Hoff Sommers*

W E HEAR A LOT today about how Johnny can't read, how he can't write, and how much trouble he is having finding France on a map. Johnny is morally confused as well, imperiling not just his own character but centuries of hard-won lessons about what makes a good person and a good society.

There is a great deal of simple good-heartedness, instinctive fairmindedness, and spontaneous generosity of spirit in our young people. Most of the students in my own classes or those I encounter in the high schools and colleges I visit strike me as being basically decent. They form wonderful friendships and seem to be considerate of and grateful to their parents—at least more than the baby boomers were. (In many ways, contemporary young people are more likable than baby boomers—they are less fascinated with themselves and more able to laugh at themselves.) An astonishing number of them are doing volunteer work (70 percent of college students, according to one annual survey of freshmen). They donate blood to the Red Cross in record numbers and deliver food to housebound elderly people. They spend part of their summer vacations working with deaf children or doing volunteer work in Mexico. This is a generation of kids that, with relatively little guidance or religious training, is doing some very concrete and effective things for other people.

## The Loss of Belief in Absolute Truth

But conceptually and culturally, today's young people live in a moral haze. Ask one of them if there is such a thing as right and wrong and suddenly you are confronted with a confused, tongue-tied, nervous, and insecure individual. The same person who works weekends for Meals-on-Wheels, who volunteers for a suicide prevention hotline or a domestic violence shelter, might tell you: "Well, there really is no such thing as right or wrong. It's kind of like whatever works best for the individual. Each person has to work it out for himself." That kind of answer, so common as to be typical, is no better than the moral philosophy of a sociopath.

The notion of objective moral truth is in disrepute. Unsurprisingly, this mistrust of objectivity in moral truth has begun to spill over into other areas of knowledge. Today, the concept of objective truth in science and history is also being impugned, for there has been an assault on the very notion that objective fact exists. Wendy Shalit, an undergraduate at Williams College, recently reported that her classmates, who had been taught that "all knowledge is a social construct," were doubtful that the Holocaust ever occurred. One of her classmates said, "Although the Holocaust may not have happened, it's a perfectly reasonable conceptual hallucination."

Kay Haugaard, a creative writing teacher at Pasadena City College, has written in the *Chronicle of Higher Education* about what it's like to teach Shirley Jackson's "The Lottery" to today's college student. This celebrated short story concerns a small American farming village that seems normal in every way; its people are hardworking and friendly. As the story progresses, the reader learns this village carries out a villagewide lottery as an annual ritual. The end of the story is truly shocking: the reader discovers that the loser of the lottery is stoned to death. It's a story about human sacrifice—but in a familiar American setting. As Haugaard explained in the *Chronicle,* English teachers of past generations have taught this story to adolescent students who are very ready to receive its message about the dangers of mindless conformity. But now teachers find that the story does not shock many of today's undergraduates. Haugaard describes a recent class discussion: "The end was neat," said one student. "Neat?" asked Haugaard, "How do you mean neat?" "Just neat, I liked it." Other students, after years learning about multiculturalism and relativism, strained to see the situation from the villagers' point of view: "They just always do it. It's a ritual." Haugaard tried to reason with them; eventually she gave up.

In effect we are raising a generation of young people who are not being given the arguments to support the ideals by which most of them instinctively live. It is today fashionable to cast doubt on what is objectively obvious. By the same token it has become unfashionable to defend these truths. It has become especially unfashionable to defend them with passion.

It was not always thus. When Thomas Jefferson wrote that "All men" have the right to "life, liberty and the pursuit of happiness," he did not say, "At least that is my opinion." He declared it as an objective truth. When Elizabeth Cady Stanton amended the Declaration of Independence by changing "all men" to "all men and women," she was not merely giving an opinion. She was insisting that, as a matter of self-evident fact, nineteenth-century America was unjust to women because it did not recognize that women were endowed with the same rights and entitlements as men. The assertions of Abraham Lincoln and Martin Luther King Jr. were made in the same spirit, as self-evident truths and not as personal judgments.

Today's young people enjoy the fruits of the battles fought by the Jeffersons, the Lincolns, the Stantons, and the Kings, but they themselves are not being given the intellectual and moral training to argue for and to justify those truths. On the contrary, it is no exaggeration to say that the education they are getting systematically undermines their common sense about what is true and right. And, again, while this sad state of affairs is not necessarily reflected in their behavior, I fear what it might mean for the future.

Men and women died courageously fighting the Nazi onslaught on civilization and democracy. Today, with the assault on objective truth in science and morals, many college students find themselves unable to say *why* the United States was on the right side in that war and in the Cold War that followed it. Some even doubt that America *was* in the right. These young people have somehow managed to live without getting a sense that there are firm moral truths. They are not even sure that the salient events of World War II ever took place at all. They lack confidence in the objectivity of history. Make no mistake: this could mean catastrophe in future conflicts where moral confidence is essential.

The young people of today are not even moral skeptics. They just talk that way. To put it bluntly, they are conceptually clueless. The problem I am speaking about is cognitive. Our students are suffering from a dreaded, infectious disease we might call CMC: cognitive moral confusion.

## The Great Relearning

What is to be done? How can we improve young people's knowledge and understanding of moral history? How can we restore young people's confidence in great moral ideals? How can we help them become morally articulate, morally literate, and self-confident?

In the late sixties, some hippies living in the Haight-Ashbury district of San Francisco decided that hygiene was a middle-class hang-up that they could best do without. The essayist and novelist Tom Wolfe was intrigued by these hippies who, he said, "sought nothing less than to sweep aside all codes and restraints of the past and start out from zero." After a while the hippies' principled aversion to modern hygiene had consequences that were as unpleasant as they were unforeseen. "At the Haight-Ashbury Free Clinic," Wolfe reported, "there were doctors who were treating diseases no living doctor had ever encountered before, diseases that had disappeared so long ago they had never even picked up Latin names, such as the mange, the grunge, the itch, the twitch, the thrush, the scroff, the rot."

The itching and the manginess eventually began to vex the hippies, leading them to seek help. Step by step, they had to rediscover for themselves the rudiments of modern hygiene. Wolfe referred to this as the "Great Relearning." The Great Relearning is what has to happen whenever earnest reformers extirpate too much, when, in order to start from zero, they jettison basic social practices and institutions, abandoning common routines, defying common sense, reason, and conventional wisdom—and sometimes sanity itself.

We are more familiar with similar but more consequential experiments of our century: Marxist-Leninism, Maoism, Fascism. Each movement had its share of zealots and social engineers who believed in starting from zero. They had faith in a new order and ruthlessly cast aside traditional arrangements. Among the unforeseen consequences of these experiments were mass suffering and genocide on an unprecedented scale. Eastern Europeans are just beginning their own Great Relearning. They now realize, to their dismay, that starting from zero is a calamity, that the structural damage wrought by the political zealots has handicapped their societies for decades to come. They are leaning that it is far easier to tear apart a social fabric than it is to piece it together again.

America, too, has had its share of revolutionary developments—not so much political as moral. We are living through moral deregulation, an experiment whose first principle seems to be that conventional morality is oppressive. What is right is what works for you. We question everything. We casually, even gleefully, throw out old-fashioned customs and practices.

We need our own Great Relearning, something that could be called moral conservationism. It is based on this premise: we are born into a moral environment just as we are born into a natural environment. Just as we have basic environmental necessities—clear air, safe food, fresh water—we have basic moral necessities. What is a society without civility, honesty, consideration, self-discipline—the basics of good character? Without a population of individuals educated to be civil, considerate, and respectful of one another, what will we end up with? Not much. For as long as philosophers and theologians have written about ethics, they have stressed the moral basics. We live in a moral environment. We must respect and protect it. We must acquaint our children with it. We must make them aware that it is precious and fragile.

The last few decades of the twentieth century have seen a steady erosion of knowledge and a steady increase in moral skepticism. This is partly due to the diffidence of many high school and college teachers, who are confused by all the talk about pluralism. Such teachers actually believe that it is not right to "indoctrinate" our children in their own culture and moral tradition.

I recently saw a PBS special on ethics in the classroom. It included interviews with high school kids from New Hampshire who were not sure why cheating was wrong. Some of the kids were in gangs and admitted to doing a lot of antisocial things. The parents seemed to agree that character education in schools was necessary, but they could not reach a consensus on several controversial moral topics. The teachers and parents sounded confused, diffident, unsure, helpless, or worse. Some believed moral education meant defending a very liberal agenda; others thought it meant just the opposite. The message was this: character education may be a good idea, but there may be no way to do it in our pluralistic, tolerant society in which everyone has his own idea about right and wrong.

Yet there is far more consensus today than the program allowed. Of course there are pressing moral issues around which there is no consensus; as members of a modern, pluralistic society we argue about gay rights, assisted suicide, and abortion. That is understandable. New moral dilemmas arise in every generation. But long ago we achieved consensus on other basic moral questions: cheating, cowardice, and cruelty are wrong. As one pundit put it, "The Ten Commandments are not the Ten Highly Tentative Suggestions." While it is true that our society must debate such controversial issues as capital punishment, assisted suicide, and the like, we must not forget there exists a core of uncontroversial ethical issues that were settled a long time ago. We must make students aware that there is a standard of uncontroversial ethical ideals that all civilizations worthy of the name have discovered. Have them read the Bible, Aristotle's *Ethics,* the Koran, or the analects of Confucius. Have them read almost any great work, and they will encounter these basic moral values: integrity, respect for human life, self-control, honesty, courage, and self-sacrifice. These are the basics of good character, and while many young people exhibit good character, they also need to understand how to conceptualize what good character is—and isn't. This conceptualization will enable them to make moral judgments, pass lessons on to future generations, and protect all the good that has been fought for through the centuries.

Children have a right to their moral heritage. High schools and college students should know the Bible. They should be familiar with the moral truths in the tragedies of Shakespeare and in the political ideas of Jefferson, Madison, and Lincoln. They should be exposed to the exquisite moral sensibility in the novels of Jane Austen, George Eliot, and Mark Twain. These great writings are their birthright.

This is not to say that a good literary and philosophical education suffices to create ethical human beings, nor is it to suggest that teaching the classics is all we need to do. What we know is that we cannot in good conscience allow our children to remain morally illiterate. All healthy societies pass along their moral and cultural traditions to their children. This is called character education.

And so I come to another basic reform. Teachers, professors, and other social critics should be encouraged to moderate their attacks on our culture and its institutions. They should be encouraged to treat great literary works as literature and not as reactionary political tracts. Pundits, social critics, radical feminists, and intellectuals from the cultural left never seem to tire of running down our society and its institutions and traditions. We are a society overrun by determined advocacy groups who overstate the weaknesses of our society and show very little appreciation for its merits and strengths. I would urge those professors and teachers who use their classrooms to disparage American institutions and traditions to consider the possibility that they are doing more harm than good. Their goal may be to create sensitive, critical citizens, but what they are actually doing is producing confusion and cynicism. Their goal may be to improve students' awareness of the plight of exploited peoples, but what they are actually doing is producing kids who are capable of doubting that the Holocaust took place—kids who are incapable of articulating moral objections to human sacrifice.

We need to take an active stand against the divisive unlearning that is corrupting the integrity of our society. Happily, the tools are at hand. We inherited a very healthy constitution. We know how to dispel moral confusion and reclaim our confidence. We need to teach our young people to understand, to respect, and to protect the institutions that protect us and preserve our kindly, free, and democratic society.

MARTIN J. CHAVEZ was the mayor of the city of Albuquerque, New Mexico, from 1993 to 1997—the first native of the city to serve as its chief executive. His focus has been on building community, including such efforts as community-based policing, the Mayor's Council on Gangs, and the Mayor's War Against Graffiti. He organized three Paint the Town days (recorded in a textbook used by cities across the nation), on which thousands of citizens volunteered their time and sweat to clean off graffiti residue. Chavez also worked with the state's senior senator, Pete Domenici, to cochair the nation's first CHARACTER COUNTS! municipal effort. For his efforts, *Newsweek* magazine named Chavez one of the nation's "top 25" mayors.

# 40

# Community Renewal Through Character Education

*Martin J. Chavez*

T HE INCIDENT SICKENED the entire community. In an attempt to add something "extra" to his football performance, a high school lineman wore a helmet on which the metal snaps had been sharpened with a grinding wheel, transforming the head gear into a nearly lethal weapon. Before the final gun sounded, a number of the players from the opposing team had become victims of his "cutting-edge" tactics. The player was thrown out of the game, suspended from school, and banned from sports. There was a court hearing. The community's shock turned into revulsion when people learned that the young player had an adult accomplice. The individual who had concocted the malicious idea and actually had done the sharpening was the boy's father.

The good news here is that horrific behavior still has the capacity to shock and to spur us to action. That capacity is evidence that we share values, some communal sense of right and wrong. To ensure a brighter future, however, communities have much work to do in passing along those values.

Even though some adults (such as the football dad) are bad role models, young people need—and have a right to—adult supervision. They need monitoring and mentoring. They need to see not just parents but also teachers, coaches, clergy, employers, and elected leaders insist on positive behavior. All these adults have a responsibility to communicate values—the ground rules of life—to children. And the community's institutions have a responsibility to support that effort.

In America today we have 57 million children who are age fifteen or younger. By the year 2006, we will have 30 million teenagers—the largest number since 1975. When you look at all of the risk factors—kids growing up in poverty, kids abused, neglected, or in single-parent families—then what these demographics come down to is that we will have a larger population of very troubled youth, very soon. While crime rates are indeed starting to come down, America's rates of lethal violence still far outstrip those of other advanced Western nations. We dare not neglect the urgent task at hand.

## What a Community Can Do

What is to be done? Albuquerque has adopted a nonpartisan, nonsectarian—but explicit—approach to teaching character to its citizens with the CHARACTER COUNTS! program, which has taken root in communities across the country as a means of renewing the values that all people of goodwill share and wish to pass on to children and promote to adults, regardless of race, class, politics, or religion.

Over the past three years, while serving as cochair of CHARACTER COUNTS! in Albuquerque, along with New Mexico senator Pete

Domenici, I have had the wonderful opportunity to visit over one hundred elementary and middle school classrooms and talk about the six pillars of character—trustworthiness, respect, responsibility, fairness, caring, and citizenship. I've witnessed firsthand that the children in these schools do yearn for standards and codes of conduct. On every one of my visits, without exception, I could count on seeing their excited faces and eager, upraised hands as they jumped at the chance to respond to the question, "All right, who can tell me what the six pillars are?"

When first proposing the idea that the city of Albuquerque officially endorse the program, I was met with a surprising variety of reactions. Although a sizable majority were supportive, the cynicism of many was startling to me. We all know it is fashionably chic to be disdainful of elected officials (read "politicians") these days. Consequently, when politicians recommend a values-based agenda, it is greeted in some quarters as a prima facie case of hypocrisy. During speeches to business audiences, I found that while no one necessarily was against the program, many didn't take it too seriously either. That early skepticism has evaporated. Three years later it is my observation that the more successful enterprises in our community are the ones that have embraced and supported the CHARACTER COUNTS! curriculum, integrating it into their own operations.

As leaders, we should not be deterred by the fear of ridicule. The positive benefits are worth the trouble. Those of us who wrestle with the myriad social problems that afflict our communities increasingly have come to understand that values do matter. City government is not just about zoning and taxes, sewers and street lights. We in government, by our speech and the manner in which we conduct our business, help to set the tone for a community. Those who today are concerned about restoring a tone of civility to government and political discourse can draw encouragement from communities' experience with CHARACTER COUNTS! Moreover, we can mobilize our communities to act by evoking a universally accepted framework of values like the six pillars. When over five thousand Albuquerque citizens came out on Paint the Town weekends to clean up the graffiti that at one time had threatened to overwhelm the city, they were acting in a spirit of responsibility, respect, caring, and citizenship. They celebrated and gave meaning to those values through their actions. They taught their children a valuable lesson. And above all, they felt like a community—and felt good about being a community—again.

Over the long haul I'm convinced that teaching and promoting values will have its greatest impact in our schools. Louis Martinez, for example, then principal at Garfield Middle School, reported on the remarkable impact that the program had immediately after his 570 students were first exposed to it in October 1994. The school is in a neighborhood that was experiencing a high level of gang activity. During the first twenty days of that school year, there were ninety-one recorded incidents of physical violence. One year later, during the same period, the number had dropped to twenty-six. At Garfield the kids made posters illustrating the six pillars of character. They discussed the "value of the month" in class and at assemblies.

These values are making a difference in children's lives by giving them practical tools—a new vocabulary—to deal with bad behavior. Mimi Stewart, a special education teacher at Zia Elementary, reported how the young children at her school, once they learned the values, began using them to resolve playground disputes. Children injected terms like responsibility and citizenship into their attempts to mediate their own interpersonal conflicts, demonstrating the positive influence of the program. It's an influence that should not be taken lightly.

Albuquerque's experience with Character Counts! has demonstrated that if we just make the effort, we can touch something rooted deep inside even the most troubled youths. Two stories underscore the power of explicitly taught values. First, consider a young Albuquerque boy (I'll call him James), abandoned by his mother, cared for by his father only briefly, then placed in foster care after the father was imprisoned for dealing crack cocaine. Returned to his mother and the boyfriend she was living with, James was unwanted by this new family and severely abused. Not surprisingly, he was diagnosed with both a behavior disorder and a learning disability. When James was called on during a classroom exercise on the six pillars, he announced that "my dad thinks this CHARACTER COUNTS! stuff is worthless." But when the teacher asked James what *he* thought about the program, James replied, "Whenever we talk about CHARACTER COUNTS! it's the safest I've ever felt."

Or take the case of a fourth grader (I'll call him Jonah) who had been sexually molested by two cousins, a boy and a girl. He reacted to the abuse by acting out at school. After four years of therapy the child still carried severe emotional scars around inside. One day Jonah was sitting on a couch in the principal's office, waiting to be punished for bad behavior, when a small group of visiting dignitaries arrived to hear about the school's CHARACTER COUNTS! program. Just above Jonah's couch was a display featuring the pictures of students who had distinguished themselves during the preceding month in some aspect of the six pillars, and one of the visiting adults asked Jonah what the display was all about. "Those kids on the wall," Jonah explained, "know what to do and they do it. I know what to do, but I don't always do it."

Our hearts can't help but be touched by Jonah's story. His and so many other stories illustrate that children, even the most troubled and abused, have an innate sense that there must be something to hold on to, a frame of reference. But in our society today, with its conflicting welter of images and messages, a community must provide that framework. That's one of the things healthy communities do. And I know that's what First Lady Hillary Clinton meant when she said, "It takes a village to raise a child."

Today, Albuquerque has also become the home of Character Comics, a small enterprise producing children's comic books dedicated to CHARACTER COUNTS! themes. Teens get together to discuss story ideas. Once stories are decided, writing, drawing, and printing tasks are assigned. The city has provided financial support to this marvelous project.

Albuquerque's Drug Awareness and Resistance Education (DARE) program incorporates the CHARACTER COUNTS! values of responsibility and caring when it teaches young children and teenagers to react appropriately to situations in which a gun unexpectedly appears. For instance, eight- to ten-year-olds learn four specific steps to take if a friend or another student takes out a gun at school: (1) don't touch the gun; (2) try to get away safely; (3) tell an adult whom you trust; and (4) tell your friend that you don't want to be around guns because someone could get hurt or killed.

Building character in the workplace is encouraged too. When Albuquerque city government employees turn on their computers each morning, the opening screen highlights the value of the month. City water bills and paychecks always feature one of the six pillars. Many of these bill and paycheck recipients are parents, and familiarizing them with the six pillars also enables them to reinforce the program's overall message when their kids start discussing what was learned in school.

## The Importance of Teaching Explicit Values

Above all, CHARACTER COUNTS! represents a direct response to one of the overarching realities of today's culture. Children today are bombarded daily with thousands of value-laden messages through television, radio, film, the Internet, and print media. However, we adults would be negligent if we assumed that the core values that make community possible will naturally emerge out of this glut of information. A random check of the violence and casual sex portrayed on TV and at the local cineplex suggests just the opposite. The sexual predators now lurking on the Internet pose further dangers to our children and their values.

We are a free society that cherishes free and unfettered speech. This of course has consequences. When children use information channels administered by adults and routinely encounter messages and images that tout destructive behavior, promote hate, or otherwise diminish human dignity, we should not be surprised that these children become confused. Adults are always right, aren't they? The flip side to living in a rich marketplace of ideas is that our culture is continually sending such mixed messages to our children.

This is why we must be explicit in our messages about values. We can't leave the communication of societal values to mere chance, lost in a vast information sea of contradictory messages. We must take time to teach, to teach clearly and to make certain that children understand. We must prepare children for the world by equipping them with the tools to discern issues of right and wrong so they can make judgments accordingly.

And this is all the more reason why we must strive to be good role models for our children. The most powerful way to communicate values is by example. Aristotle had it right. We become virtuous, and thus truly happy, by the practice of virtue.

## Language, Democracy, and Citizenship

In a larger sense, what's at stake in character education is our democracy—our capacity to live together peacefully as a community of free and self-governing people.

It is said that America is different because, unlike most other nations, its citizens are not bound together by soil or blood, by a dominant race, religion, or ethnicity. As we talk about values and ideas, we should remember that America is uniquely an idea. Here we must learn to love and respect one another; it's not naturally wired into our genes. The founders constituted this nation on a set of values, and it is the responsibility of each generation to transmit these values to the next. It is these shared values that make civility possible—and it is civility that enables democracy to function.

Democracy, to survive, must have an educated, fully informed, and active citizenry. Every individual matters, every individual is important, every individual has rights—and responsibilities. Czech president Václav Havel identifies the "principal challenge of our time, a challenge for the third millennium," as the "rehabilitation of the human dimension of citizenship." Quite rightly, citizenship is one of the six pillars of character.

But again, it is explicitness that is so essential. Teaching and talking about the six pillars over and over again is important precisely because language is so important. Through the language we use, we encourage habits of the mind and heart in ourselves and others. If we neglect to engage in responsible discourse, then the irresponsible will hold sway uncontested.

A half century ago, the novelist George Orwell foresaw a dark future where an ubiquitous tyranny destroyed the meaning of life by destroying the meaning of language. Happily, we have avoided that fate. Today our challenge is to keep the language of human values—the vocabulary of ethics and character—from being overwhelmed in the relativistic information marketplace.

We must continually return to our roots by actively and consciously renewing our common, valued traditions. As G. K. Chesterton said: "Conservatism is based upon the idea that if you leave things alone you leave them as they are. But you do not. If you leave a thing alone you leave it to a torrent of changes. If you leave a white post alone it will soon be a black post. If you particularly want it to be white you must be always painting it again. . . . Briefly, if you want the old white post you must have a new white post."

EDWARD A. WYNNE has been professor of education at the University of Illinois at Chicago for more than a quarter of a century, during which time he has published, coauthored, or edited ten books and more than 120 articles. Many of his writings deal with character development and draw on his extensive studies of more than three hundred public and private schools. Founder of two national periodicals on character education, he was also principal organizer and editor of "Developing Character, Transmitting Knowledge," a national statement signed by twenty-seven prominent Americans.

# 41

# Managing the School Environment to Build Character

*Edward A. Wynne*

THROUGH MOST OF human history and prehistory, the first goal of education has been to raise morally wholesome citizens. Teaching facts, skills, and theories was also appropriate. But they all were taught in a philosophical setting. Even today, morality is the prime instructional aim of typical education. The change over time has not been from a concern with morality to a concern for facts. Instead, education has shifted its focus over the centuries from teaching character plus facts and ideas to teaching, at this time, individualistic behavior plus some facts and ideas.

## What Character Is

Our word *character* comes from an ancient Greek term meaning to "visibly and permanently mark," as by scratching the face of stone.

A person's character is the permanent and visible sign of his or her inner nature. The signs can be acts, words, or the failure to act or speak. The quality of courtesy, for instance, is a compilation of signs that total up to the entire person in words or deeds, and sometimes tact, or the failure to act or speak. Courteous people act appropriately. We know this not from looking into their heads but in terms of their acts and words.

Of course it is possible for people to say one thing and feel another thing. But from a character perspective, visible acts or words are what count. Individuals learn good character by being taught good habits—ways of regularly doing the right things in challenging situations. This character instruction process begins in the family, when individuals are infants, and proceeds as they learn about the habits of infancy, childhood, adolescence, and so on.

The principles of character education have been the foundation of education since—and even before—education philosophy began with Plato and Aristotle in classical Greece. Starting in the early eighteenth century, the Romantic movement produced new principles of moral shaping. They placed much greater emphasis on individual self-expression and gradually increasing popularity. By the mid-twentieth century, they had somewhat replaced principles of character education as the prime goal of American education. One can term the education guided by these new-wave principles romantic education. Many of the principles of romantic education are indirectly derived from modern philosophy.

Modern, or romantically oriented, education assumes that virtuous conduct will arise in men and women if they are largely left free to follow their own devices. For reasons that are self-evident, these assumptions about natural virtue are increasingly falling into public disfavor. Simultaneously, the character approach has steadily revived as its basic assumptions about people become increasingly attractive. Here are some of these assumptions:

- Without careful monitoring and instruction, many people may be disposed to exploit and abuse one another.

- People usually find meaning through affiliation with social groups (for example, families, jobs, religions, nations, and political and social communities). To join such groups, individuals must possess or learn the character traits and behaviors appropriate to such groups. For example, fast-food workers must be polite and energetic.

- Long-term groupings—families, clubs, religions, nations—devise recruitment and training systems to ensure that appropriate new members affiliate with the group norms.

- Because people are often disposed to exploit each other, it is hard work to habituate individuals to good behavior. The likelihood of successful habituation is greatly increased if the examples, incentives, and precepts placed around people are colorful, strong, and imaginative and form a coherent network of reinforcement.

- Lists of desirable character traits—for example, honesty, obedience, kindness, diligence—can be useful tools when planning campaigns of moral habituation. If charity, say, has a high priority, we can examine the surrounding environment to see if it provides appropriate occasions for the practice of charity. If it lacks such occasions, then the responsible adult(s) can undertake efforts to restructure it.

- People of goodwill often differ on how to teach moral behavior. Some focus on making sure everyone in a given group will be a moral citizen. Other instructors give greater emphasis to protecting the rights and dignity of individuals against potential abuses committed by the group. America has lately focused on the rights of individuals rather than of the group (the family, school, community, and so forth). We may be experiencing a lack of groups (ranging from villages to schools and families) that teach character effectively.

- Children are not the moral or intellectual equal of adults and therefore should not be given the responsibilities and authorities of adults.

*Controversies About Character Formation.* In general the character tradition assumes that institutions such as families, schools, and long-lived organizations will act more wisely than individuals and also that individuals who have lived through a variety of experiences have learned things that many young people do not yet know. Large formal institutions have institutional memories, complex and elaborate experiences and structures that facilitate deliberative decision making. This does not mean that organizations are always right or can do no wrong. It simply recognizes that individual judgments are often incorrect and even selfish. Given such widely recognized tendencies, it is unrealistic to expect that human beings will reflexively do the right thing without the influence of strong institutions. The moral is: institutions designed to mobilize and transmit time-tested experience will generally lead to improved (and more moral) decision making.

Systems of reward and punishment are needed to encourage people—especially children and adolescents—to develop good habits. Even when such incentives seem lacking, careful observers will recognize the contrasts between traditional and modern systems of moral education. In other words, even the supposedly self-determining learner is often really responding to habits developed from earlier reward structures. Our first lessons about courtesy, obedience, and avoiding physical dangers were embedded in us by the powerful incentives and punishments available to parents of very young children.

In our highly egalitarian culture, rewards and punishments are often the targets of great scrutiny and criticism. In my fieldwork in education research, I have often met parents and educators who actively believe it is a bad thing to deliberately encourage academic competition among pupils. These critics say that "providing rewards for excellence makes pupils less self-motivated." Sometimes such objectors cite formal education research in support of their position. To my mind, this research is of limited relevance. However, the objectors are undoubtedly right in one important particular: there are powerful forces, including the ideas of many American intellectuals, that tend to stifle efforts to elevate the character of American pupils.

Yet the concept of good character is deeply associated with the virtue of excellence, and all the intellectuals and their studies cannot argue that away. We respect Martin Luther King Jr. and Mother Teresa for their character, the kind of character that the Nobel Peace Prize was created to celebrate. Such prizes serve an important role, reminding us what the ideal is, what we should all strive for, even though the circumstances of our own lives may differ from the circumstances of those whom history has made heroes.

Beyond prizes, there are other, more modest ways we can encourage the development of good character. Certainly we should unabashedly encourage our public and private institutions—religious agencies, schools and colleges, political institutions, families, and so forth—to commit themselves to making good character a goal of the highest order. We must recognize—and manage—the power of each of these environments to shape the human character.

***The Importance of Managing Environments.*** Environment greatly affects behavior for good or bad.

- Environments can establish and maintain systems of recognition and punishment. These systems can encourage individuals to try harder to practice desired behavior and to avoid practicing bad behavior. One mechanism is public or private praise for excelling individuals or groups. Praise can be transmitted by rewards, memorials, ceremonies, gold stars on report cards, athletic letters, titles or decorations, and so forth. Punishments can range from dismissive frowns to prolonged imprisonment.

- Environments can identify, praise, or otherwise honor certain people as notable heroes or villains—and thus encourage other community members to copy good, and scorn bad, role models.

- The length of time people spend in intimate connection with a particular environment and its members has much to do with environmental effects on character—for example, how much time does the family spend at meals together? How often do individual students shift among different schools, classes, or particular teachers?

- Environments teach people to identify and honor moral conduct in the past and present and to practice it in the future. What national holidays should be recognized, and to what effect? What legacies have been passed to us from our predecessors? How do we hope the future will regard our achievements?

## What Teachers Can Do to Build Character

Character education happens all the time, in each of the many environments that we occupy, in each of the groups with which we are affiliated. But to give kids the best chance of developing strong character, is there anything we can do to structure an environment they share—namely, school? Yes. There is much teachers and other adults who influence young people can do to structure, or restructure, the school environment as a character-building institution. The best place to start, of course, is always with one's own example. Beyond that, the only limit is one's imagination. One helpful resource is a list of one hundred specific and low-cost ideas for schools, published in *Reclaiming Our Schools: Teaching Character, Academics and Discipline*, by Kevin Ryan and Edward A. Wynne (1997). Here are ten examples from that list:

1. Encourage students to admire and emulate heroic men and women. Hang pictures of such people in classrooms and halls; describe their achievements.

2. Ensure that school and class recognition systems (for example, report cards, honor rolls, public address announce-

ments, school paper articles) praise both academics and character.

3. Prohibit vulgar language at school. Explain to students that it is a form of air pollution.

4. Write, call, or visit parents to express praise or criticism of their children.

5. Assign older students to help younger ones. Train these "mentors" in ways they can be helpful.

6. Design student recognition systems that honor both successful individuals and groups (for example, give recognition to the "most improved class").

7. Choose a personal motto for yourself and explain it to your class. Help individual students and also the class as a whole develop personal mottoes.

8. With the help of other faculty, establish a code of behavior for everyone in the school community—teachers, administrators, parents, and students. Have everyone affected sign a receipt for his or her copy of the code. Explain the code to pupils each year and ensure it is enforced.

9. Consider starting, supervising, or coaching a club or team in your school. Such activities give faculty extra opportunities to affect students' character formation.

10. Foster student diligence. American high school students complain about being underworked (yes, it's true!). And scientific studies reach the same conclusion. Conduct a homework census; if students are not putting in at least six hours of homework per week (not counting study hall), then teachers should increase assignments.

# INDEX

## Photo Credits